Henry James and the Abuse of the Past

Henry James and the Abuse of the Past

Peter Rawlings

First published 2005 by
PALGRAVE MACMILLAN
Houndmills, Basingstoke, Hampshire RG21 6XS and
175 Fifth Avenue, New York, N. Y. 10010
Companies and representatives throughout the world

PALGRAVE MACMILLAN is the global academic imprint of the Palgrave
Macmillan division of St. Martin's Press, LLC and of Palgrave Macmillan Ltd.
Macmillan® is a registered trademark in the United States, United Kingdom
and other countries. Palgrave is a registered trademark in the European
Union and other countries.

ISBN 0–4039–4652–3

This book is printed on paper suitable for recycling and made from fully
managed and sustained forest sources.

A catalogue record for this book is available from the British Library.

Library of Congress Cataloging-in-Publication Data

Rawlings, Peter.
    Henry James and the abuse of the past / Peter Rawlings.
        p. cm.
    Includes bibliographical references and index.
    ISBN 1–4039–4652–3
    1. James, Henry, 1843–1916–Knowledge–History. 2. United States–
History–Civil War, 1861–1865–Literature and the war. 3. James, Henry,
1843–1916–Knowledge–United States. 4. Literature and history–United
States. 5. History in literature. I. Title.

PS2127.H5R39 2005   2004051335
813'.4–dc22

10   9   8   7   6   5   4   3   2   1
14 13 12 11 10 09 08 07 06 05

Printed and bound in Great Britain by
Antony Rowe Ltd, Chippenham and Eastbourne

For Carol and Alexander

The *whole* of anything is never told
(Henry James)

Contents

Acknowledgements

I acknowledge the support of the Arts and Humanities Research Board and the University of the West of England for research leave in 2002–3. Sections of Chapters 3 and 4, here substantially rewritten and extended, first appeared, respectively, as 'Henry James, Delia Bacon, and American Uses of Shakespeare', *Symbiosis* 5 (2001), and 'Grammars of Time in Late James', *Modern Language Review* 98 (2003); I am grateful for permission to draw on this material.

Note
For the List of Abbreviations, see pages 164–5.

Introduction: 'We Want None of Our Problems Poor'

This book is organized around Henry James's use and abuse of an event and context to which he returned compulsively: his 'obscure hurt' and the American Civil War. In his 1879 study, *Hawthorne*, James observed that 'it takes a great deal of history to produce a little literature', and 'that it needs a complex social machinery to set a writer in motion' (320). He went on to specify the Civil War as a primal scene of lost innocence,[1] choosing to construct it as a precipitator of and pretext for the complications, ambiguities, and moral turpitude on which much of his writing was to depend:

> The subsidence of that great convulsion has left a different tone from the tone it found, and one may say that the Civil War marks an era in the history of the American mind. It introduced into the national consciousness a certain sense of proportion and relation, of the world being a more complicated place than it had hitherto seemed, the future more treacherous, success more difficult. (427–28)[2]

Available henceforth are ramifying senses of a present predicated on a thickened past reaching uncertainly into the future. Complication, or its fabrication at least, is the literary imperative here; and this was the case for James at both the national and personal levels. It was James, as much if not more than Nathaniel Hawthorne, who had now 'eaten of the tree of knowledge' (428). The war became a *felix culpa* for him not just for what it was, but also for what it was not; not because he enlisted and distinguished himself on the field of battle, rather because he singularly failed to do so.[3] Whether James was either unable or unwilling to take up arms is less significant than the use to which he put his negative experience of the Civil War in terms of the discourse of fiction-compelling obscurity it enabled. This, and not simply his unwillingness or inability to fight as such, determined the trajectory of his senses of the past, present, and future, and shaped much of the writing to come.

The telling feature of the 'obscure hurt' that seemingly incapacitated James as he worked with other volunteers to extinguish a fire in Newport on 28 October 1861, is not the injury itself, nor even so much James's insistence on how obscure it was, but the utter obscurity of the account to which it gave rise in *Notes of a Son and Brother*.[4] 'It might be argued', suggests Gordon in relation to this event, 'that truth in its humdrum sense doesn't apply to the fecundities of the developed imagination' (64–5). In a description that ultimately fails to describe, descriptive excess abounds: pre-modifications and qualifications cluster around any sign of burgeoning clarity as a concrete experience is mutilated by abstraction, leaving the reader dangling between the impalpable and the inconceivable. A 'passage of personal history', a 'private catastrophe or difficulty, bristling with embarrassments' has, in James's 'consciousness' a 'queer fusion or confusion' not 'clearly expressible' with the 'firing on Fort Sumter' (414). This tenuous asymmetrical combination of individual and collective experience, of the private and the public, became for James a myth of his own origins. It stemmed from his pre-existing and developing theories of consciousness and knowledge, generated by and partly generating the grammar of his theory and practice as a writer.

James commented in 1897 on the 'incalculable angle at which experience may strike' ('Hubert Crackanthorpe' 841); and his subsequent reflections on the intensities and wounds of Newport is similarly shaped by a keen sense of the surprising tangents of experience:

> Jammed into the acute angle between two high fences, where the rhythmic play of my arms, in tune with that of several other pairs, but at a dire disadvantage of position, induced a rural, a rusty, a quasi-extemporised old engine to work and a saving stream to flow, I had done myself, in face of a shabby conflagration, a horrid even if an obscure hurt. (*HJA* 415)

It is a measure of the rhetorical success of a progressively more baffling account that commentators such as C. P. Snow concluded that 'no good writer could write so deplorably, or obfuscate so clumsily, unless he had something to cover up' (200).[5] Post-lapsarian cover-ups, however, are the stuff of James's fictional world. They are central to the elements of secrecy, concealment, and ignorance that constitute his principal epistemological tenets, control his senses of the past and, variously defined, determine his attitude towards written history. The challenge for James is ever in those 'memories in truth too fine or too peculiar for notation, too intensely individual and supersubtle—call them what one will' (*HJA* 426). Demonstrated by the 'obscure hurt' is Bergson's contention in *Creative Evolution* that 'the negation of a thing implies the latent affirmation of its replacement by something else, which we systematically leave on one side':

> Thus is formed the idea of the void or of a partial nought, a thing being supposed to be replaced, not by another thing, but by a void which it leaves, that is, by the negation of itself. (295–6)

'Our life is thus spent', continues Bergson,

> in filling voids, which our intellect conceives under the influence, by no means intellectual, of desire and of regret, under the pressure of vital necessities.[6]

'We are constantly going from the void to the full', for 'such is the direction which our action takes' (298).

To argue, as a range of critics have, that James suffered some kind of castration, physical or psychical, resulting in a 'passional death' (Rosenzweig 88) and the birth of a capacity for producing art, that he experienced a Swedenborgian vastation like his father's, thus compensating for a sense of inferiority with a wound equivalent to Henry James Senior's amputated leg, or that this was the initiation of a masochistic aesthetic determined in part by an ambition to achieve a domination over a brother, William, whose marriage was the 'obscure hurt' for Henry given the homoerotics of his fraternalism, is to miss the point that the fictional and autobiographical dynamic is in the availability, for use and abuse, of a seminal obscurity.[7] Consonant with this, the emphasis in James tends to be on what is not, rather than what is, not on what can be represented, but on what cannot. The illusion of an unrepresentable essence, a reality beyond appearances, is one of the enabling fictions produced by this emphasis.

All the world's a stage for James, a theatre of war, and an arena for the performance of accidents and contingent senses of the self, for 'that is what it is really to *have* style—when you set about performing the act of life' (Rev. of *George Sand* 779). To engage directly in the war would, in part, be to forgo the more rewarding uses to which it could be put, and to evacuate in advance the peculiar vantage point from which he as a writer could inspect the corresponding illusions, however necessary, of life and art. In a view expressed in 1868, three years after the end of the war, the self-serving and the pertinent coalesce:

> In every human imbroglio, be it of a comic or a tragic nature, it is good to think of an observer standing aloof, the critic, the idle commentator of it all, taking notes, as we may say, in the interest of truth. (Rev. of *The Spanish Gypsy* 956)

'Even prisons and sick-rooms have their special revelations', insisted William James ('On a Certain Blindness' 860), and 'invalids', Henry agreed, 'learn so many secrets,' for 'the health of the intellect is often promoted by physical disability' (Rev. of *The Earthly Paradise* 1191).

The production of obscurity on which James's writing in part depends involves an unspeakable appropriation of the suffering of others, and of the Civil War in general. The war was not, however, simply a pretext for a self-fashioning aesthetic; it was also the means by which James dramatized throughout his fiction and other writing, as it returns again and again to war and its environs, the destruction of essentialism possible there. For Kaplan, the Newport injury is 'carefully calibrated', and 'one of its effects was to enable' James 'to heighten his consciousness about himself, to create an interesting personal history to substitute for the war experience that apparently he preferred not to engage directly' (56). This is certainly part of the story; but like many of the numerous commentators on the incident, Kaplan's horizon is restricted to biography: he fails to excavate the epistemological and discursive depths plumbed by Henry James himself. As James uses his 'obscure hurt' to assimilate and engross aspects of the Civil War, he notes that the 'interest of it', of the hurt, that is, 'I very presently knew, would certainly be of the greatest, would even in conditions kept as simple as I might make them become little less than absorbing'. In this account, the war is peripheral, and his accident central:

> Circumstances, by a wonderful chance, overwhelmingly favoured it—*as* an interest, an inexhaustible, I mean; since I also felt in the whole enveloping tonic atmosphere a force promoting its growth. Interest, the interest of life and of death, of our national existence, of the fate of those, the vastly numerous, whom it closely con-

cerned, the interest of the extending War, in fine, the hurrying troops, the transfigured scene, formed a cover for every sort of intensity, made tension itself in fact contagious—so that almost any tension would do, would serve for one's share. (*HJA* 415–16)

In wittingly stressing the 'interest' of it all, James signals his position as a usurer of a kind. The interest is not in things as they were or are, but in how they present themselves to the consciousness of a 'man of the imagination' (*PA* 1307), whose ascendance over the man of action, of whom the soldier seems emblematic, is in a scepticism that extends not only to whether any facts of experience can be presented, as distinct from represented, but to the very notion of an objective reality.

In a move consistent with an apparent disavowal of written history, James railed against the 'fatal futility of Fact' (*PSP* 1140); and there are at least four possible dimensions to what could be described as his life-long fear of and resistance to facts. First of all, there is the original event of his not enlisting in the Union army. Secondly, there is the question of the extent to which his homoerotic proclivities had to be carefully coded. Thirdly, in the final ten years or so of his life especially, James's fiction and other writing encrypts increasing anxieties about publicity, exposure, and revelation; and towards the end, this surfaced in attempts to stifle posthumous biographical penetrations. The plausibility or otherwise of these approaches, and how they impinge on, interact with, and produce readings of a range of James's texts, represent the spine of my overall argument. It will be contended, however, that the fourth dimension subordinates the first three, and that this was also James's principal perspective.

What James feared in this fourth dimension were not facts as such, but certain paralyzing facts about facts. It is not the revealing of secrets that unleashes chaos, but the discovery that there are none to reveal: hence the vital importance of a paradigm of contrived and actual obscurity. Obscurity is mobilized in the interests of preserving an instrumental ignorance that can save appearances, and this process is intimately connected with the homoerotic discourse of much of the fiction. The way out of a potential abyss of meaninglessness in a world of appearances for which there is no corresponding reality—more accurately, a way of averting and diverting the gaze from such an abyss—is either the representation of negative experience, or the circulation of negative utterance, or (in what amounts to the same thing) the multiplication of secrets and the perpetuation of obscurity. Similarly, if experience and identity are in essence performances, the carnival, or theatre, of war is the *urtext*. Refusing to perform, or enlist, and occupying the nominally passive terrain of the observer and writer, as distinct from pitching into fervent activity conventionally defined, is a form of hyper-performance that contains and vanquishes all others. Hence the supremely ironic pose and poise of those narrators in the fiction of Henry James most closely involved with war and the Civil War.

The context of the first chapter, '"The Exquisite Melancholy of Everything Unuttered": History and the Abuse of the Past', is James's critique not just of what, by the end of the nineteenth century, was a fading vogue for scientific history increasingly under attack from a variety of anti-positivists, but his wariness of all attempts, historical, biographical, and fictional, to offer the illusion of an accessible past in the guise of its reconstruction.[8] The first section of the chapter scrutinizes early reviews, with their hostility towards the specious claims for objectivity made by historians such as Leopold von Ranke, and looks at the doom awaiting the compromise made between history and the imperatives of fiction in 'The Art of Fiction' (1884). By the time James collected and augmented the travel pieces known as *Italian Hours* (1909), the subject of the second section, he had little interest in accommodating historians in the house of fiction. In *Italian Hours*, the relics and documents on which history depends hover in the margins of the text as objects of irony, satire, and comedy. 'The Aspern Papers' is at the centre of a third section which argues that the New York Edition preface (1907–9) to that tale is a crystallization of James's thinking on narration, representation, fiction, and history. Some of the ideas and concepts of Henri Bergson, William James, Henry Adams, and contemporary critics and theorists such as Hayden White and Michel de Certeau, are brought to bear on the pathological narrator of 'The Aspern Papers', and the significance of his futile pursuit of what he believes, in the shape of documents, survives of the past. The chapter concludes with the Henry James of *The American Scene* standing on the banks of the Concord River musing over the limited reach not only of narration and representation, but also of any discursive mediation of the past.

Chapter 2, 'Wars and Rumours of Wars: Among the Soldiers', focuses more narrowly on the Civil War context of the 'obscure hurt'. Whereas the impossibility of history is central to the first chapter, homoeroticism and the performance of masculinity shape the second. Given that an atmosphere of moral panic, gender confusion, and traumatic desire often pervades James's fiction at the turn of the nineteenth century, it seems reasonable to look for its determinants not just in the Cleveland

Street scandal (1889–90) and the trials of Oscar Wilde (1895), but at a possible aetiology that reaches back through *Roderick Hudson*, the early Civil War tales, and the staging of the 'obscure hurt' itself.[9] Speculations about James's sexual proclivities in themselves, however, are not the issue. Sex, as an arena of intense representation, is introduced to demonstrate the much greater importance for James of the discoveries he makes about fiction and reality in realms of strenuous masculinities, only apparently so, such as soldiery and war. In this respect, we are back with the contrived obscurity of the 'hurt' and the opportunities it provides. 'The Story of a Year,' *Roderick Hudson*, and *Notes of a Son and Brother* are the main texts under scrutiny.

Three short stories, the first two of which have been neglected by critics, figure prominently in the third chapter, 'Shakespeare and the Long Arras': 'The Birthplace', 'The Papers', and 'The Private Life'; and what connects this chapter with the second, in part, is the heavy inflection of anxious homoeroticism in 'The Papers' and, to an extent, in 'The Private Life'. Shakespeare, in a variety of guises and roles, has an acute bearing not only on these tales, but also on James's more general uses of obscurity and the past. The chapter begins, taking its cue from James's introduction to *The Tempest*, by examining aspects of Delia Bacon's attempts to deprive Shakespeare of his plays and attribute them to Francis Bacon, among others, within the context of nineteenth-century American negotiations with and commercial appropriations of the bard. Correspondingly, 'The Birthplace' rehearses the competing attractions of 'the roar of the market and the silence of the tomb' ('Dumas the Younger' 291) as James locates incoherently held terrors reaching back to the Civil War about publicity and exposure on what was already, by the beginning of the twentieth century, the American mass cultural site of William Shakespeare. With his own bio-critical fate in mind, James is extremely ambivalent about the enigma of Shakespeare's life and the marauding biographers to which it consigned him.

The final chapter, 'Grammars of Time, Senses of the Past', returns, like James himself in much of his fourth-phase writing, to wars and rumours of wars.[10] It concentrates on 'The Jolly Corner', 'The Diary of a Man of Fifty', *The Sense of the Past*, the autobiographical writings, and some of the essays written at the time of the Great War, notably 'The Long Wards' and 'Within the Rim'. Perspectives on time, the very grammar of senses of the past, present, and future, are at the core of 'The Jolly Corner' and of this book's concluding examination of Henry James and the abuse of the past. James became increasingly intrigued, and eventually obsessed, with the possibilities at the logical, grammatical, and narrative levels of complicating the present by including a tangible past and a conjecturable future. His sense of time and the past were shaped in part by William James's speculations in *The Principles of Psychology* on the 'saddle-back' nature of the 'specious present' (573), and connections between this conception of space and time and aspects of the thinking of F. H. Bradley, J. Ellis McTaggart, Otto Jespersen, and others, pursued throughout the chapter.

James's 'obscure hurt', then, broadly interpreted and freely construed, serves throughout this book as a point of departure and return for an exploration of aspects of the theory and practice of James as a historiographer, epistemologist, and grammarian and philosopher of time as he everywhere registers the extent to which, as Strether has it, 'we want none of our problems poor' (*The Ambassadors* 273).[11] These areas involve meditations on what can, cannot, and must not be said and, more widely, on what the permissions and prohibitions fundamental to discourse function as and signify. Crucial to James's encounter with a physician after the injury,[12] and very much the *leitmotif* of this book, is the obscure and obscuring language in which he reports the far from useless medical opinion pronounced:

> It was not simply small comfort, it was only a mystification the more, that the inconvenience of my state had to reckon with the strange fact of there being nothing to speak of the matter with me. (*HJA* 417)

More than usually so, James is 'suspended in webs of significance he himself has spun' (Geertz 5).

1
The 'Exquisite Melancholy of Everything Unuttered': History and the Abuse of the Past

> For the letter killeth, but the spirit giveth life.
> (2 Corinthians 3: 6)

(i) The arts of fiction and history

In one of the earliest critical studies of Henry James, Rebecca West commented on an 'odd lack of the historic sense' in his work and an 'estimate of modern life' consequently 'confused' (27); but in offering this judgment, West mistook the sometimes indeterminable, and often oblique, nature of James's sense of the past for its absence. T. S. Eliot was much more interested, on the other hand, in establishing the distinctiveness of a historical sense once removed that he saw as all-pervasive in James. Both Hawthorne and James 'had that sense of the past which is peculiarly American, but in Hawthorne this sense exercised itself in a grip on the past itself; in James it is a sense of the sense' ('On Henry James' 129).[1] On its own idiosyncratic terms, James's sense of history was acute, and his shifting reactions to the turbulence of the philosophies and methodologies of history in the nineteenth century arise from and give shape to his autobiographical ruminations and his fictional projection of senses of a sense of the past.[2] For James, as for Trilling, 'the refinement of our historical sense chiefly means that we keep it properly complicated' (*The Liberal Imagination* 185).

By the close of the nineteenth century, and at a time, as Leon Edel has it, 'when men are...unusually conscious of the clock and the calendar' (*Henry James: The Treacherous Years* 329), James on the brink of what Georges Poulet has called his 'bygone future' (353), became obsessed with a past, his own and that of others, as it yielded to his pensive, imaginatively charged, apprehensions. James's relation to the past, however, and his senses of it, and senses of those senses, were far from static: he configured and reconfigured them endlessly as he everywhere sought to indulge in what de Certeau terms those 'arcane crafts' disowned by the nineteenth-century scientific historian: 'resurrection, animation, and even ventriloquism' (viii). Nowhere in James do questions of history and the past press more than in his 'fourth phase' (McWhirter, '"A Provision Full of Responsibilities"' 149), that period towards the end of his life when he concentrated on autobiography, cultural criticism, and aesthetics, and which culminated in a return to *The Sense of the Past*, a novel he had begun at the end of the nineteenth century and whose dictation he resumed just before his death. At issue there for Ralph Pendrel is the poverty of history by contrast with a sense of the past, however nebulous, which the narrator of 'The Aspern Papers' lacks utterly: his 'historic faculty, clumsily so to dub it, or in other words his sense of the past', is 'the thing he has always wanted to have still more than historic records can give it' (*N* 504). In line with his characterization of Pendrel, James defines the 'queer museum of history' in terms of 'human relations' in *William Wetmore Story and His Friends* (2: 103–4; 1: 226); and he sees it throughout as embodied in particular people on whom he can exercise his imagination, rather than in documents or texts. James proposes a definition of the 'historic sense' quite different from that of the nineteenth-century German school:[3] 'What is the historic sense after all', he asks in relation to Balzac, 'but animated, but impassioned knowledge seeking to enlarge itself?' (Introduction, *Two Young Brides* 110).

At the age of twenty-three, when James's future was anything but 'bygone', he penned a review of two now forgotten novels by Anne E. Manning.[4] By 1867, the date of the review—and as science, with its growing emphasis on positivistic, law-seeking, approaches to data, was becoming the model for history—James can be whimsical about Walter Scott and a first half of the century dominated, in the realm of fiction, by the later eighteenth- and early nineteenth-century romantic enthusiasm for the past.[5] By contrast, 'history and romance are so much more disinterested at the present moment than they were during Scott's lifetime....The great historians nowadays are Niebuhr and Mommsen, Guizot and Buckle, writers of a purely scientific frame of mind' ('Historical Novels' 1154).[6] The focus on particularity in Romantic discourse that informed Scott's novels had generated the paradigm within which Leopold von Ranke (1795–1886), whose work is a major part of the founding discourse of nineteenth-century historiography, operated.[7] Despite an emphasis in practice and theory on the importance of moving from the 'investigation and observation of particulars to a universal view of events' (Ranke 59), Ranke's most notorious statement entails a devotion to facts and an innocence about the perils of representation abhorrent to James:

> To history has been assigned the office of judging the past, of instructing the present for the benefit of future ages. To such high offices this work does not aspire. It wants only to show what actually happened (*wie es eigentlich gewesen*). (57)[8]

In ways that fully anticipate Nietzsche's contention that 'there are no facts in themselves. It is always necessary to begin by introducing a meaning in order that there can be a fact' (Barthes 16), James recoils from the 'vast fabric of impenetrable fact...stretched' over the historian's 'head'. The historian, relegated by James to the underworld of industrial production, 'works in the dark, with a contracted forehead and downcast eyes, on his hands and knees, as men work in coal-mines' ('Historical Novels' 1154). Not for James was Niebuhr's dogmatic wresting of scientific history from what he called 'fiction and forgery' (Niebuhr 48), and he was to have only contempt for Mommsen's naïve assertion that 'history...is nothing but the distinct knowledge of actual happenings' anchored in 'the available testimony' (192).[9] James valued Hawthorne especially because 'he has none of the apparatus of an historian', his 'shadowy style of portraiture never' suggesting 'a rigid standard of accuracy' (*Hawthorne* 321). As for 'forgery', James anticipates in *A Small Boy and Others* that his critics will castigate him as an 'artful dodger' given that he has put the past to 'criminal use', 'falsifying its history' and 'forging its records even'. His defence is to argue, however, that senses of the past, as distinct from the desiccations of most historical writing, are phenomenal: they are affairs of the 'intelligence', or consciousness, and survive there in forms for which there are no 'traceable grounds'. His concern, however convenient it might be, is not with the facts, but with the 'mental history after the fact' (*HJA* 125). Henry Adams, for one, would have approved:

> The historian must not try to know what is truth, if he values his honesty; for, if he cares for his truths, he is certain to falsify his facts. (1137)

For a writer who was a life-long votary of the oblique, indeed opaque, incomplete, and barely uttered, registration of what the imagination aesthetically intensified encounters in experience, the 'poor, bare, shabby facts of things' (Preface, *Port Tarascon* 250) were at best merely the beginning, and at worst, a paralyzing kind of finality. They are merely the 'odds and ends' which might be 'recovered' and 'interpreted' as the 'story', or history, is transposed by the artist into a 'subject' that is 'expressive' ('The Story-Teller at Large' 286). Niebhur, Mommsen, and Buckle were committed to the yield of an empirical method early disavowed by James. Buckle went even further in that he attested to the burden on history to discover 'regularity in the midst of confusion' (124–5), the 'vast majority of historians' filling 'their works with the most trifling and miserable details' (133). For Buckle, the aim should rather be that of discovering, in the spirit of Comte, the determining laws of the universe as they shape historical events. But 'miserable details' and general laws alike were an anathema to a James who revelled in 'the presence of what is missing' and the 'history of there being so little' ('Old Suffolk' 256). James had little affection for what he frequently regarded as German pedantry, and he attacked *Romola*, the most historical of George Eliot's novels, for smelling too much of the 'lamp'; 'it has always seemed to me', he complained, as 'the most Germanic of the author's productions', and a 'twentieth part of the erudition would have sufficed' ('The Life of George Eliot' 1006); and Count Vogelstein, 'an intelligent young German' in 'Pandora', has a 'mind' containing 'several millions of facts, packed too closely together for the light breeze of the imagination to draw through the mass' (816–17).[10]

After his 1867 review, 'The Art of Fiction' (1884) is James's next most sustained articulation of the relation between fiction and history. That essay, of course, is also an impassioned insistence on the imperative of novelistic freedom and, thereby, an emphatic repudiation of positivist history and its law-seeking proclivities. If Macaulay, in his 1828 essay, 'History', suggests the extent to which historians are, and ought to be, under the pressure of fiction, he focuses in the process on those elements of historical discourse that become for James, in 'The Art of Fiction' and the prefaces to the New York Edition, the very elements that distinguish the novel from history.[11] History, for Macaulay, is an affair of representation: 'no picture is exactly like the original', and 'no history can present us with the whole truth' (76); or as James was to express it in his notebooks, 'the *whole* of anything is never told' (*N* 15). In a principle that was to control James's theory and practice of fiction and its epistemological grammar, the significance is in the 'management' of 'perspective' (77), in the exhibition of

> such parts of the truth as most nearly produce the effect of the whole. He who is deficient in the art of selection may, by showing nothing but the truth, produce all the effect of the grossest falsehood. (76)

There is a symmetry between aspects of Macaulay's essay and some of the contours of James's preface to *The Spoils of Poynton*, both writers detecting a fluid boundary between history and fiction. For Macaulay

> facts are the mere dross of history. It is from the abstract truth which interpenetrates them, and lies latent among them like gold in the ore, that the mass derives its whole value. (78)

Similarly, James declares in one of his first reviews an unwillingness to succumb to the Gradgrindery of a reductive empiricism he sees as factitious:

> Like Mr. Gradgrind in Dickens's *Hard Times*, what the novel-reader craves above all things is *facts*. No matter how fictitious they may be, so long as they are facts. (Rev. of *Two Men: A Novel* 616)

'The facts of history are bad enough', wrote James in *A Little Tour in France*, but 'the fictions are, if possible, worse' (64).

James has little truck with an 'imponderable dust' of a past (*HJA* 147) consisting of the 'sandbank of fact' ('She and He: Recent Documents' 750), or with what he derides as 'shining facts, grouped and piled like… Alpine ice-masses' (Rev. of *Hours of Exercise in the Alps* 1357); and in the preface to *The Spoils of Poynton*, he contrasts canine bone-sniffing and its ultimately destructive unearthing of the 'fatal futility of Fact' (*PSP* 1140) with an art that results in the alchemical transformation of skeletal remains into gold nuggets:

> Life being all inclusion and confusion, and art being all discrimination and selection, the latter, in search of the hard latent *value* with which alone it is concerned, sniffs round the mass as instinctively and unerringly as a dog suspicious of some buried bone. The difference here, however, is that, while the dog desires his bone but to destroy it, the artist finds in *his* tiny nugget, washed free of awkward accretions and hammered into a sacred hardness, the very stuff for a clear affirmation, the happiest chance for the indestructible. (1138–9)

In an implicit attack on Ranke and his school in 'The Art of Fiction', James appears, nevertheless, to arrange a reconciliation between what he had to acknowledge as the contiguous realms of history and fiction: 'the subject-matter of fiction', he observes, 'is stored up likewise in documents and records, and if it will not give itself away…it must speak with assurance, with the tone of the historian' (46). That 'tone' connects James with Macaulay, though, rather than with scientific history, and reveals the extent to which he is in the business of appropriation rather than affiliation. The approval of history and its methods begins in its correlation with the art of fiction, and it intensifies where the former converges with the latter. James's subsequent move demonstrates the potential enormity of the chasm between history and fiction, as he practises it at least:

> A novel is in its broadest definition a personal, a direct impression of life: that, to begin with, constitutes its value, which is greater or less according to the intensity of the impression. (50)

Facts, indeed the very data of experience, are, problematically, the material of both history and fiction; but James fears the stifling plenitude of facts coveted by the empirical researcher and the concessions extorted from art by life. That anxiety and exposure are ever proximate in James to facts emerges from the terms in which he eventually confronts the data of America in his own *The American Scene*:

> There would be a thousand matters—matters already the theme of prodigious reports and statistics—as to which I should have no sense whatever, and as to information about which my record would accordingly stand naked and unashamed. (353–4)

James squirms over Balzac's 'passion for exactitude', for '*all* the kinds of facts', and his being 'perpetually moved by the historian's impulse to fix, preserve and explain them', and he concludes that the 'artist of the Comédie Humaine is half smothered by the historian' (Introduction, *Two Young Brides* 93–4). Fearsome in Balzac, as he 'sees and presents too many facts', is a 'portentous clearness' alien to James's sense of art and of the past ('The Lesson of Balzac' 124).[12] For James, 'the image is thus always superior to' a 'thing itself' that is never the significant reality (Introduction, *Madame Bovary* 340), and he yearns not for facts as such, but for germs, traces, fractured anecdotes, and the like, as imaginative stimuli for the indeterminate reaches of fiction constituted as much, if not more, by what cannot be uttered and represented as by what can. Story-tellers in London society, regretted James, were besotted with delivering 'the greatest possible number of *facts*...facts, facts, and again facts'; they are 'the thing dearest to the English mind'. His craving is for 'some other school of talk' which handles 'the fact rather as the point of departure than as the point of arrival' (*William Wetmore Story and His Friends* 2: 204–5). Historians, for James, shared with photographers a destructive urge for completion, for an overwhelming aggregation of detail and, consequently, a shrinking of usable margins for the imagination:

> In this day of multiplied photographs and blunted surprises and profaned revelations none of the world's wonders can pretend, like Wordsworth's phantom of delight, really to 'startle and waylay'. ('Siena Early and Late' 513)[13]

The commitment of the scientific school of history, for James, was to the sterilities of restoration. The pursuit of the past in the interests of retrieval and the struggle for an objectivity that can only be specious, together with all attempts at completion, or even utterance, have dire consequences for the imagination: 'the work of restoration', he notes in *A Little Tour in France*, 'has been as ingenious as it is profuse, but it rather chills the imagination' (42). The usefulness of the past, or of what survives of it in the present, exists in inverse proportion to the degree to which its fragments and relics can be assembled and pondered, and this is the persistent refrain of the autobiographical writings. In surveying his own past, James acknowledges what had become by then a convenient plight:

> the historic imagination, under its acuter need of facing backward, gropes before it with a vain gesture, missing, or all but missing, the concrete *other*, always other, specimen which has volumes to give where hearsay has only snippets.

'*Complete* examples of the conditions' which inform present conceptions of the past are 'irrecoverable', so James is free to draw lines 'just where' he 'might most profit from' them (*HJA* 598). In 'Siena Early and Late', the emphasis at the outset is on a 'waiting scene' whose principal feature is the 'shallow horseshoe' of a Palazzo Pubblico 'void of any human presence'. The real significance of the 'waiting scene', present or past, however, is in the 'waiting'. Exploited is an alliance between grammar and state whereby a tenseless verb is transposed into a compound substantive forever suspended in realms of vacancy and the liminal (513).

The aims and methods of scientific historians, assured only of 'certain certainties' (T. S. Eliot, 'Preludes' 23), are rejected by James both on their own terms and as a rationale for fiction. He announces in 'The Art of Fiction' that

> experience is never limited, and it is never complete....It is the very atmosphere of the mind; and when the mind is imaginative—much more when it happens to be that of a man of genius—it takes to itself the faintest hints of life, it converts the very pulses of the air into revelations. (52)

There can only be speculations about how consternated Niebuhr, Mommsen, and especially Buckle would have been if invited to entertain their kinship with a writer who affirms that the 'novel is history' (46) and yet relies on the mystical process of converting the 'very pulses of the air into revelations', claiming the power of guessing 'the unseen from the seen' (53). But however much an adversary he makes of the scientific historian, James is still anxious to recruit and protect broader senses of history for novelistic purposes. This is the case, problematically, at least, in 1884; by the time of the 'fourth phase', history and senses of the past in general are sites of intense ambiguity and irony. In 'The Art of Fiction', although James states that the 'novel is history', the controlling analogy is between painting, the novel, and history. All three forms, in line with Macaulay's 'History' and its affinities with James's essay, are determined not by laws and facts, but by the contingencies of 'representation'. The 'only reason for the existence of a novel is that it does attempt to represent life', and in this respect James declares (leaving aside the question of what can be complete about any analogy) that 'the analogy between the art of the painter and the art of the novelist' is 'complete'. In what follows, history enters only to be subordinated to art and fiction by a carefully situated 'also' and 'allowed':

> as the picture is reality, so the novel is history. That is the only general description (which does it justice) that we may give of the novel. But history also is allowed to represent life. (46)

The historian is soon to be evicted, however, from this inhospitable accommodation.

In his attack on Trollope's 'terrible crime' of confessing to his readers that he is only 'making believe' (46), James appears to seek an alliance not only with the Macaulay of 'History' but also with Edward Gibbon, another historian whose literary, social, and moralizing aims were very different from those of the nineteenth-century German school. 'Such a betrayal of a sacred office', James argues in a passage worth examining at some length, 'shocks me every whit as much in Trollope as it would have shocked me in Gibbon or Macaulay'.

> It implies that the novelist is less occupied in looking for the truth (the truth, of course, I mean, that he assumes, the premises that we must grant him, whatever they may be), than the historian, and in doing so it deprives him at a stroke of all his standing-room. To represent and illustrate the past, the actions of men, is the task of either writer, and the only difference that I can see is, in proportion as he succeeds, to the honour of the novelist, consisting as it does in his having more difficulty in collecting his evidence, which is so far from being purely literary. It seems to me to give him a great character, the fact that he has at once so much in common with the philosopher and the painter; this double analogy is a magnificent heritage. (46–7)

A sequence of seemingly casual rhetorical gestures results here in the removal of history from James's poetics of fiction and a denial of what has just been so confidently proclaimed: the 'novel is history'. The novel and history are precariously united by a twin commitment to the pursuit of truth and the task of representation; but this position comes under siege from a battery of parenthetical equivocations. For the German school, truth is the destination of history; and for a second or two, it appears that James, too, is 'looking' for it. For James, however, truth is an initiating assumption: its premises have to be granted at the outset rather than validated by argument. Proximate is a principle he regarded as inviolable for the critical reading of novels aspiring to art: 'We must grant the artist his subject, his idea, his *donnée*: our criticism is applied only to what he makes of it (56). The process is teleological in that 'truth', like Aristotle's 'final cause', is both the end and the beginning, a terminal purpose that initiates.[14]

Small is the distance, however, between these manoeuvres and the idea that truth, often impenetrable in James's fiction and autobiographical writing, is an affair of contingencies available only to the artist, the corollary being that the past is there to be used and abused as a function of premises that cannot be challenged. The affinities are with Michel de Certeau's contention that 'History furnishes the empty frame of a linear succession which formally answers to questions on *beginnings* and to the need for *order*'. 'History', therefore, is 'less the result obtained from research than its condition' (12), and 'analysis' chooses '"subjects" conforming to its place of observation' (31). Elsewhere in this passage, James fractures a dependence on common evidence by insisting on the superiority, because there is 'more difficulty in collecting it', of the novelist's use of unspecified material beyond records and documents (the 'purely literary'); and 'representation' and the 'past', as bonds between historian and novelist weaken with the shift to 'illustration' and the 'actions of men'. James draws on the authority of Aristotle to prepare the way for the historian's demise at the hand of the philosopher. Aristotle posited that the 'objects' of '*mimēsis* are people doing things' (*Poetics* 92), and 'action' is at the centre of both Aristotle's and James's definition of 'mimesis'.

In substance, James's distinction between history and fiction, or 'narrative art', is similar to Aristotle's. For Aristotle, history differs from the 'narrative art' of 'epic' and 'tragedy' partly in terms of the more static requirements of the former: 'plots' in 'narrative art ... should not be like histories; for in histories it is necessary to give a report of a single period, not of a unified action' (*Poetics* 123). Although he was a jealous custodian of the need for particularity in fiction, James subscribes to the overall scheme whereby Aristotle is able to elevate poetry, or narrative fiction, over history. 'The essential difference' between poetry and history, held Aristotle:

> is that the one tells us what happened and the other the sort of thing that would happen. That is why poetry is at once more like philosophy and more worth while than history, since poetry tends to make general statements, while those of history are particular. (*Poetics* 102)

The power of poetry over history lies partly in its potential for dealing with probabilities bearing on the present rather than simply with moribund facts fixed in the past.

In 'The Art of Fiction', then, disappearance is the ultimate fate of the historian. What began as a triple analogy between history, painting, and the novel—history being subordinate, even so, to the other two—turns, by a process of prestidigitation, into the 'magnificent heritage' of what is now only a 'double analogy' between 'philosopher and painter'. In 'The Present Literary Situation in France', James takes an even longer 'stride':

> It is distinctly when we come to novelists—for I must make a long stride over historians, philosophers, and poets, sustained by the reflection that the best novelists are all three—that we remain rather persistently more aware of what is gone than of what is left. (118–19)

(ii) A 'stroll upon the Lizza'

By the time James collected his Italian travel writing in 1909—revising and extending previously published pieces, and adding new material—he was even less interested in making a space for historians in the house of fiction. Indeed, 'The Jolly Corner', published in 1908, a year before *Italian Hours*, the posthumously published and incomplete *The Sense of the Past* (1917), and the three volumes of autobiographical writings (1913, 1914, and 1917), the last volume of which, again, is incomplete and posthumous, all take issue with the low return for the imagination and critical interest in large-scale investments in history and the past, as distinct from senses of the past.[15] It is in these texts, as will become evident here and in subsequent chapters, that the use of the past more than occasionally turns to abuse as James forages and forges in the 'backward reach' of time ('Frances Anne Kemble' 1073).

In *Italian Hours*, documents and the history to which they have given rise appear and retreat, hovering in the margins of the text as the objects of irony, satire, and comedy. They offer at best but a limited communion with those residues, deposits, and relics available for conjecture rather then analysis and narrative. Such remains are worthless without the vitalizing capacity of the imagination. Even then, the affair is one of appropriation and fabrication rather than of the pursuit of facts and of the truth. What matters for James are the ways he evolves, on different occasions and in disparate genres, for putting the past to use. In any event, the historians, librarians, and archivists scattered throughout *Italian Hours*, as well as the writers of guide-books, like John Ruskin, who aspire to loftier forms, are projected as lacking in an imagination mitigated against by the very procedures they adopt. The result is a severing of the past from the present; it has become useless, in part, because too much rather than too little is known about it.

Nothing for James, and certainly not discursive mediations in the shape of history or historical records, could compare with a prolonged experience of Italy: 'Reading Ruskin is good; reading the old records is perhaps better; but the best thing of all is simply staying on' ('Venice' 289). With more than a hint of facetiousness at the expense of historians, and glancing back to 'The Altar of the Dead', James muses over a 'high historic house, with such a quantity of recorded past twinkling in the multitudinous candles' ('Two Old Houses and Three Young Women' 350). Places, above all relics and ruins—'sentient' ruins ('Roman Rides' 441)—and not records, license an appropriation of the past as a site of imagination and the imaginary, with its 'old voices, echoes, images' and 'endless strange secrets, broken fortunes and wounded hearts'

('Two Old Houses and Three Young Women' 352). But the location of the sentience, together with its quality and uses, is in the observer, in 'the principle of observation animating the mass' ('Balzac' 147), and not in the data. Here, with its inflection of sentimental fiction, is the 'element of the history of Venice' that preoccupies James. 'It is behind the walls of the houses', beyond the range of historians and the popular manifestation of their work in guidebooks, 'that old, old history is thick and that the multiplied stars of Baedeker might often best find their application' ('Two Old Houses and Three Young Women' 351, 356).

Such places, or so James likes to believe as he ponders an idea that dominates *The Sense of the Past*, can 'lead him back to the thing itself' ('A Few Other Roman Neighbourhoods' 486), and there 'one might live over again...some deliciously benighted life of a forgotten type' ('From a Roman Note-book' 483). Time consumes, and records fade, but what remains for the predisposed inquisitor in Arezzo is the 'after-taste of everything'; there, James was more than content, not carelessly, but 'systematically', to leave 'the dust of ages unfingered on the stored records' in the interests of a 'general impression' ('A Chain of Cities' 510). On the previous day, on the site of Hannibal's victory over Rome, a similar note is struck: imaginative senses of the spectral past survive and displace written history and its insubstantial collateral of dim records:

> Dim as such records have become to us and remote such realities, he is yet a passionless pilgrim who doesn't, as he passes, of a heavy summer's day, feel the air and the light and the very faintness of the breeze all charged and haunted with them, all interfused as with the wasted ache of experience and with the vague historic haze. (508–9)

James casts himself in the role of Richard Searle (a progenitor of Ralph Pendrel in *The Sense of the Past*), the passionate pilgrim whose 'latent preparedness' for 'English life' propels a thwarted obsession with the possibility of his, and an American, repossession of an Old World consisting of, like much of Italy for James, 'memories and ghosts and atmosphere' ('A Passionate Pilgrim' 543–44). At Hampton Court, Searle observes that

> There is a rare emotion, familiar to every intelligent traveller, in which the mind, with a great passionate throb, achieves a magical synthesis of its impressions. You feel England; you feel Italy. (554)

In a recuperative parody also at work in *Italian Hours*, this tale mocks the reading skills of a sentimental tourist whilst investing in the yield of his imaginings as the story develops into an American tragedy.

Its parsonage, retained to my modernized fancy the lurking semblance of a feudal hamlet. It was in this dark composite light that I
had read all English prose....'Well', I said to my friend, 'I think there
is no mistake about this being England'. (554–5)

The ironic tone of 'A Passionate Pilgrim', with the instabilities, masks,
and the shifting distances it produces, intensifies in James's fourth-
phase explorations of senses of the past. James adopts Searle's persona
of the sentimental tourist to challenge the arrogations of history by
alluding to and deploying a rhetoric of fiction (Searle's light is 'dark' and
'composite') that subordinates the data of the past to his own purposes.

The culmination of these moves, and James's belief in the superiority
over scientific historical methods of his own way with the past, is in
'Siena Early and Late'. There is an explicit attack on histories stemming
from those German sources identified by James as early as 1867 in
'Historical Novels':

The casual observer, however beguiled, is mostly not very
learned....But such as it is, his received, his welcome impression
serves his turn so far as the life of sensibility goes, and reminds him
from time to time that even the lore of German doctors is but the
shadow of satisfied curiosity. ('Siena Early and Late' 515)

James considers, momentarily, that he 'ought...to have plunged into the
Siena archives' (528), but his preference is for that 'pervaded or mildly
infested air in which one feels the experience of the ages' (529). The
'after-taste of experience' (528) he requires has to involve a reciprocal
relation between past and present. This reciprocation is critical to his
sense of the past as variably useful for, or susceptible to the designs of,
the present, and is there in the overheard snatches of life which the
letters, notebooks, and prefaces to the New York Edition suggest, if
problematically, as the origins, pretexts, and paratexts of the fiction.

For the scientific historian, this assimilation of the past for the purposes of the present—more than occasionally entailing, in the case of
James, its strategic reconfiguration by the present—is transgressive,
compromising as it does canons of objectivity and the pursuit of what
really happened. The mining image of 'Historical Novels' recurs in
'Siena Early and Late' as James associates the industriousness of the historian with less noble forms of production in cavernous depths. Having
stood 'at the mouth of' the 'deep, dark mine' of the archives, he
informs his readers that he 'didn't descend into the pit'. 'Instead', he
writes, bypassing the carbon and arriving at the diamonds more surely
thereby, 'I simply went every afternoon...for an amusing stroll upon

the Lizza'.[16] What follows is a deceptively languorous, slightly intoxi-
cated, account of a historical method which, although at some distance
from Ranke and the German school, is predicated on a systematic aesthetic position that cannot be detached from James's art of fiction as a
whole. Wandering in the town

> had its own unpretentious but quite insidious art of meeting the
> lover of old stories half-way. The great and subtle thing, if you are
> not a strenuous specialist, in places of a heavily charged historic
> consciousness, is to profit by the sense of that consciousness—or in
> other words to cultivate a relation with the oracle—after the fashion
> that suits yourself. (528)

In 'The Art of Fiction', James concludes that the 'deepest quality of a
work of art will always be the quality of the mind of the producer' (64),
and what he seeks in 'Siena Early and Late' are synergies between the
consciousness of the artist 'on whom nothing is lost' ('The Art of
Fiction' 53), and for whom the 'air-borne' particles of 'experience [are]
never limited' (52), and the 'heavily charged historical consciousness'
of Siena. What signifies, however, is less the historical consciousness
with which Siena has been imbued, more the 'sense of that consciousness'. It is this that the mining of the records and, by association, the
written history produced, stifles. Where 'experience at large' is the aim,
'the fine distilled essence of the matter, seems to breathe, in such a case,
from the very stones and to make a thick strong liquor of the very air'.

> You may thus gather as you pass what is most to your purpose;
> which is more the indestructible mixture of lived things, with its
> concentrated lingering odour, than any interminable list of num-
> bered chapters and verses. (528)

Not just history then, but its medium of language, its organization
in 'chapters and verses', and the records on which it depends, are
disavowed. In *Italian Hours*, decay appeals to James because it is a sign,
in the cadaverous image close to paradox employed here, of the 'indestructible mixture of lived things', of entities beyond intelligibility
whose vehicle can only be that of discourse.

Far from being excessively at ease with words, James struggled ceaselessly to demonstrate their limits. If 'a man's reach should exceed his
grasp' (Browning, 'Andrea del Sarto' 200), then ultimately, neither the

reach nor the grasp of language and its modes of representation can be commensurable with the reciprocities of the present and the past. The power of what cannot be uttered or represented always exercised a much greater influence on the theory and practice of James's fiction than the mere utterance of which historical writing was an 'interminable' example. At the Boboli Gardens in Florence, James's 'sense of *history*' is produced not by copiousness, but by a general air of silence, idleness, and abandonment:

> In the wide court-like space between the wings is a fine old white marble fountain that never plays. Its dusty idleness completes the general air of abandonment. Chancing on such a cluster of objects in Italy—glancing at them in a certain light and a certain mood—I get (perhaps on too easy terms, you may think) a sense of *history* that takes away my breath. (James, 'Florentine Notes' 567)

'Heard melodies are sweet, but those unheard/ Are sweeter',[17] for 'silence is articulate after all' (James, 'Browning in Westminster Abbey' 787).

(iii) The 'act of retrospect' and 'The Aspern Papers'

The preface to 'The Aspern Papers' expresses the main tenets of James's position on history, the past, and fiction at the turn of the century. It is because 'penetration fails' in the presence of Italy's 'great historic complexity', with the observer left scratching at the 'extensive surface', hanging about in the 'golden air' (*PAP* 1174), that James feels compelled to calculate the respective yields of the historian and the 'man of the imagination' in this predicament. The historian extracts less than the 'man of the imagination' in that the former uses, effectively, little of what overwhelms him, hindered as he is by the plethora of material that serves only to obstruct his access to the past; the latter, however, requires few facts, perhaps none at all, to stimulate that faculty of the imagination without which there can be no sense of the past, let alone a sense of that sense. The allegory of 'The Aspern Papers' is organized, then, around these realizations. The 'odd law' is that

> which somehow always makes the minimum of valid suggestion serve the man of imagination better than the maximum. The historian, essentially, wants more documents than he can really use; the dramatist only wants more liberties than he can really take. (1175)

In the presence of these obstacles and the inability of the methods of history to overcome them, James goes on to express his 'delight' in 'a palpable imaginable *visitable* past—in the nearer distances and the clearer mysteries', for with 'more moves back the element of the appreciable shrinks' (1177).

The more remote the past, then, the less useful or usable it is. James was fond, however, of exploiting the concrete and abstract reaches of what is 'appreciable', or 'valuable'. The association of 'appreciation' with 'interest' casts the writer, like the narrator in 'The Aspern Papers', in the role of a usurer, one for whom there are flimsy partitions between use and abuse. What the usurer shares with the writer of fiction and the painter, rather than with the historian, is an interest not in things as they are or were, not in merely 'what happened', but in how all this material presents itself to the consciousness of the 'man of imagination'.

The value, so to speak, of 'appreciation' is in its being 'after the fact'. It is a name

> we conveniently give, after the fact, to any passage, to any situation, that has added the sharp taste of uncertainty to a quickened sense of life. (*PDM* 1285)

In his preface to *The Princess Casamassima*, James writes close to the parable of the talents,[18] attracting for himself and the narrator of 'The Aspern Papers' the ambiguous moral and ethical position of the successful investor of other people's wealth:

> But the affair of the painter is not the immediate, it is the reflected field of life, the realm not of application, but of *appreciation*—a truth that makes our measure of effect altogether different. My report of people's experience—my report as a 'story-teller'—is essentially my appreciation of it, and there is no 'interest' for me in what my hero, my heroine or any one else does save through that admirable process. (*PPC* 1091)

The 'main condition of interest', as James further exploits mercantile senses of interest and appreciation in his preface to 'The Altar of the Dead', is the 'appreciable rendering of sought effects' (*PAD* 1258).

The events and actions of *What Maisie Knew* are of no consequence to James until they becomes part of Maisie's 'bewilderment'. At that point, in a novel that specializes in fabricating moral dubieties, it all becomes 'appreciable' (*PWM* 1163). Nothing detaches James more fully from the putative project of the scientific historian, and connects him so closely as autobiographer and writer of fiction to the mendacious world of 'The Aspern Papers, than the terms of his definitive statement on 'appreciation', the 'Beautiful Gate itself of enjoyment' (*PLM* 1234), in the preface to *What Maisie Knew*:

> To criticise is to appreciate, to appropriate, to take intellectual possession, to establish in fine a relation with the criticised thing and make it one's own. (*PWM* 1169)

Similarly, the documentary source of Browning's *The Ring and the Book* amounted to a 'mass of matter', but it is

> at the same time wrapped over with layer upon layer of contemporary appreciation; which appreciation, in its turn, was a part of the wealth to be appreciated. ('The Novel in *The Ring and the Book*' 793)

James's 'man of imagination', unlike the historian, possesses a 'thickness in the human consciousness that entertains and records, that amplifies and interprets' (*PAD* 1259). It is in this sense that the historian is consigned to boredom while James can experience the excitement of taking perilous liberties. The 'prose-painter of life, character, manners', suggests James in *William Wetmore Story and His Friends*, 'licensed to render his experience in his own terms, might do more justice' to his subject 'than the mere enumerator, to whom liberties, as they are called, are forbidden' (2: 196–7). James delighted in 'the intellectual extravagance of the given observer', especially 'when this personage is open to corruption': 'he may have to confess that the group of evident facts fails to account by itself for the complacency of his appreciation' (*The American Scene* 417).

In the narrator of 'The Aspern Papers', however, James combines a pathological historian—in the form of a literary critic, or editor—with a treacherous 'man of the imagination'.[19] He is cast in a Faustian guise: the quest for knowledge, as with so many of James's characters (Isabel Archer, Maisie, and the governess in 'The Turn of the Screw', among others), is presented as a transgression of limits and an indecorous mingling of the erotic and the scientific. There are reciprocal displacements in desires for and denials of access to the past and to the body, means and ends folding into each other, as attempts at penetration are made in both domains. The possibility of 'violating a tomb' (314) for papers Juliana Bordereau decided not to consign there after her death is equivalent to violating Miss Tita for the same purpose. In an economy of the search for knowledge carnal and historical, Tita, Juliana, and the papers are, at one level, concrete elements in the pursuit of Aspern and the past and metonyms of both. 'Miss Tita'

> had lived for years with Juliana, she had seen and handled the papers and (even though she was stupid) some esoteric knowledge had rubbed off on her. That was what the old woman represented— esoteric knowledge; and this was the idea with which my editorial heart used to thrill. (254–5)

What propels the tale is a failure to retrieve and represent the past constituted, in part, by the narrator's unwillingness or inability, to submit himself to the principles of sentimental fiction; a marriage with Miss Tita and access to the papers would have plunged 'The Aspern Papers'—which thus depends for its negative success on the narrator's failure as editor, historian, and fictional character—into the mire of melodramatic closure.[20] The narrator's rationalization of his refusal to marry Tita, as distinct from the possibility of less fettering forms of violation, results in a brutal evaluation of Tita and a whimsical, self-serving reassessment of the papers: 'I could not, for a bundle of tattered papers, marry a ridiculous, pathetic, provincial old woman' (316). Tita, Juliana, and the papers converge (the possessive pronoun of in 'their fate', in what follows, having ambiguous referents) as worthless commodities in the present rather than seminal vestiges of the past as the narrator indulges in sordid reflections on the state of his balance sheet:

> As my confusion cooled I was lost in wonder at the importance I had attached to Miss Bordereau's crumpled scraps; the thought of them became odious to me and I was as vexed with the old witch for the superstition that had prevented her from destroying them as I was with myself for having already spent more money than I could afford in attempting to control their fate. (317)[21]

Ultimately, Tita is scrapped, Julia bewitched, and an interest in the papers construed as mere superstition. Necessarily, for James's tale, the narrator has benefited neither from Macaulay's 'History'—advising, as it does, that a 'truly great historian would reclaim those materials which the novelist has appropriated' (87)—nor from that emphasis of James's, in 'The Art of Fiction', that the 'deepest quality of a work of art will always be the quality of the mind of the producer' (64). Inept, scurrilous, and highly limited in perception and intelligence, he is a carefully constructed target of the story's ironies, for he fails to realize the first principle of any discourse of the past: in the presence of the inexpressible, the writer must have the imagination to 'reconstruct and reconstruct of course' (*HJA* 79).

For Juliana Bordereau, the narrator is more and less than a composite historian and man of the imagination, he is a 'publishing scoundrel' (303) for whom writing about is always a prying into ('Do you write about *him*—do you pry into his life?' 269); he is 'like the reporter of a newspaper who forces his way into a house of mourning' (280). Gatekeeper of the past, custodian of the papers, and mortuary attendant of a kind, Juliana Bordereau (as borderer) patrols the line between the past and the appropriative designs of the present, denying access to the summit of any historical endeavour and thus preserving an absence which is the life of fiction and the death of history: 'The truth is God's', she insists, 'it isn't man's; we had better leave it alone. Who can judge of it—who can say?' (285). Relevant are de Certeau's observations that 'discourse about the past has the status of being the discourse of the dead'. The 'object circulating in it is only the absent', the 'dead' being 'the objective figure of an exchange among the living'.

> Through these combinations with an absent term, history becomes the myth of language. It manifests the very condition of discourse: *a death*. It is born in effect from the rupture that constitutes a past distinct from its current enterprise. Its work consists in creating the absent, in making signs scattered over the surface of current times become the traces of 'historical' realities, missing indeed because they are other. (46)

In 'The Aspern Papers', the past cannot yield to research, of whatever variety, the art of fiction or, ultimately, to any form of representation; the story itself as an artefact is predicated like language and discourse on the unavailability of the real.[22] The narrator's fetishization of the papers is a sign of the very absence of the past they signify, and on which the plot and story depend. What the story demonstrates is the 'gap' that exists 'between the silent opacity of the "reality"' that history 'seeks to express and the place where it produces its own speech' (de Certeau 3). The narrator experiences the extent to which the 'imaginary structures' that make up the 'signified' of his narrative, or 'historical discourse', are 'affected by a referent outside of the discourse that is inaccessible in itself' (de Certeau 42).

The narrative of 'The Aspern Papers' defeats the historical project of the plot and severs itself from that truth of the past suspended by Juliana Bordereau and left as such. Part of the aim of the story, as J. Hillis Miller has argued, is to explore longstanding relations between narrative and history and to demonstrate in the process the 'impossibility of knowing and possessing the historical past through narrative' ('History, Narrative, and Responsibility' 199). 'All that can be narrated', Miller continues, 'is the failure to see, know, possess, or uncover the actual events of the historical past' where those events, like the 'presumed affair between Juliana Bordereau and Jeffrey Aspern ... cannot be known from the outside' (202). Marrying Tita would have been no solution to the problem, for the narrator would then have been under the injunction of secrecy that results from being inside rather than outside. Miller's diagnosis of the problem is convincing as far as it goes, but it depends on a reductive sense of what constitutes an 'event'.

'A true historical event', reasons Miller

does not belong to the order of cognition. It belongs to the order of performative acts, speech acts or acts employing other kinds of signs in a performative way. Such an event makes something happen. It leaves traces on the world that might be known, for example the Aspern papers if they were published and read, but in it itself it cannot be known.

There are 'two kinds of knowledge':

One is the kind obtained from historical research or from seeing something with one's own eyes. That kind can be narrated. The other kind is that blind bodily material kind that cannot be narrated. We can only witness to it, in another speech act. (203)

Miller's commitment to the possibility of knowledge outside discourse is fundamental to his theory of semiotics. For Miller in *Hawthorne and History*, as for J. L. Austin, 'speech acts' unite language and the real, recuperating the 'blind bodily material kind' of experience otherwise erased in its narration. His account of the 'material embodiment' of signs bears interestingly on 'The Aspern Papers', but again, Miller has much more confidence in the real existence of events already constituted as meaningful, as distinct from their representation, than does James:

The exploding star and the earthquake are in this no different from the story. What is true of all three is true of historical events in general. The star and the earthquake too are signs, in the heavens, on the earth. They are signs that have a material embodiment, like all signs. They become history when those signs are read. (*Hawthorne and History* 114)

But earthquakes depend for their unity and identity as coherent events on the sign 'earthquake'. An earthquake moves into visibility as an 'earthquake' only when signified as such; it cannot be the 'material embodiment' of a sign: the sign embodies, or constructs, the earthquake. Signs, in ways neither Miller nor the narrator of 'The Aspern Papers' can acknowledge (initially, at least), are both the after-effects of an event and the means by which it is reconstructed and replaced. 'Signs' cannot 'become history' merely when 'read' as signs: a sign in isolation is not history; equally, signs in the aggregate require a narrative if history is to emerge. The history of an earthquake is twice-removed from the real occurrence it thereby doubly expunges: once by the sign 'earthquake' and again by a narrative which can never resemble, or reassemble, the real it impersonates or incorporates. A skewed representation of a real that is not only an over-plus of its sign, 'earthquake', but a spectre evacuating its meaning together with the narrative of which it might be a constituent, is ultimately as valueless as the papers incinerated at the end of James's tale.

Aspects of Miller's argument are similar to Joseph Roach's in his 'Culture and Performance in the Circum-Atlantic World'. For Roach, 'social memory and history as different forms of cultural transmission...function as forms of forgetting'. The alternative is to adopt a performative strategy in which the focus is on 'restored behavior...bodily knowledge, habit, custom'. Both Miller and Roach overlook the extent to which any retrieval or restoration of the performative has to be in a discourse that replaces and eradicates the past. It is less that 'cultures select what they transmit through memory and history', and more a question of the deletion such a transmission entails (Roach, 47). Roach suggests 'genealogies of performance' involve 'the study of restored behaviors in their diachronous dimension', and that this results in an 'approach' to 'literature as a repository of the restored behaviors of the past' (48). But 'restored behavior' is a contradiction in terms: 'reconstructed behavior represented in discourse' is closer to what might, or might not, be achievable.

Miller and Roach, unlike James, live in a world where the past has a curious potential for a non-textual existence. In reality, both Miller's knowledge of the past as history and his unknowable 'speech acts' of a 'blind bodily material kind' ('History, Narrative, and Responsibility'

203), and Roach's 'restored behaviour' are, like the past itself, nothing but textual refractions and refractory texts. What is 'refracted' is diverted or deflected (as in a ray of light through a lens) whereas 'refractory' elements are perverse and unmanageable, or untreatable in the case of a disease (*OED*). James's sense of the past involves a merging of these senses of 'refracted' and 'refractory' in that he sees discourse as refracting (supplying a mediating angle) what is also refractory or unyielding unless depicted in terms of absence and obscurity. The past, for James, is a patient with an obscure, often refractory, hurt which nevertheless (and productively so) compels refraction.

If Miller's difficulties in *Hawthorne and History* arise from his mistaking the 'veil' in Hawthorne's tale as a 'potentially unreadable' sign, or a sign whose readings are 'unverifiable' (97), they are compounded by his conflating of 'real', 'material', and 'sign'—'the real material sign'—and an unwillingness to recognize that 'the piece of black crape' (120), as distinct from its discursive representation, is as far from his grasp as Aspern's papers are from the tale's narrator. Whatever the incoherencies of Miller's position, however, it eventually leads to a definition of effectual allegory relevant to James and his way with the past: 'the most successful allegorical signs are those...that resist successfully any conceptual formulation of their meaning' (120). For James, however, the reality beyond the sign, which Miller mistakenly sees as always already significant, is suspended by a discourse that constitutes a sign with which it is necessarily and generatively incommensurable. The real is displaced or concealed by its speculative penumbra of multiple interpretations; far from resisting 'allegorical meanings' (120), the real of the past is a boundless site of construction interminably available. 'Actual events' and their amenability to representation are intensely problematic in James: he is much less willing to presuppose, or take as a given, the notion of a discourse-free event. On the evidence of *Italian Hours*, reinforced by his impressions in *The American Scene*, events have an elemental position in James's hierarchies of ontology and epistemology. For Hayden White, histories differ from chronicles in that the former consist of narratives which transform mere 'contiguity' (*The Content of the Form* 15) into meaningful structures and a moralized reality. Narrative is not, as Miller comes close to implying, an all but invisible vehicle of representation; it constructs the very events under narration and promotes them into meaningful structures.

De Certeau's approach to 'events' in *The Writing of History* has clear resonances with the James of *The American Scene*, and with his contention in his review of 'The Journals of the Brothers de Goncourt' that 'the effort of our time has been, as we know, to disinter the details of history' (422). History for de Certeau is a virtual tomb of the past, and in an interesting qualification of Miller's position, he argues that the function of 'language', or any talk about the past, 'is to introduce through *saying* what can no longer be *done*' (101). Out of the 'moving and complex mass' of the past, 'events' appear as a function of 'historiographical delimitation'. This 'procedure...allows the arranging of the unknown within a blank square prepared for it ahead of time and named "event"' (98). A body of history, with its periods, events, facts, and documents, is a function of 'setting aside' that which returns, like the repressed, to erode the very grammar of its narratives (72). In similarly setting aside documents that are a result of the same process, 'The Aspern Papers' offers a powerful analysis of these structures and of the extent to which the 'real', however illusory an entity, as distinct from the fiction that is the substance of the tale, is beyond the reach of its discourse. Commenting on the 'fatal *cheapness*' of the '"historic" novel' to Sarah Orne Jewett in 1901, James offers, in effect, some belated advice to his narrator:

> You may multiply the little facts that can be got from pictures & documents, relics and prints, as much as you like—*the* real thing is almost impossible to do. (5 October 1901, LL 360)

James's negotiations with the past, uncertain and self-serving as they often are, involve the centrality of his own superfine consciousness in an extension of the principle that observation animates 'the mass' ('Balzac' 147); and this is very much the basis on which he felt able to write *William Wetmore Story and His Friends*, a work in which his associations with the material, however distant and limited, and his treatment of the subject displace Story and his friends in a structure that anticipates the relationship between James and his brother Wilky in *Notes of a Son and Brother* (discussed in the next chapter):

> A subject is never anything but his who can make something of it, and it is the thing made that becomes the property....it is to the treatment alone that the fact of possession attaches....The treatment...is the man himself. (2: 234–5)

This allows James, in ways unavailable to the narrator of *The Aspern Papers*, to have designs on a past he can reconstruct, or construct. James acknowledges in *The Middle Years* 'how little I shall be able to resist' the 'force of persuasion expressed in the individual *vivid* image of the past', and an '*apparent* transfer from the past to the present of the particular combination of things' which is only ever an 'illusion...of the recording senses' (*HJA* 551–2). Correspondingly, Hawthorne's trade with Italy in *The Marble Faun* is condemned as 'factitious and unauthoritative' because this is

> always the result of an artist's attempt to project himself into an atmosphere in which he has not a transmitted and inherited property. (*Hawthorne* 445)

James abominated writing that combined an 'abundance of research' with a 'paucity of personal observation' (Rev. of *England, Literary and Social, from a German Point of View* 950), and he allocates forms of association and consciousness lacking in Hawthorne to Spencer Brydon in 'The Jolly Corner', and especially to Ralph Pendrel in *The Sense of the Past*. It is the intensity of their speculations about a past in which they have been involved, through forsworn alternatives and ancestry respectively, that enables its tenuous reanimation.[23] Both characters, like James himself, delight in the 'associations awakened by things', and in the extent to which the 'the magic of the arts of representation' trace 'these associations into the most unlighted corners of our being, into the most devious paths of experience' ('Alphonse Daudet' 230). In a move critical to James's art, such associations are to no avail unless a murky and obscure past has been fashioned from the outset, a past implied in part by senses of a 'smothered, unwritten, almost unconscious private history' (*The American Scene* 593). For the James of Newport, if in ways not quite intended by Emerson, 'history is an impertinence and an injury' ('Self-Reliance' 42). In any event, the 'act of retrospect', and the attempt to 'remount the stream of time', require 'one's imagination itself' to 'work backward' so that what is found can live again in the 'intelligence' (*PR* 1194). In *The American Scene*, this immediately becomes 'a question...of what one' reads '*into* anything, not of what one' reads 'out of it' (412) for history, as an affair of 'spectral animation',

> is never, in any rich sense, the immediate crudity of what 'happens', but the much finer complexity of what we read into it and think of in connection with it. (*The American Scene* 506)

Barthes's identification of the 'paradox which governs the entire question of the distinctiveness of historical discourse' has an acute bearing on James's conception of the tautological nature of historical representation:

> The fact can only have a linguistic existence, as a term in a discourse, and yet it is exactly as if this existence were merely the 'copy', purely and simply, of another existence situated in the extra-structural domain of the 'real'. (17)

In de Certeau's paraphrase of Barthes, the Aspern papers, artefacts and tale, seem even more proximate:

> The *signified* of historical discourse is made from ideological or imaginary structures; but they are affected by a referent outside of the discourse that is inaccessible in itself. (42)

If in *The American Scene*, the 'bleeding past' can be 'woundedly rescued from thieves' (632) and the task of history is to resist 'fatal penetration' (692), for de Certeau, similarly, historical narratives are structured by excluding the 'real' beyond its boundaries; but the body produced by this process, without which there would be no history, is wounded by the excisions of the past and continues to haemorrhage:

> The structure of a composition does not retain what it represents, but it must 'hold' enough so that, with this escape, the past, the real, or the death of which the text speaks can be truly staged— 'produced'. Thus is symbolized the relation of discourse with what it designates through losing it; that is, its relation with the past which it is not—but which could never be conceived without writing. (98–9)[24]

The disjunction between events and the past, and narratives and 'what happened', together with the conviction that historians presuppose the scheme of the past that determines their history, has its corollaries in the realms of representation and language in James's texts. Facts, events, and narratives are the means by which the world is fabricated, not the paraphernalia of its neutral representation. If history replaces the flux of the past with its own discourse, then language renders the 'real' variably intelligible by substituting its apparent coherence for the chaos beyond. Discourse, like historical narrative, assumes in advance the objects of its attention. With this realization, the lines dividing non-fiction from fiction, and use from usury, become thin indeed.

(iv) 'Rabid usury' in *The American Scene*

'The Aspern Papers' is part of a prolegomenon not only to James's deep scepticism about the possibility, or desirability, of historical knowledge, but to his growing suspicion of discourse, whatever the object realm. His preoccupation with the inarticulate relation between language and the real takes many of its inflections, rarely acknowledged, from the dark turns of science, philosophy, and the philosophy of history at the *fin-de-siècle*.[25] Henry Adams, concluding that the 'world' was 'no longer simple and could not express itself simply', (1010) resorted to the explanatory potential of force, 'satisfied' that as 'time-sequences' were 'the last refuge of helpless historians' (803)

> the sequence of men led to nothing and that the sequence of their society could lead no further, while the mere sequence of time was artificial, and the sequence of thought was chaos. (1069)

Consonant with the stress in Barthes and de Certeau on history's trade with the 'imaginary', Adams contemplates the 'staggering problem' of the 'despotism' exercised by 'an artificial order which nature abhorred' (1138).

If the real is 'a primary world of forms resisting intelligible practices' (Conley xvii), it corresponds with senses of that chaotic world beyond appearances which scientists such as Karl Pearson and Ernst Mach[26] unleashed towards the end of the nineteenth century. Order was only apparent; the intelligible world was the function of language in the form of synthesizing concepts or categories. In a hierarchy stretching from the turbulence of things as they are to an ordered universe, language bears the same relation to the real as narrative history to the past: both substitute symbols for a world that, ultimately, can neither be coded in language nor narrated. History and fiction have an equivalent status; they differ only in the claims they make on the real. Pearson launched a direct attack on positivist history, seeing it as 'all facts and no factors'.

> History can never become science, can never be anything but a catalogue of facts rehearsed in more or less pleasing language, until these facts are seen to fall into sequences which can be briefly resumed in scientific formulae....Only when history is interpreted in this sense of natural history does it pass from the sphere of narrative and become science. (301–2)

By the time of *The American Scene*, James's commitment to the power and originality of his own impressions, together with his sense of the conflicting relations between language, representation, and the real, was developing into what Henry Adams called the 'tragedy' of 'introspection' (1114), a solipsistic perspective whereby the compromise involved in acts of communication becomes more and more resistible. The burden is on the impossibility of utterance. What cannot be said conspires with what must not be said as the past is construed as a 'negative quantity' in a process far from unfamiliar to the Newport James (*The American Scene* 400). There is more in play than self-indulgence when James wryly informs his brother William that 'one has always a "public" enough if one has an audible vibration—even if it should only come from one's self' (23 July 1890, *HJL* 3: 300).

As early as 1879, in 'The Sentiment of Rationality', William James anticipated a central tenet of Bergson's in arguing that categories are a 'most miserable and inadequate substitute for the fulness of the truth'; and he is proleptic of de Certeau in concluding that such systems are a 'monstrous abridgement of things which like all abridgements is got by the absolute loss and casting out of real matter' (975). For Bergson, similarly, the intellect is allied to the discontinuous rather than to the flux of the real: 'just as we separate in space, we fix in time' (*Creative Evolution* 163). But whereas William James escapes 'gleefully' from the 'gray monotony' of linguistic abstractions into 'the teeming and dramatic richness of the concrete world' (976), Bergson's emphasis, like Henry James's, increasingly after 1900, is on the enisled condition of each consciousness.[27]

In *Creative Evolution* Bergson is at one with William James in concluding, generally, that 'life transcends intellect' (46), but his specific focus is on the overflow of the intelligible world by 'the state of consciousness' (200). The only reliable analogue for reality, whose 'very stuff' is 'duration' (272), is that 'mobility of being' that 'escapes the hold of scientific knowledge' (337):

> There is one reality, at least, which we all seize from within, by intuition and not by simple analysis. It is our own personality in its flowing through time—our self which endures. (*An Introduction to Metaphysics* 24)

What James registers, as he contemplates American history on the banks of the Concord River in *The American Scene*, and from which he unsuccessfully attempts to retreat in *The Sense of the Past*,[28] are the penalties and rewards for the artist of a self-communing detachment from language no longer regarded as mapping easily on to the real. A scepticism about the validity of history in all its guises has developed into a linguistic nihilism in which 'the letter killeth';[29] and all that survives, pendulously, is James's isolated consciousness.

At this carefully selected site of New World historical density, James recalls the minute-men episode, the effective initiation of the American War of Independence.[30] 'The Fight', reflects James, 'had been the hinge ...on which the large revolving future was to turn' (568). Now, though, routes to that past seem blocked: what is palpable no longer leads to the visible and visitable. The focus is on how little this scene, and the facts of history, can reveal, on the eventual imponderability of the experience, and on the impenetrability and silence of this data of the real:

> I hung over Concord River then as long as I could....It had watched the Fight, it even now confesses, without a quickening of its current....Not to be recorded, at best, however, I think, never to emerge from the state of the inexpressible, in respect to the spot, by the bridge, where one most lingers, is the sharpest suggestion of the whole scene—the power diffused in it which makes it, after all these years, or perhaps indeed by reason of their number, so irresistibly touching. (569)

The overwhelming impression, in a scene reminiscent of the 'inexpressive chaos' specified by William James as the stuff of the real (*The Principles of Psychology* 277), is of what little survives other than the simplifying residue, in all its ineffability, of what was: 'the small aspect, and the rude and the lowly, the reduced and humiliated'. Instead of the minute-men and what they immeasurably represent, the visitor has only 'the rude relics...of greatness' (570):

> I was much more struck with the way these particular places of visitation resist their pressure of reference than with their affecting us as below their fortune. Intrinsically they are as naught—deeply depressing, in fact, to any impulse to reconstitute. (571)

What would the meaning of these, or any other relics, be without a shaping foreknowledge pursuing a reciprocal response, imbuing them with a significance illusorily intrinsic for the scientific historian? James is in the presence here, in de Certeau's terms, of that 'blank square prepared for it ahead of time and named "event"' (98). Such events are modalities 'of the present' (292), 'interpretation' being 'constructed as of the present time' (4), and do 'not explain, but' permit 'intelligibility' (96):[31]

> The truth being perhaps that one wouldn't have been so met half-way by one's impression unless one had rather particularly *known*, and that such knowledge, in such a case, amounts to a pair of magnifying spectacles....Would the operative elements of the past...with the rest of the historic animation...have so lingered to one's intelligent after-sense, if one had not brought with one some sign by which they too would know; dim, shy spectralities as, for themselves, they must, at the best, have become? (*The American Scene* 566–7)

Acknowledged here is just how unrepresentable representative moments of the past are. For James, ultimately, as for Bergson, 'what is not determinable is not representable' (*Creative Evolution* 307). Forms of representation and narration, de Certeau's 'delimitation' (98), are mere substitutes for the overplus of what was, and the work of this discourse takes place in the present. If the real has no place in the symbolic order, relics are incommensurable with narrative representation; they function as the return of the repressed to evacuate the site of writing from which they have been excluded, reintroducing 'the real that was exiled from language' (de Certeau 42). But these relics, like Aspern's papers, are now only the 'present' signs of 'dead' things (Barthes 18); their 'sense' is always an 'after-sense', for 'relics are apt to be dead' ('Frances Anne Kemble' 1074).

'The Aspern Papers' defies Church's conclusion that the 'possession of the letters—either to have them or to eliminate them...would signify' the narrator's 'return to a position of mastery' (28). It is less that 'the letters' represent 'a text through which the narrator could incorporate and identify with his god' (Person, 'Eroticism and Creativity in *The Aspern Papers*' 28), more that this is the empty illusion exposed by the tale. The residues of the past are available for the use and abuse of the present entirely because 'the real is never any more than a meaning, which can be revoked when history requires it' (Barthes 18); in themselves, the remains of the past are void of all significance. A void, however, 'whether it be a void of matter or a void of consciousness', is '*always a representation which is full*' (Bergson, *Creative Evolution* 283). 'There is no essential difference between a past that we remember and a past that we imagine', suggested Bergson (*Creative Evolution* 294), and this is a view to which James subscribes, but with important modifications: an imagined past is much more serviceable, and the one can easily fold into the other.[32]

James is deeply ambivalent, however, in ways also to become apparent in his autobiographical writings, about an appropriative sense of the past seen as mingling liberation and loss. The symptomatic concept, again, is that of 'appreciation' (on which the New York Edition prefaces expatiate so extensively). The 'warm flood of appreciation', available only to a 'prepared sensibility' (566)—or to a writer pursuing the 'appreciable rendering of sought effects' (*PAD* 1258)—is accompanied by allusions, in the form of Shylock, to Shakespeare's *The Merchant of Venice* in which the homologies between appreciation, interest, and usury are made clear. For any reconstructor of the past

> there is a thing called interest that has to be produced for him—positively as if he were a rabid usurer with a clutch of his imperilled bond. (*The American Scene* 648)

Projected is an interest in the past at the expense of the dead that amounts to casting the historian as a necrolater. At issue is a use of the past, a sense of its relation to the present, from which the minute-men have been 'precluded' (569), and the fissure between their 'disinterested sacrifice' (570) and the virulent forms of interest now at work. The historian prospers only when the interests of the past in the future are subordinated to his own or ignored. But there is unease in *The American Scene* over accepted conventions for rationalizing a sacrifice of life in the past for the grasp of the present and future, and this is also the means by which the cultural work of history is metaphorized. In a double sacrifice, lives are lost for American independence and displaced for the purposes of historical discourse. Palpable, in de Certeau's terms, is history's need to constitute the past as a corpse; visible, too, is the vertiginous temporality of 'The Jolly Corner' and *The Sense of the Past* as the historian lurks in a future-oriented present baiting a trap for the past:

> Which all comes indeed, perhaps, simply to the most poignant of all those effects of disinterested sacrifice that the toil and trouble of our forefathers produce for us. The minute-men at the bridge were of course interested intensely, as they believed—but such, too, was the artful manner in which we see *our* latent, lurking, waiting interest, like a Jew in a dusky back-shop, providentially bait the trap. (570)

In the 'major phase', the energy is for the exploration of linguistic silences and absences, fractures and incoherencies, for testing the limits of signifying processes at all levels; in the fourth phase, as James finds himself pushed and pulled by the 'stream of time', these emerge as the penalties, rather than the rewards, of discourse.[33] What begins as a mild strain in James—his occasional references, for example, to objects which say 'more things to you than you can repeat' ('A Roman Holiday' 418), and to the 'incommunicable spirit of the scene' ('Lichfield and Warwick' 74)—becomes, in 1909, a plangent acknowledgement of the extent to which the past is both 'irrecoverable and unspeakable' ('A Few Other Roman Neighbourhoods' 487) as he resorts to 'mute eloquence' (Rev. of *Italian Journeys* 477). We are back, and much more urgently so, with the world of 'The Aspern Papers': language cannot be the means of any neutral, or objective, access to a past which it produces and from whose real absence it derives. The 'local present of proper pretensions' can only 'invent a set of antecedents', and

> to turn attention from any present hour to a past that has become distant is always to have to look through over-growths and reckon with perversions. ('Mr. and Mrs. James T. Fields' 162–3, 165)

If Stonehenge represents the 'pathless vaults beneath the house of history' ('Wells and Salisbury' 104), the relics of Concord, like the remains of Pompeii, momentarily appear to James as the 'immaterial, inaccessible fact of time' at last 'transformed' into tangible 'soils and surfaces' ('A Roman Holiday' 420). The stones of England can no more be interrogated, however, than the minute-men of Concord, and the soil of Italy requires that very narrative mediation which detaches it from the real.

> You may put a hundred questions to these rough-hewn giants as they bend in grim contemplation of their fallen companions; but your curiosity falls dead in the vast sunny stillness that enshrouds them, and the strange monument, with all its unspoken memories, becomes simply a heart-stirring picture in a land of pictures. It is indeed immensely vague and immensely deep. ('Wells and Salisbury' 104)

Agatha, in 'Longstaff's Marriage', has a much less intractable problem than James: 'But when I am dead...You can speak of me in the past. It will be like a story' (306). For Agatha, death is the beginning of a tale of the past; but for James and de Certeau, such discourses are the end of a real that can never be narrated as an incorrigible past susceptible to abuse may also, in turn, be abusive.[34] If 'Carlyle's expression was never more rich than when he declared that things were immeasurable, unutterable, not to be formulated' (Rev. of *The Correspondence of Carlyle and Emerson* 244), then for James there is 'official history' and a panoply of 'commemorative objects' which 'somehow leave the exquisite melancholy of everything unuttered' (*The American Scene* 569). But in the presence of the 'ineffable', of what is 'too deep and pure for any utterance' (*N* 109), and the 'unspeakable', 'unutterable', and 'abysmal' (*N* 240), James continued, however fitfully, to believe that 'you may in a particular case be eloquent without articulation', muffling thereby 'the ache of the actual' ('London Notes', 3 March 1897: 1397; 31 July 1897: 1400).[35]

2
'Wars and Rumours of Wars': Among the Soldiers

> And ye shall hear of wars and rumours of wars: see that ye be not troubled: for all these things must come to pass, but the end is not yet.
>
> (Matthew 24: 6)

> It was horrible leaving the court day after day and having to pass through a knot of renters (the younger Parker wearing Her Majesty's uniform—another form of female attire).
>
> (Max Beerbohm, Letter to Reggie Turner, 3 May 1895)

(i) Among the soldiers

'I am grossly ignorant of military matters', announced James in 'The British Soldier', 'yet...I am always very much struck by the sight of a uniform' (5). The 'close-fitting uniform of a soldier'—of 'clear blue toggery imperfectly and hitchingly donned' (*HJA* 456)—appears to have given him the same 'peculiar feeling' as that experienced by Jacobus X in the *Crossways of Sex* (1: 94). His admiration for the Horse Guards in particular suggests a severe case of what was popularly known as 'scarlet fever' (Weeks, *Sex, Politics, and Society* 113).[1] 'I never see two or three of them pass without feeling shorter by several inches':

> When, of a summer afternoon, they scatter themselves abroad in undress uniform—with their tight red jackets and tight blue trousers following the swelling lines of their manly shapes...it is impossible not to be impressed, and almost abashed, by the sight of such a consciousness of neatly-displayed physical advantages. (8)

Reflecting further on this 'heavy-handed picture', James observes that it is when he is 'armed and mounted' that the guardsman is at his most 'picturesque', and that on such occasions 'I am sure to make one of the gamins who stand upon the curbstone to see them pass' (9).[2] Towards the end of 'The British Soldier', and its continuous lingering over the tidiness of the soldiers' 'accessories' and the 'brightness and tightness of uniforms' (11), the ambivalent delights of soldiering are considered; but James fears that having 'too many masters' would weigh 'heavily against the assured comforts and the opportunity of cutting a figure'. He then recollects

> being told by a communicative young trooper with whom I had some conversation that the desire to 'see life' had been his own motive for enlisting. He appeared to be seeing it with some indistinctness: he was a little tipsy at the time. (11)

As rhetorical and ocular associations between James, street-boys, and military men give way to actual contact, the reader may be left wondering quite what this cultivated American, this sometime Brahmin Bostonian, was doing in the company of a drunken soldier in Aldershot.

The contention that soldiers were 'notorious from the eighteenth century throughout Europe for their easy prostitution' (Weeks, *Sex, Politics and Society* 113–14) is borne out by Mark André Raffalovich.[3] Acting as an informant in Havelock Ellis and John Addington Symonds's *Studies in the Psychology of Sex*, he writes:

> The number of soldiers who prostitute themselves is greater than we are willing to believe. It is no exaggeration to say that in certain regiments the presumption is in favour of the venality of the majority of men.[4]

Ellis reports that 'there is a perfect understanding in this matter between soldiers and the police, who may always be relied upon…for assistance and advice'. On 'summer evenings Hyde Park and the neighbourhood of Albert Gate is full of Guardsmen…plying a lively trade, and with little disguise—in uniform or out' (10n-11n).[5] 'Soldiers are no less sought after in France than in England or in Germany', correspondent 'Z' informed Symonds, 'and special houses exist for military prostitution both in Paris and the garrison towns' (*A Problem in Modern Ethics* 19).[6] 'The common soldier', Xavier Mayne[7] believed, 'likewise the soldier of better than humble grade, in almost every country, every military administration and garrison town, exercises largely clandestine prostitution' (*The Intersexes* 212). 'The skeptic'

> has only to walk around London, around any English garrison-center, to stroll about Portsmouth, Aldershot, Southampton, Woolwich, large cities of North-Britain or of Ireland, to find the soldier-prostitute in almost open self-marketing. (220)

This is not a state of affairs confined to Britain, for 'the Anglo-Saxon American is certainly highly homosexual, and when he is a soldier he does not lose that quality' (221). 'So far as I can see', wrote Jack Saul in his *The Sins of the Cities of the Plain*, 'all the best gentlemen in London like running after soldiers' (86):

> There are lots of houses in London for it....The best known is now closed. It was the tobacconist's shop next door to Albany Street Barracks, Regent's Park....The old lady would receive orders from gentlemen, and then let us know. (89–90)

There is little doubt that soldiers represented for James sites of com-promised authority, unstable boundaries, and furtive desire. That, at least, is often the effect of how he positions 'dusky soldiers of every shade clad in crimson and white' (Rev. of *Ismailia* 732). In the intro-duction to Kipling's *Mine Own People* (1891), he salivates over Kipling's 'love of the inside view, the private soldier and the primitive man' (1124), and admires, in particular, Mulvaney, 'a six-foot saturated Irish private' (1126) who provokes him into asking:

> are not those literary pleasures after all the most intense which are the most perverse and whimsical, and even indefensible?...Many a reader will never be able to say what secret human force lays its hand upon him when Private Ortheris...goes mad with home-sickness by the yellow river and raves for the basest sights and sounds of London. (1129)

The 'taste' and 'opportunities' 'for foreign contacts and free manners, for the natural, personal life', which 'are among soldiers and sailors common enough', are features of Pierre Loti's life to which James draws particular attention ('Pierre Loti' 489). Elsewhere, Venice has its 'tightly-buttoned officers' ('Venice' 291) and Milan its 'swarming red-legged sol-diery' and 'blue-legged officers' ('From Chambéry to Milan' 365, 367).

But in part, soldiers are seen as relics of the past, elements in a collage of the perversely picturesque and grotesque.[8] 'The soldiers, the mounted constable, the dirt, the dreariness, the misery' conjure up 'a mental image of the dark ages' in Rome ('Roman Neighbourhoods' 450); and in France, James finds himself in a 'barrack', with its 'extreme nudity and a very queer smell' (*A Little Tour in France* 236), reflecting on an earlier visit to Rheims that

> the net result of any little tour that one may make just now is a vivid sense of red trousers and cropped heads. Wherever you go you come upon a military quarter, you stumble upon a group of young citizens in uniforms. It is always a pretty spectacle....it is pictorial to be always *sous les armes*. ('A Little Tour in France' 744)[9]

The 'pretty spectacle' is usually, however, close to the unspeakable, or what cannot be named; and in the case of British soldiers, imperial contours, compromised and rendered intriguing by theatrical and feminizing elements, as in 'The British Soldier', are also part of what is ambiguous, admirable, and desirable. On Blackheath Common, James stumbles across a 'British soldier...with his cap upon his ear, his white gloves in one hand and his foppish little cane in the other'. Discovering that this soldier, who 'wore the uniform of the artillery', hails from Woolwich, and 'inspired again by vague associations', James hastens to the arsenal. He reflects on quite why a 'sentry-box' should 'set one thinking of the glory of this little island'; and this, he concludes, 'is more than I can tell' ('London at Midsummer' 143–5).[10]

It would be facile to conclude that an enthusiasm for uniforms and a propensity for lurking in areas notorious for male prostitution could reveal much about any individual's sexual orientation, but it has long been evident that Leon Edel was strategically over-cautious in his treatment of a sequence of intimate letters from James to Hendrik Andersen written in the early years of the twentieth century.[11] These letters, Edel tells us, along with those to Morton Fullerton, Howard Sturgis, A. C. Benson, Hugh Walpole, Jocelyn Persse, and others—'use words hitherto absent from his epistolary vocabulary—phallus, penis, bottom, *derrière*' (*HJL* 4: xvii). But Edel lowers the erotic temperature with his 'psychosexual', physical encounters as such being relegated to the safe territory of the 'imagination':

> At this distance it is perhaps less important to know the exact form James's psychosexual life took than to know that he was open to

feeling. He could now reach out to his younger friends, be loving and tender and embracing. Old inhibitions, old cautions had in part given way to what he himself called 'the imagination of loving'. (*HJL* 4: xx)[12]

Questions about the genital activity of a James 'probably ambivalent about sex' (*HJL* 4: xix) are ultimately imponderable and now largely redundant within the paradigm of 'de-essentializing currents in recent gender theory' (Sedgwick, *Tendencies* 73); although as Chapter 3 will argue, James's own anxieties about his posthumous reputation exploit the contours of bio-critical assumptions held at the time.[13] A 'gay' James is as anachronistic as a 'homosexual' one is historically limiting; and both imply that sex is what one is rather than something one might do from time to time. Sedgwick defines 'queer', however, a mobile category more appropriate for the textual if not the corporeal James, in terms that could apply to much of his fiction.[14] It refers to:

> the open mesh of possibilities, gaps, overlaps, dissonances and resonances, lapses and excesses of meaning when the constituent elements of anyone's gender, of anyone's sexuality aren't made (or *can't* be made) to signify monolithically. (*Tendencies* 8)[15]

But in relation to James, the problem is not simply one of 'homosexual', 'gay', or 'queer' sexual categorization or identification.[16] In circulation are illusions about the reach of language and the very possibility of meaningful utterance as compelled by those senses of mobility uncovered by a rhetoric of performance whose futile function is the preservation of a notion of an appearance-saving domain, essentially, of the real. The contiguities of the discourses of gender and sexuality with those of obscurity, secrecy, and privacy as constituted by a rapaciousness for the real are much more important than speculations about the uses to which James may have put any available orifices. In *Epistemology of the Closet*, Sedgwick commits herself to 'the performative aspects of texts' and to an underlying assumption directly relevant to my pursuit of the reciprocities between obscurity, the use and abuse of the past, and the homoerotic in James:

> the relations of the known and the unknown, the explicit and the inexplicit around homo/heterosexual definition—have the potential for being peculiarly revealing, in fact, about speech acts more generally. (3)

In part, as D. A. Miller has it, the mechanism involves the role of secrecy in the 'subjective practice in which the oppositions of private/public, inside/outside, subject/object are established' (207).

The uncoupling of sex and gender, or at least a realization that the body can be made to incarnate, represent, and perform gender in multiple ways only arbitrarily connected with sex, should move the business of performance, and considerations about who achieves forms of mastery over it, into the centre of any discussion of James and soldiery. As Sedgwick reminds us:

> the question of gender and the question of sexuality, inextricable from one another though they are in that each can be expressed only in the terms of the other, are nonetheless not the same question. (*Epistemology of the Closet* 31)

For Judith Butler, more fundamentally, 'gender is a kind of persistent impersonation that passes as the real' (viii)

> When the constructed status of gender is theorized as radically independent of sex, gender itself becomes a free-floating artifice, with the consequence that *man* and *masculine* might just as easily signify a female body as a male one, and *woman* and *feminine* a male body as easily as a female one. (6)

In this context, James between the lines, rather than between the sheets, is both more ponderable and more significant given that his fiction is not only a vehicle for performance but the supreme means, for him, by which grammars of performance, identity, and discourse are constructed and excavated: 'expression is creation', 'it *makes* the reality,' and it is altogether a performance superior to any 'reality' in that 'everything is saved' by novels whose style produces an 'image...always superior to the thing itself' (Introduction, *Madame Bovary* 340). Fiction is one of the principal 'discursive means' specified by Butler by which the 'fabrications' of the gendered self are 'manufactured and sustained' (136). 'Gender is always a doing', and '"the doer" is merely a fiction added to the deed' (24). 'There is no gender identity behind the expressions of gender' and 'identity is performatively constituted by the very "expressions" that are said to be its results' (25). In such a world, then, 'are we not moreover—and let it pass this time as a happy hope!—pretty well all novelists now?' (James, Introduction, *Madame Bovary* 346).

James's writing does not only, or even mainly, encode (or decode) sexual proclivities criminal at the time. He mobilizes mythologies of secrecy and privacy not merely, if at all, to conceal his sexuality, but to explore the question of whether illusions of secrecy and meaning, of a real beyond the world of appearances on which meaning and communication are predicated, can withstand the potentially destructive sense of all-pervasive indeterminacy released by a discovery that the real, experience, and performance not only conspire and coalesce, but are simply conterminous. Philip Horne has argued that just because there are instances of the unnameable in James, and that 'homosexuality has often been spoken of as the unnamable', it does not necessarily follow that James 'means homosexuality when he refers to something unnamable' ('The Master and the "Queer Affair" of "The Pupil"' 120). Leaving aside the quite considerable problem of what 'means' can itself mean here, I would argue that James's preoccupation with gaps, silences, perhaps the unnameable, and the like, are always more significant (as such) than the local business of sex or the homoerotic in themselves. Nevertheless, in a period (towards the end of the nineteenth century and beyond) when 'homosexuality' and 'silence', and its cognates, had become something of a collocation, James's investment in the former, however intriguing in itself, has its most telling yield in the terrain of the latter.[17] James is preoccupied with the malleability of the past, and productive barriers to disclosure, not because he is in the closet, bedroom, or barracks with men; he occupies these spaces, discursively if not actually, because they are as close as he can get to the tree of knowledge.

(ii) Telling tales

The significance of James's preoccupation with military uniforms cannot be detached from his oblique experience of Civil War combat. Saul Rosenzweig's analysis of the Newport incident focuses in part on the extent to which James's 'obscure hurt', more 'psychological' than 'physical',

> coming as it did at a time when *men* were needed by the country and were, like his own brothers Wilky and Robertson, answering the call...more surely constituted a proof of his powerlessness and crystallized a sense of impotence from which he never fully recovered. (84)

Rosenzweig's James is a patient in need of recovery who turns 'to the art of fiction' (85) for therapy, a fiction whose 'avoidance of passion' and 'overqualification' are 'largely traceable to such an implicit attitude of combined guilt and inferiority', expiation coming in part by his 'participation in World War I' (84).[18]

This is a comprehensive misunderstanding of the powerful tactics adopted by James to subordinate the Civil War to his own purposes, and its continuing consequences for the theory and practice of his fiction, a subordination partly predicated on the complex mobilization of his vague injury. Guilt and self-recrimination seem utterly remote from James's ecstatic recollections during the First World War of one supine Civil War experience. There is all of the passion of which Rosenzweig deprives him, and no sense whatsoever, even under the pressure of world war, of an earlier 'failure of masculinity',[19] or of any kind of compensatory imperative:

> I even invest with the color of romance, or I did at the time, the bestowal on me...of the precursory pages of Matthew Arnold's *Essays in Criticism*....I can still recover the rapture with which, then suffering under the effects of a bad accident, I lay all day on a sofa in Ashburton Place and was somehow transported, as in a shining silvery dream, to London, to Oxford, to the French Academy, to Languedoc, to Brittany, to ancient Greece. ('Mr. and Mrs. James T. Fields' 172)[20]

It is apparent from the notebooks just how pivotal James thought this moment in the essay; but whatever the severities of the accident, they are obliterated by Arnold in the preparatory note:

> don't drop above all the Matthew Arnold reference, and how he gave me the English pages of *Essays in Criticism*, then just out...to read in Ashburton Place, and with what intense emotion I read 'em. (*N* 537)

Occlusion and excision certainly characterize the handling of Ashburton Place and its demolition in *The American Scene*; but the overwhelming impression is one of enabling preterition. James alludes to

> the history of two years of far-away youth spent there at a period— the closing-time of the War—full both of public and of intimate vibrations. (543)

For Ashburton Place in particular, erased and therefore all the more alluring, James reserves an embroidery that enables him to 'tangle up' its associations with 'retrospect and make the real romantic claim for them' (542). There are 'old secrets to keep and old stories to witness for' concerning the onset of his 'literary career', but the absent house, as a convenient metonym of James's Newport wound, has left a 'gaping void' (543). Although there is a sharp 'sense' of a 'rupture', which leaves James with his 'early impression of the place' on his 'hands, inapt, as might be, for use', he is able as a consequence to 'try...to fit it to present conditions' (544).

The deep structure of the 'obscure hurt', in terms of empowering omissions and intricate covertures, appears as the house collapses—'success in life', we are informed in *A Small Boy and Others*, 'may perhaps be best defined as the performance in age of some intention arrested in youth' (HJA 50)—and because 'the interval back cannot again be bridged', James indulging in modest onanistic pleasures at its expense,

> we simply sit with our enjoyed gain, our residual rounded possession in our lap; a safe old treasure, which has ceased to shrink, if indeed also perhaps greatly to swell, and all that further touches it is the fine vibration set up if the name we know it all by is called into question—perhaps however little. (*HJA* 574)

When bemoaning the 'unsurvivable *back* of those...years' in his notebook (as memory and the corporeal coincide and conspire on the ambiguous site of that 'back'), James considers the 'strange little intensities of history' and the 'delicate little odd links in the long chain, kept unbroken for the fingers of one's tenderest touch' (*N* 239). More carnally, he relishes the prospect of being able to 'plunge'

> my hand, my arm, *in*, deep and far, and up to the shoulder—into the heavy bag of remembrance—of suggestion—of imagination—of art—and fish out every little figure and felicity, every little fact and fancy that can be to my purpose. (*N* 237)

In *Notes of a Son and Brother*, the 'tension' that arises out of the 'obscure hurt' has its homology in the war, which forms a 'cover for every sort of intensity, made tension itself in fact contagious—so almost any tension would do, would serve for one's share' (416). Conventional priorities, involving the individual and the community, and art and war, are inverted as the American Civil War, with its 'enveloping tonic atmosphere' (415), becomes a fortuitous arena in which the dimensions of James's Newport accident can be endlessly extended. For Paul Eakin, who finds it difficult to exorcise the ghost of Saul Rosenzweig, the 'obscure hurt'

> was principally a psychological event in which the young man earned for himself the right to what he had always been, one of life's noncombatants, and he did so, paradoxically, in the most heroic terms available to him at the time, those of the Civil War. (*Fictions in Autobiography* 108)

But however valid some kind of psychological paradigm might be in this context, it is far from the only one, or the most significant; and James's theory and practice as a writer, and especially the uses to which he put his accident, everywhere belie the ascription to art of a passive, 'noncombatant', status. For James, conscientious objection in the realm of the art of fiction was an anathema. The self-absorbed centralization of his injury is the means by which he both marginalizes the conflict and seizes on it, in a move he was to make repeatedly in the proximity of soldiers and war, as a delightfully serendipitous convenience.[21] It was also an indispensable context for an analysis of the performance of gender, and of performance in general, as all things military were arrogated in order to trumpet the superior might of fiction.

'All wars are meditations on masculinity' (Kimmel 72), and the American Civil War, far from being an exception to David Leverenz's proposition that 'manhood begins as a battlefield code' (73), is a defining example of the extent to which war is a theatre not only for testing and contesting gender, but a place in which some of its best performances can be seen.[22] At this level, the 'contagiousness' of war is relevant to James's campaign as a writer not only because he is able to fabricate a powerful, self-serving, alliance between his own predicament and the wounded soldiers he visits after the Newport incident, but also because both areas of experience, and experience in general, are constituted by a rhetoric of performance that discourses of war have a masculine interest in denying. But as an examination of William James on manhood and effeminacy demonstrates, gender and performance tend to figure prominently in any discussion or representation of war whatever the nominal agenda of a writer.

Drawing on ideas that first appeared in *The Varieties of Religious Experience*, where war is offered as a 'school of strenuous life and heroism' (332), and on a turn-of-the-century jeremiad promulgated by Theodore Roosevelt, among others, William James's 'The Moral Equivalent of War' considers widely held views that the battlefield is 'the only alternative' to 'degeneration' (1287), and that its '"horrors" are a cheap price to pay for rescue from' a world 'of clerks and teach-ers...of industrialism unlimited, and feminism unabashed' (1285).[23] In a qualified fashion, William James aligns himself with the 'anti-militarist party' (1289); but he remains firmly committed to the breed-ing of a 'martial type of character' (1292) under threat from a 'pacific civilization' (1291). He does not believe that

> peace either ought to be or will be permanent on this globe, unless the states pacifically organized preserve some of the old elements of army-discipline. (1289)

Conventionally enough, war is projected as the primary domain of masculine, heroic action; beyond it, there is merely a civilian, domestic sphere controlled by women amidst rampant feminization at the indus-trial, commercial, and cultural levels. Confident senses of the boundary between the masculine and the feminine come under siege, however, as the military life is characterized in terms of that very non-production, writing and art in general, that have made the regeneration of war, or its equivalent, so imperative.

In *The Varieties of Religious Experience*, the soldier is glorified as a 'man absolutely unincumbered' (291); he is free to act, therefore, in a 'theatre for heroism' (330) where there is not only 'war and adventure', but the 'beauty' of war (331), for 'war is the romance of history' ('The Moral Equivalent of War' 1284). Army-life has many 'elements of charm' ('The Moral Equivalent of War 1287), not least as embodied in soldiers who 'as ends in themselves', like works of art untrammelled by ques-tions of utility, are 'pure pieces of perfection' ('The Moral Equivalent of War' 1285). The 'higher aesthetic feelings' are juxtaposed in *The Principles of Psychology* with 'festivities, ceremonies, ordeals', and the 'solemn rites and exercises' of 'military power', 'the formation of armies and the undertaking of military expeditions' being among the ripest 'fruits' of man's sense of play (1045).[24] War and the aesthetic, then, together with fiction, performance, and the fluidities of gender, consort here in ways that are vital to an understanding of Henry James's con-tinuing encounters with soldiers and soldiering, and to a sense of the specific tactics of the Civil War stories of the 1860s. For William, as for Henry, the discursive strategies of 'soldiering', which lies 'always latent in human nature', are as central to the sphere of art as they are to a military one they ultimately conquer (William James, 'On Some Mental Effects of the Earthquake 1221).

'The Story of a Year' appeared in the same year, 1865, as James reviewed Walt Whitman's *Drum-Taps*. Whitman's poetry, and what he sees as its strident, vulgar, and opportunistic treatment of war, is subjected to intense vitriol and vicious irony. In tone and substance, we are some way in this early essay from Edmund Wilson's view that James's 'not taking part' in the war increased his 'tendency to dream and to brood, to be content to note personal impressions' (645). For James, Whitman is much more than one of the 'rhetorical time-servers and polished conventionalists' attacked in John Weiss's 1862 essay 'War and Literature' (199). His review is a vigorous condemnation of the 'violent sympathy' and haste with which Whitman, 'like hundreds of other good patriots', had sought to transpose the 'tumult' of 'battle' into verse and prose ('Mr. Walt Whitman' 629).

What emerges here is the extent to which James's accident, and certainly his subsequent meditations on it, were not simply a contrivance for avoiding the war to become a writer, but the means by which he could compel obscurity and cultivate that discourse and thematics of irony already more than embryonic in the first short stories. In what was soon to become a familiar refrain, as identified in the first chapter, James repudiates the relevance of mere facts to literature, but here the act of repudiation is at least as important as its object. There are homologies between James's non-combativeness in the narrow, military, sense, the peculiar detached engagement with the war he orchestrates in *Notes of a Son and Brother*, and an insistence that the finest art is dependent on a writer's occupying elevated vantage-points, even if that should be a sofa in Ashburton Place, from where distance and perspective can be organized. War is a formulaic experience best avoided given the ease with which its crudities can be transferred into fiction and poetry:

> *Of course* the tumult of battle is grand, the results of a battle tragic, and the untimely deaths of young men a theme for elegies. But he is not a poet who merely reiterates these plain facts *ore rotundo*.[25] ('Mr. Walt Whitman' 629)

For James as a writer, battles and casualties are the mere incidents and incidentals of war, and like the so-called facts and events of history, demand to be abused, reversed, and even perverted, if anything worthwhile is to ensue. In a contradiction of the idea that he felt 'war-making' contained no 'hidden sources of value' (Rose 237n), Whitman is berated for exactly this kind of myopia:

> for the poet, although he incidentally masters, grasps, and uses the superficial traits of his theme, is really a poet only in so far as

he extracts its latent meaning and holds it up to common eyes. ('Mr. Walt Whitman' 629)

In staying close to the front line, as James's metaphor implies, Whitman has overlooked a superior war for which actual fighting should only be the pretext. This, rather than 'private guilt and misgivings', is the 'flavour' (Aaron 113), James far from proposing that 'art', his art that is, 'was but a makeshift substitute for life' (Beebe 521): 'A great deal of verse that is nothing but words has, during the war, been sympathetically sighed over...because it has possessed a certain simple melody.'

> But Mr. Whitman's verse, we are confident, would have failed even of this triumph, for the simple reason that no triumph, however small, is won but through the exercise of art, and that this volume is an offence against art. (632)

James engrosses sacrifice and a nobler form of patriotism as he tells Whitman that 'art requires, above all things, a suppression of one's self, a subordination of one's self to an idea' (633). A treacherous space is constructed for the poet in which his writing, after a 'monstrous war', is the greater monstrosity: his poetry is 'spurious', a betrayal of a 'stern and war-tried people', and 'aggressively careless' (634).

In reviewing *Azarian* (again in 1865), James attacks Harriet Prescott Spofford for using 'far too many words' and for possessing 'in excess', and with some uncertainty as to what or who is the fatality, 'the fatal gift of fluency' (610) he detected everywhere in women's fiction in the 1860s and 1870s. The incontinent expression of *Drum-Taps* is seen as having something of this popular, vulgar, femininity: James sneers at Whitman's military credentials, disparages his nursing, and makes a self-fashioning assertion of the irrelevance to art of an active involvement in the war:

> it is not enough to have served in a hospital (however praiseworthy the task itself)....It is not enough to be rude, lugubrious, and grim. You must also be serious.

Having deprived Whitman of his manhood, James removes it from his equation of art and war altogether, along with the attributes that might propel a man into the army or, conventionally speaking, be acquired there:

> Your personal qualities—the vigor of your temperament, the manly independence of your nature, the tenderness of your heart—these facts are impertinent. (634)

Six months after the gender acrobatics of his 'The Story of a Year', then, re-forming 'masculinity' is offered as the main task for a writer in the realm of war. What James sought to avoid was that conception of 'heroes' developed, as Howells had it, by 'young-lady writers in the magazines' to fight 'the late campaigns over again, as young ladies would have fought them' (Rev. of *Miss Ravenel's Conversion from Secession to Loyalty* 121). 'To become adopted as a national poet', he informs Whitman's readers, 'it is not enough....to discharge the undigested contents of your blotting-book into the lap of the public'. The reader 'delights in the grand, the heroic, and the masculine; but it delights to see these conceptions cast into worthy form' (633).

The Civil War features prominently in three of the stories with which James began his literary career: 'The Story of a Year' (1865), 'Poor Richard' (1867), and 'A Most Extraordinary Case' (1868). Given James's emphasis in his review of *Drum-Taps* on the importance of 'latent meaning', his deliberate indirection, muted tones, and refusal to represent conventional heroism cannot be disposed of as merely the adoption of a 'Civil War...background' (Edel, *Henry James: The Untried Years* 236).[26] Carefully tangential, these tales are more an abuse than a use of the war, making it subservient to a campaign in which popular fiction, common assumptions about the unproblematic nature of representation, and torrid zones of gender come under a reviling scrutiny. Critical approaches to these tales are mired by biographical moves in which the 'obscure hurt' figures as the central recruit of reductive readings. John Ford in 'The Story of a Year', the Richard of 'Poor Richard', and Mason ('A Most Extraordinary Case') are versions for Saul Rosenzweig, again seminal in this domain, of that 'passional death' (88) which diverted James into a life of art and which was more or less the result of unconscious motivations whose aetiology is in psychological forces at work in his family. This line of argument, as far as it goes, is not without interest or pertinence; but there is little support for it in the fiction itself.[27]

Of the three tales, 'The Story of a Year' has both the greatest proximity to the war and greatest distance from it.[28] As Ford joins his regiment, the narrator declares:

I have no intention of following Lieutenant Ford to the seat of war. The exploits of his campaign are recorded in the public journals of the day, where the curious may still peruse them. My own taste has always been for unwritten history, and my present business is with the reverse of the picture. (34)

Like Charles H. Doe, the author of *Buffets* (1874), James has in his own purposive fashion 'brought the war into his tale, but he has left it standing at the door' (James, 'Recent Novels' 38). But if 'The Story of a Year', and much of the rest of James's fiction for Saul Rosenzweig, exists only as an indirect, or coded, manifestation of an inability to enlist and the 'passional' cost involved, it would be a meagre return on the discursive contrivance of the 'rich cover of obscurity' (*HJA* 414) and what it can be read as signifying. James has lived to tell a tale that disavows *Drum-Taps* and the sentimental war fiction of the popular magazines. More importantly, however, he is also able to disclaim 'the public journals of the day' and all forms of written history. What controls the story are anxieties in evidence from the outset about the representation and performance of gender and the proliferation of masks involved.

These specific corollaries of James's negative experience and the perspectives it enabled matter much more than a turn he was already taking towards the writing of fiction. The nature of James's encounter with the war sharpened his focus on the limits of language, on what can and cannot be uttered, and on the perils of too convenient a trust in appearances and their representation. This is the force of James's conclusion that his 'season of some retirement' at Harvard, which became a 'beauty' through the 'haze of time',

> was at least a negative of combat, an organised, not a loose and empty one, something definitely and firmly parallel to action in the tented field. (*HJA* 417)

'The truth is doubtless, however, much less in the wealth of my experience', wrote James in an extension of his use of 'negative' here, 'than in the tenacity of my impression' (*HJA* 60).

William James criticized these early stories for their 'want of blood' (Letter to Henry James, 4 March 1868: 37) and their lack of a 'warmth of feeling' and 'generosity of intention' (Letter to Henry James, 13 April 1868: 47) But in his comments on 'A Most Extraordinary Case', he came close to identifying the epistemological basis of his brother's commitment to the 'negative', and to seeing how it related to his ambition to achieve a detachment from what he regarded as the representational excesses (in particular) of women's writing:

> the scepticism and as some people wd. say impudence implied in your giving a story which is no story at all is not only a rather *gentlemanly* thing, but has a deep justification in nature, for we

know the beginning and end of nothing. (Letter to Henry James, 13 April 1868: 47)

Shortly after Ford goes into battle, Lizzie (the two are engaged as Ford joins his regiment) visits the 'great manufacturing town of Leatherborough' (40), where she attracts the 'tall, sallow' (41) Mr. Bruce. She learns from him that Ford has been seriously wounded. Divided in loyalties, she has a dream in which walking with a tall dark man who calls her his wife, she encounters the corpse of a wounded soldier who opens his eyes to say 'Amen':

> Then she and her companion placed him in the grave, and shovelled the earth over him, and stamped it down with their feet. (49)

If the 'villagers', initially, 'stamped' Jack 'a very Hector' (23), then here is stamping of a different kind as his body (in a fate similar to Hector's) becomes the object of his survivor's gaze. Lizzie has done no more than to take Jack at his word, even at the risk of burying him prematurely:

> I want you to beware of that tawdry sentiment which enjoins you to be 'constant to my memory'....There are some widows and bereaved sweethearts who remind me of the peddler in that horrible murder-story, who carried a corpse in his pack. (26)

After the dream, 'he of the dark eyes and he of the wounds were the two constantly recurring figures of Lizzie's reveries' (49).

Donning his uniform at the outset of the story, Ford experiences a 'sudden rush of manhood' (24), but Lizzie thinks about how he will look after the war is over. Ford has designs on a beard and masculinity, but another, more gender-compromising, fate is hinted at:

> 'I shall be all incrusted with mud and gore. And then I shall be magnificently sun-burnt, and I shall have a beard.'
> 'Oh, you dreadful!' and Lizzie gave a little shout. 'Really, Jack, if you have a beard, you'll not look like a gentleman.'
> 'Shall I look like a lady, pray' says Jack.
> 'Are you serious?' asked Lizzie. (25)

There is more to Ford's uniform than might usually meet the masculine eye. James arranges a revealing juxtaposition between a theatrical patriotism and the stuff of cheap romance, the 'great brightness' and 'blue and gold' of flamboyant military dress, and Lizzie's stockings:

> What blinding ardor had kindled these strange phenomena: a young lieutenant scornful of his first uniform, a well-bred young lady reckless of her stockings? (23)

If Ford is cross-dressed and feminized, then the manner of Lizzie's capturing and captivating Mr. Bruce completes a process whereby the 'reality of war' (23) involves not only a radical reversing of the 'picture' (34), but a realization that a picture, a performance of a rather indifferent kind, is all the war can be in a story where distinctions between war and romance, especially in terms of gender, collapse in the discourse of fiction. In asking 'might she not play the soldier, too, in her own humble way?' (36), the narrator mingles the feminine and domestic with the masculine and the military; however distinct they seem, both are intensely histrionic domains, war being 'operetta, at best, with guns' (James, 'American Literature', 7 May 1898: 679).

Railing against the sentimental grammar that constitutes her passive role sitting 'by the window knitting soldiers' socks' (35), Lizzie extracts herself from a popular story now moribund, and plans a battle of her own:

> John Ford became a veteran down by the Potomac. And, to tell the truth, Lizzie became a veteran at home. That is, her love and hope grew to be an old story. (39)

In a scene that parallels the tale's opening and foreshadows its end, Lizzie appears richly adorned and ready to enlist.[29] Ford and his battles are rendered peripheral in a campaign ultimately resulting in humiliation, the effective loss of his uniform there eventually giving way to its removal.

> Her skirt was of voluminous white, puffed and trimmed in wondrous sort. Her hair was profusely ornamented with curls and braids of its own rich substance. From her waist depended a ribbon, broad and blue. White with coral ornaments....One by one Lizzie assumes her modest gimcracks: her bracelet, her gloves, her handkerchief, her fan, and then—her smile! (41)[30]

At the party for which Lizzie has so meticulously prepared, and where she encounters Mr. Bruce, war and dancing, fighting and flirting, and uniforms and fancy dresses, are all of a piece:

> At eleven o'clock she beheld them linked by their finger-tips in the dazzling mazes of the reel. At half-past eleven she discerned them charging shoulder to shoulder in the serried columns of the Lancers. At midnight she tapped her young friend gently with her fan. (41–2)

According to Fahs, 'war romances became' such 'a staple' of 'numerous...monthlies and story papers' during the Civil War that by 1864, the Northern *Round Table* was condemning the vogue. The 'one thread of a plot' it describes is exactly what James rejects in 'The Story of a Year':

> They began with a heroine initially objecting to a lover's enlistment, 'weeping "bitter tears" upon his coat collar and murmuring—always murmuring—"I cannot spare you *now*!"' After his enlistment there followed news of a battle, in which the hero was 'reported killed, or there would be no little wholesome agony to depict'. Finally, at the end of the story he miraculously returned, so that the plot ended 'with a wedding on the part of the couple, and a yawn on the part of the reader'. This 'tissue of flimsy plot, dreary platitude, and sickly sentiment', the *Round Table* complained, 'floods the market of to-day, and gives us a healthy fear of opening the popular magazines'. (131)[31]

On his death-bed, Ford sanctions the union with Mr. Bruce which Lizzie has foresworn; and wearing the bloody army-blanket in which the wounded soldier returned, she prepares to take on that 'career of duty' (31) hitherto shirked. The narrator, however, has other intentions which, in keeping with the tenor of all three stories, are communicated negatively. 'I forbid you to follow me!' Lizzie tells Mr. Bruce. 'But for all that', the tale concludes, 'he went in' (66). The story ends by denying the validity of the question with which it begins—'for, when the hero is despatched, does not the romance come to a stop?' (23)—and Ford is mortally wounded as much in the successful campaign fought by Lizzie and the narrator as in battle. Ford dies cuckolded and unaware, far away from the dubious heroisms of war, and under the ironic gaze of Lizzie as Artemis, the virgin goddess of the wilderness, the hunt, and fertility:

> Poor Ford lay, indeed, not unlike an old wounded Greek, who at falling dusk has crawled into a temple to die, steeping the last dull interval in idle admiration of sculptured Artemis.
>
> 'Ah, Lizzie, this is already heaven!' he murmured. (64)[32]

In the three tales of the 1860s, the focus is on heroines rather than heroes, any battles are off-stage, and wounded, dying, soldiers, find themselves thwarted in a genre of sentimental fiction purged by unconventional shifts in plot, inversions of character-type, and coruscating narrators. Only the shabby tokens of war surface: enfeebled veterans are now hopelessly dependent on women who, more often than not, neglect or scorn them. These stories bear little resemblance, then, to Rebecca West's characterization of James's early work as 'pale dreams' which 'might visit a New England spinster looking out from her snuff-coloured parlour on a grey drizzling day' (24).

Major Luttrel in 'Poor Richard' has the role of a stock villain who cheats and lies in a bid to win Gertrude's hand and wealth; and it is Richard, a disintegrated love-sick farmer, who becomes 'abundantly a man' in Gertrude's eyes (207). 'A Most Extraordinary Case' opens with Mason, now only 'half a man' and therefore unable to 'fall in love' (275), 'undressed, unshaven, weak, and feverish' receiving his aunt in 'the uppermost chamber of one of the great New York hotels' (263). If Captain Severn in 'Poor Richard' attempts to capitalize on his largely bogus, certainly rather short, war record, then Mason has been totally enervated rather than masculinized, by the Civil War. In the world of romance, with its oppressive gender denotations, as well as in James's fiction at large, where predatory women like Lizzie and Miss Hofmann ('A Most Extraordinary Case') abound, the experience of soldiering counts for little. Mason's pursuit of Miss Hofmann is ineffectual entirely because of his heroic mutilations:

> 'He must be a strong man who would approach her', he said to himself. 'He must be as vigorous and elastic as she herself, or in the progress of courtship she will leave him far behind....She needs a man...complete, intact, well seasoned, invulnerable'. (284–5)

Mason's defeat is James's victory, however: he it is that authorizes Miss Hofmann's impenetrability in the presence of such an impotent siege.

That the emasculation of soldiers is not a capricious, incidental feature of these stories, and especially of 'The Story of a Year', is evident in a remark made by James to Thomas Sergeant Perry in which the tale, as a tail, takes on phallic dimensions:

> Do not expect anything: it is a simple story, simply told. As yet it hath no name: and I am hopeless of one. Why use that vile word novelette. It reminds me of chemisette. Why not say *historiette* outright? Or why not call it a bob-tale? (25 March 1864: *HJL* 1: 50)

Genre, gender, masculinity, and castration are figured and reconfigured here as pen and sword become inseperable. 'Chemisette' and 'historiette' imply a tale gendered feminine in which a soldier is smothered by a woman's chemise and cut down to size by an artful mastery of war and fiction. 'Unwritten' is the 'history' ('The Story of a Year' 34) of Ford's military exploits: they are confined to a 'historiette' which bob-tails them. If a bob-tail is erect, it is far from tall; and it depends for its existence on an act of mutilation uncomfortably close to castration.[33]

(iii) 'The last refinement of romance': Roderick Hudson and Wilky James

Even without the context of war, for a man to embark on the writing of fiction as a career in the 1860s would have been widely thought of as a queer move. As William Dean Howells noted in his infamous assessment of the situation, the professional writer was frequently ridiculed as a 'kind of mental and moral woman, to whom a real man, a business man, could have nothing to say after the primary politeness' (Lynn 283). 'At any time in the nineteenth century', Tony Tanner tells us:

> the American writer might have worried that his practice of writing fiction should be considered...unprofitable or useless (when compared with the manual and mercantile work which was building America), or degenerate or effeminate (when measured against some vague but strong notion of virility nourished by both the Puritan's and the pioneer's idea of what a man's work consisted of. In both cases some kind of mastery was believed in, mastery over the wilderness, over the community, over impulse, over the wayward fantasies of the imagination....) (*Scenes of Nature, Signs of Men* 48–9)[34]

Kimmel's emphasis is also on 'manhood' within a context of what he calls 'producerism', an 'ideology that claimed that virtue came from the hard work of those who produce the world's wealth' (29). Within the environment of war, Tanner's 'vague but strong notion of virility' takes on highly specific contours for the 'sons of the college professors, and of the city clergymen', not that distantly related to Henry James, of John W. De Forest's Civil War novel *Miss Ravenel's Conversion from Secession to Loyalty*. There is a resonance, at least, between the snobbery De Forest depicts and the revulsion against Whitman's vulgarity expressed in the *Drum-Taps* review: 'Not martial nor enthusiastic in character', they 'held aristocratically aloof from the militia and...from every social enterprise which could bring' them 'into contact with the laboring masses':

> It needed two years of tremendous war to break through the shy reserve of this secluded and almost monastic little circle, and let loose its sons upon the battlefield. (82)

William James's *The Principles of Psychology, The Varieties of Religious Experience*, and 'The Moral Equivalent of War' were written some decades after the start of the Civil War, yet the intensifying fears over degeneration and the feminization of culture registered there are part of a matrix of anxieties visible in the period immediately preceding the war and heightened by its outbreak. Before Confederate armies fired on Fort Sumter, and the advent of Henry James as a writer, hostilities in the marketplace of fiction tantamount to open war of a kind had been raging for some time. This, at least, was the perception of writers such as Hawthorne; and it is very much the perspective on the period offered by Alfred Habegger.

In a notorious letter to William D. Ticknor in 1855, Hawthorne wrote that

> America is now wholly given over to a d—d mob of scribbling women, and I should have no chance of success while the public taste is occupied with their trash—and should be ashamed of myself if I did succeed. (304)

Similar sentiments are also evident in Orestes A. Brownson's 'Literature, Love, and Marriage' (written in 1864 when the fate of the North was still very much in the balance), where the weakness of the American novel as presided over by women is all but identified as a cause of the Civil War itself:

> Not a man amongst us was found, at the breaking out of the present formidable Rebellion, able to solve a single one of the great problems it presented for practical solution.

'We have any quantity of fictitious literature', Brownson continues:

> fictitious in all the senses of the term, produced chiefly by women, and therefore weak, sentimental, preventing instead of aiding high national culture. We prize woman as highly as do any of our

contemporaries, but we have no great liking for feminine literature, whichever sex has produced it. (220)

That commentators such as Brownson located gender in the fiction, rather than in the author, was hardly likely to have diminished the problems of a Henry James arriving as a fledgling writer in a culture of 'producerism' antipathetic in any event to professional writing. To set foot in this territory was to be effeminate by definition; and to begin, in part, by writing Civil War stories in the wake of a lingering, perhaps malingering, state of invalidism was to compound the problem yet further.

'The fifties', Habegger contends, 'was the one decade in American history in which women wrote practically *all* the popular books'.[35] He sees, rather perversely and against the grain of the facts, both William Dean Howells and Henry James—sissies in a world of men, war, and business—as stemming exclusively from and writing entirely in opposition to what he calls 'the maternal tradition of Anglo-American women's fiction', rather than that of 'Hawthorne, George Eliot, Balzac, Flaubert, or Turgenev' (ix). James was unable to engage with the American male in the raw, especially the businessman, his early renown being for the 'meticulous study of American girls' (60). To write within and take on the female-dominated fiction of the 1850s, whatever the adversarial intentions, is for Habegger, 'always' to be seen as 'somehow feminine' (ix). The crux of his polemic, in which the validity of some of the parts is vitiated by the incontinent edifice of the whole, is established when Habegger concludes that 'James was so detached, so uninitiated' that 'early in life he failed to earn masculinity' and 'grew up a genderless man with a dark suspicion that all sexual roles and functions are sinister' (255).

Habegger offers little evidence for speculations that recuperate in a vertiginous mixture the psychological hypothesis proffered by Saul Rosenzweig and the crude castration theories of the 1920s and beyond. He posits a relationship—as did Rebecca West, Stephen Spender, Van Wyck Brooks, Hemingway, and others among the earlier critics—between the wounded body, within the context of gender and war, and a pathological set of fictional and stylistic preoccupations. Now, however, castration has given way to a less fevered sense of simple 'deformity': 'James's aborted masculine initiation...was finally a type of deformity, and...this deformity impaired his writing' (255). Habegger settles on three soldiers in particular in an effort to clinch his argument: the statue of Bartolommeo Colleoni in 'The Aspern Papers', Rowland Mallet

in *Roderick Hudson*, and Henry's brother, Wilky; these emblems of val-
our are contrasted with the effete, effeminate, and passive narrators of
'The Aspern Papers' and *Roderick Hudson*, both of whom are simply read
as surrogates for James.

But when the narrator scrutinizes the statue of Colleoni in 'The Aspern
Papers', there is much more in play than a 'parasitical young man', as
a Henry James surrogate, 'looking up at the tall warrior, who ignores
him' (262). Quick to consign James's style, with its intricate ironies, to
perverse, useless, unmanly categories, Habegger is then unable to avoid
conflating the narrator of 'The Aspern Papers' and Rowland Mallet in
Roderick Hudson first of all with the author of each text, and then with
the biographical Henry James. The passage on which Habegger dwells
comes towards the end of the story:

> I was standing before the church of Saints John and Paul and look-
> ing up at the small square-jawed face of Bartolommeo Colleoni, the
> terrible *condottiere* who sits so sturdily astride of his huge bronze
> horse, on the high pedestal on which Venetian gratitude maintains
> him. The statue is incomparable, the finest of all mounted
> figures...but I was not thinking of that; I only found myself staring
> at the triumphant captain as if he had an oracle on his lips....But
> he continued to look far over my head, at the red immersion of
> another day...and if he were thinking of battles and stratagems they
> were of a different quality from any I had to tell him of. (317)

It can only be 'as if' Colleoni has 'an oracle on his lips' and 'as if' he
were 'thinking of battles' now that he survives merely in bronze as a
work of art. In any event, as a victorious *condottiere*, he has more in
common with a Henry James who aligns himself with the Venetian soldier and the 'different quality' of his campaigns. The narrator is on the
brink of being vanquished for his mendacious and naïve mistaking of
the Aspern papers for the real, and for entangling himself in a badly
executed sentimental fiction in the process. Colleoni, in ways available
to Habegger if not to the narrator, is twice removed here: once by
'Venetian gratitude' and again by James into the masterful discourse of
his tale.

For Habegger, *Roderick Hudson* is the active, 'romantic conqueror'
pursued by a Rowland Mallet (in an obsession similar to the narrator's
for Aspern) who represents, at this stage, James's continuing desire to
become 'a man like other men'. Yet there is a form of parapraxis here
that reveals how intense the synergies are between art, war, and the

homoerotic, for Rowland's passivity is aligned with the 'homosexual, or at least the homophilic' (262).[36] In a move Habegger has long wanted to make, James the 'sissy' has now become 'homosexual', Habegger endorsing the generational, producer-driven, ideology within which the professional male writer was originally condemned in nineteenth-century America. As Foucault reminds us, gender and sexual orientation were inseparable from the imperative of production, and Habegger's approach demonstrates the enduring intensity of these connections:

> A single locus of sexuality was acknowledged in social space as well as at the heart of every household, but it was a utilitarian and fertile one: the parents' bedroom...sterile behavior carried the taint of abnormality....Nothing that was not ordered in terms of generation or transfigured by it could expect sanction or protection. (*History of Sexuality*, Vol. 1: 3–4)

Habegger's intention is to argue that as James was not a proper man (the defining characteristic of which is, of course, heteronormativity) his work evolved within traditions of sentimental realism in the 'feminine fifties' and, secondly, it was logical for him, subsequently, to retreat into anti-realism and symbolism with its self-consuming complexities and wilful isolation from the pragmatics of action and production. But in reality, James's writing is not a function of his compromised masculinity or his homosexuality for Habegger: he writes queerly, so he must be queer. This is the context of the founding castration myth in the 1920s during which Van Wyck Brooks 'laid the ground-work for linking James's removal to Europe and his "preciousness"', on the one hand, with his '"castration" or demasculinization, on the other' (Haralson, *Henry James and Queer Modernity* 195).

Habegger's use of 'naturalism' here, and the happy relation it has with the 'natural', is reminiscent of Lionel Trilling's attack on the lionization of the 'peasant' Dreiser at the expense of a James whose style, his 'awareness of tragedy, irony, and multitudinous distinctions', where there is a 'political fear of the intellect', consigns his work to the category of useless art (*The Liberal Imagination* 22–3). Obscurity, as in the 'obscure hurt', was always already, however, the means by which James took up arms against the sea of a culture valorized exclusively in terms of production, especially against what he believed was an inundation of women's writing. In a sense, we are back with correspondences between homosexuality and silence, or what cannot (or must not) be uttered, or communicated. Intercourse and discourse are near allied, and whatever is construed as being transgressive in the former will takes us to the limits of the latter. It was all irresistible for James, given his preoccupation at all levels with thresholds of experience, representation, and language.

Habegger tarries but little over his contention that the 'Civil War gave young men a supreme opportunity to validate their male prowess'; he pauses only to note that 'the closest' James 'came to war was by reading Wilky's fine letters written from the front' (261). He came, in fact, a little closer than that. Wilky's letters are the focal point of *Notes of a Son and Brother* in which his military exploits are transposed into an art that James has lived to master in a victory above and beyond more literal battlefields.[37] That James had no compunction in exercising an editorial abuse of the past, involving the appropriation of Wilky for aesthetic purposes in his autobiographical writing, is clear from one of the final letters to his nephew, Henry James III.

Harry protested against his Uncle Henry's carving up and arranging of the family letters to suit his own narrative purposes. James's position, in effect, was that 'what a man thinks and what he feels are the history and character of what he does' (*PPC* 1092). 'My own ethic', he pleads, with more than a slight shudder at the possibility of his having had to enmesh himself in facts, 'with no aesthetic whatever concerned in the matter, would have been the ideal of documentary exactitude, verbatim, *literatim et punctuatim*'. But as an artist (rather than a soldier or historian, say), James is not free from the obligation to live 'back imaginatively' into his 'unspeakable', Civil War 'contemporaneities' with Wilky. What happened—in any case now irretrievable unless one were, like the narrator of 'The Aspern Papers', to mistake documents for the real—could never take the reader of *Notes of a Son and Brother* to the truth of what was now, in any case, 'unspeakable'. What is 'unspeakable' is, in part, the aesthetic use to which James has now been able to put Wilky and the past. The 'editing of those earliest things, other than "rigidly"', has an 'exquisite inevitability' for James: it is a culmination of his realization that the abuse of the past is all there is, however convenient this may at times have been for him, given that its retrieval is unimaginable, impossible, and undesirable. (Letter to Henry James III, 15–18 November 1913, *HJL* 4: 800–1)

What Habegger ignores in *Roderick Hudson*, however pertinent his tracking of Rowland's sexuality, is the extent to which James relished rather than regretted, or treated as a humiliation, the 'throbbing affair' (*HJA* 475) of his vicarious Civil War experiences and the 'fairy-tale' of Wilky's military exploits (*Notes of a Son and Brother* 456). From the earliest short stories and *Roderick Hudson*, through to *The Bostonians*, 'Owen Wingrave'—who dodges the army 'not from cowardice, but from suffering' (*N* 67)—and the autobiographical writings, James's was no passive appropriation of the Civil War experience of others, but an active expropriation.[38] In *Roderick Hudson*, it is the possible correspondence between Wilky, as a type of the Civil War veteran James could never have been, and Roderick's brother Stephen that is critical, together with a specious connection, established only to be ruptured, between James and Roderick (rather than with Rowland) as artists. Rowland, confined and protected by his utter lack of imagination and possessing no artistic propensity, is able to submit to the entailment of a patriotism here ironically re-nominated as 'the great national discipline which began in 1861' (32).

In 'James Russell Lowell' (1892), James opposed 'patriotism', a 'purely practical...prescription of duty in a given case', to a world much too 'various and universal' to be circumscribed by its precepts (532–3).[39] The resonance here is with that first review of Whitman's *Drum-Taps*. In searching for a correlative for patriotism in everyday experience, James suggests that it is less an element of heroic adventure, more a simple reflex that has no 'place' in 'the foreground of the spirit', like 'a knack with the coiled hose when the house is on fire' (533). James returns, however unconsciously, to the very scene of the Newport fire; his failure to extinguish the flames without injury now represents a repudiation of a patriotism relegated from its potential proximity to the spirit, to art and the imagination, to the lower reaches of a mere manual dexterity. Similarly, that war as the 'romance of history' ('The Moral Equivalent of War' 1284) for which William James yearned is, for Rowland, merely the fulfilment of a 'duty' which was 'obscure' (as the war and Newport, again, become interchangeable) with 'ideal precision' (32).

Stephen's New England blood (Mrs. Hudson is from Massachusetts, but her husband was Virginian) 'ran thicker in his veins' (40), by contrast with Roderick whose voice was a 'soft and not altogether masculine organ' (36); but the reward for his early 'commission' is to be despatched by the narrator in the most perfunctory, formulaic, of fashions: 'He fell in some Western battle and left his mother inconsolable' (40). For the duration of this novel at least, the aesthetic adventures of the feminized Roderick are to displace the tedious adventures of war. From the perspective of New England and the result of the war, and especially for contemporary readers familiar with the usual grammar of popular Civil War fiction and its aftermath, the novel divides along perverse generic, gender, and national lines. The veteran is prosaic and dead, whereas the non-combatant who lives on has all the 'madness of art';[40] but Roderick's ultimately unsuccessful campaign as a sculptor in Europe is haunted by the unwritten memorial of his dead brother's war exploits. Roderick, 'who has a good share of the old Southern arrogance' (41), and Stephen represent a form of reversal that was to become associated with the 'myth of the lost cause' and the romantic construction of the Old South: war and victory are relegated to the North, whereas the South has the poetry of defeat.[41] The outcome for Henry James, however, is altogether another affair, and he organizes a deft transposition for Roderick in which he experiences a victory which, unlike the author's, is only fleeting.

One strand of the narrative, in ways which appear to correspond with the analysis of James's own predicament offered by Rosenzweig and Habegger, involves the notion that Roderick disintegrates as an artist partly in the wake of a weakly sublimated guilt over the death of his brother and a broad failure both to substitute for Stephen and to undertake, for his mother, the respective military and artistic roles of each. 'I have to fill a double place', he tells Rowland, 'I have to be my brother as well as myself'. That Roderick names the place where Stephen was mortally wounded immediately distances him from a narrator too aloof to do so, and it is the management of distance in James's narratives that so eludes Habegger:

> When he was brought home from Vicksburg with a piece of shell in his skull, my poor mother began to think she hadn't loved him enough....I have been very different from Stephen. (48)

That 'difference', in an echo of James's Ashburton Place idyll as he read Matthew Arnold in 1864, takes the form of those apparently degenerate, effeminate, alternatives to war castigated by William James, Roderick 'dreaming of the inspiration of foreign lands—of castled crags and historic landscapes' (65). James, with his cryptic experience at Newport hovering, suggested more than three decades after the war that 'our individual perception of human accidents insists on its perversities and may even disconcert our friends' ('Hubert Crackanthorpe' 841). Similarly, the occlusion of Stephen and his military adventures from the narrative, Roderick's abandonment of his mother for art and Europe, and his inability to confront the complexities of his part in a triad of relationships which include Rowland, Christina Light, and Mary Garland, are the cause and effect of what can be taken as one gloss on James's arts of fiction and autobiography: he has a 'strangely irresponsible way of looking at harmful facts' (162). He can reside only temporarily in any pantheon of art erected by James, however, in that he is unaware of art's predication on silence, withheld utterance, and obscurity: Roderick is disabled, in the main, by an 'extraordinary insensibility to the injurious effects of his eloquence' (287). Roderick finds himself more at ease with Christina Light, destructively so, than he does with mundane Rowland and the dutiful Mary Garland, for Christina has an appealing propensity (not unfamiliar to her author) for abusing the past to suit herself:

> She had a fictitious history in which she believed much more fondly than in her real one, and an infinite capacity for extemporized reminiscence adapted to the mood of the hour. (193)

Roderick's failure to compensate for his dead brother by occupying a 'double place' (48) results in a malaise whereby he is suspended between an exiled pursuit of art for which his powers are fading and a conventional marriage in Northampton, Massachusetts, to Mary Garland. But a rivalry in which Stephen can no longer participate between a 'New England' veteran soldier and a Southern non-combatant artist is re-calibrated in the final section of the novel as a contest between Rowland Mallet and Roderick over who has suffered, and is suffering, the more. Rowland's disapproval of Christina Light, and his exhorting Roderick to honour his engagement with Mary Garland, masks his erotic investment in both Roderick and Christina, the conduit for which survives in frequent visits to Mary Garland after Roderick's death. Rowland Mallet may have been the soldier, but he has had 'no occasion to play the hero', and Roderick has all the wounds. It is not so much that 'Mallet teaches Hudson to live' (Zacharias 119), more that Roderick Hudson eventually learns how to die:

> 'I have suffered, sir!' Roderick went on, with increasing emphasis and with the ring of his fine old Virginian pomposity in his tone....there are certain things you know nothing about. (335)

The feminized artist overpowers Rowland on his own ground, condemning him as a pacifist and a coward when it comes to women.[42] Victorious in a battle of a kind over Rowland, Roderick occupies at the last, and only momentarily, the position of soldier and artist. With audacious irony, he calls into question the normative sexuality of a man once a soldier in a war Roderick chose to avoid, implying that successful heterosexuality requires imagination rather than military prowess. However distant Roderick is from his author, and especially along this axis of romance and women, here is a victory organized, in turn, by a Civil War non-combatant who adopts the language of war in the camp of an enemy he, as an unsuccessful sculptor at best, turns into a gelding ('nothing to be touched'):

> Women for you, by what I can make out, mean nothing. You have no imagination—no sensibility, nothing to be touched!...There is something monstrous in a man's pretending to lay down the law to a sort of emotion with which he is quite unacquainted—in his asking a fellow to give up a lovely woman for conscience's sake when *he* has never had the impulse to strike a blow for one for passion's! (335–6)

That Rowland is now the victim, rather than the victor, is reinforced by the narrative's allocating to him that language of the 'lost cause' which the South had begun to adopt immediately after its defeat:

> he had an insufferable feeling of having been placed in the wrong in spite of his excellent cause. (341)

'Roderick had beaten him', and Rowland has become the ignominious Southerner (342). What kills Roderick, however, is not war, but his suicidal plunge; but Newport-like, the narrative obfuscates the injury to achieve a fictional transfiguration:

> He had fallen from a great height, but he was singularly little disfigured....An attempt to move him would show some hideous fracture, some horrible physical dishonour, but what Rowland saw on first looking at him was only a strangely serene expression of life. The eyes were those of a dead man, but in a short time, when Rowland had closed them, the whole face seemed to awake. (348)

If Roderick defeats Rowland on his own terms, then there are further and more enduring victories in meta-fictional realms for an author who re-masculinizes the genre of the romance at the expense of 'scribbling women', and challenges in the process the conventional gendering of war and writing.[43] More specifically, whatever the real fabrications on which Roderick's illusory victory depends, he did not, unlike Henry James, achieve an artistic mastery over his brother in the medium of a memorializing autobiography. *Notes of a Son and Brother*, which includes a sketch of 'G. W. James brought home wounded from the assault on Fort Wagner', dwells at length on Wilky's Civil War experiences, defying the chronology of events, before moving, like *Roderick Hudson*, to a climax in which Henry commandeers Wilky's 'heroism' by expatiating on his own injury. In any event, Henry's autobiography has become the sole means by which Wilky's exploits can be transmitted; and he is even allowed to benefit, as Henry's letter to Henry James III details, from an editorial hand that treats him as a compositional device. James may have lamented 'knowing' the war in an 'indirect and muffled fashion', but he nevertheless explains that Wilky's letters have to be organized so that there is no 'leakage in their characteristic tone' (*HJA* 382), and earlier reminds his reader: 'I like ambiguities and detest great glares' (*HJA* 299). Disingenuously presented is a contrast between 'outwardness' and 'living inwardly' (*HJA* 383) by a writer whose fiction constantly celebrates the dividends of the latter.

In *Notes of a Son and Brother*, not just the 'obscure hurt', but the obscurity of its representation, are altogether more interesting, because more enigmatic and fiction-compelling, than Poor Wilky's letters and wounds. As in the tales of the 1860s and *Roderick Hudson*, we are a long way from a guilt-ridden James squirming in the presence of soldiers. James interrupts his account of Wilky and the war, otherwise unfathomably, to give his impressions of an encounter with Charles Dickens in 1867. The only cowering 'military pressure' he comes under is from a fellow writer of fiction and his enigmatic reserve:

> But the offered inscrutable mask was the great thing, the extremely handsome face, the face of symmetry yet of formidable character, as I at once recognised, and which met my dumb homage with a straight inscrutability, a merciless *military* eye, I might have pronounced it. (*HJA* 389)

James recovers and constructs in his autobiography an 'intensity' the nature and power of which only he by virtue of his contrived vantage-point could have experienced; an intensity dependent, unlike the raw eloquence of Wilky's letters, on obscurity and the indescribable, on the 'obscure hurt', in fact. If 'living' is unavailable, what better than the 'act of living' (*HJA* 382):

> All of which, none the less, was not to prevent the whole quite indescribably intensified time—intensified through all lapses of occasion and frustrations of contact—from remaining with me as a more constituted and sustained act of living, in proportion to my powers

and opportunities, than any other homogeneous stretch of experience that my memory now recovers. The case had to be in a peculiar
degree, alas, that of living inwardly—like so many of my other cases;
in a peculiar degree compared, that is, to the immense and prolonged outwardness, outwardness naturally at the very highest
pitch, that was the general sign of the situation. (*HJA* 382–3).

James's 'appreciation' of the war is in the extent to which he has continued to use or abuse it, refining its horror into an exquisite romance
in which he projects himself as the hero. This is not James as 'elegist
and mourner', a 'rueful preserver of selected memories' (Aaron 115), or
the victim of Rosenzweig's 'passional death' (88):

> My appreciation of what I presume at the risk of any apparent fatu-
> ity to call my 'relation to' the War is at present a thing exquisite to
> me, a thing of the last refinement of romance, whereas it had to be
> at the time a sore and troubled, a mixed and oppressive thing.

What Wilky enabled then, as in the now of the autobiographical
act,[44] is a 'generalised pang of participation…all but touched' with 'full
experience' (*HJA* 383). In the notebooks, the mention of 'Poor Wilky'
immediately entails reflections on the 'grievous trial' of James's own
'ill-health' and 'physical suffering' (*N* 225); and pondered in *Notes of a
Son and Brother* is a 'risk' happily taken of 'appearing to make' his 'own
scant adventure the pivot' (*HJA* 284) of the early Civil War. 'The value
of everything' here, James posits, gains 'by me keeping my examples
together' (*HJA* 394). Some thirty or forty pages after Wilky's war-injured
return, as anachronies are exploited for the purposes of suspense and
self-glorification—'I jump considerably forward, for its (privately) historic value' (*HJA* 381)—James opens the wound of his 'obscure hurt',
declaring amidst the usable past he has moulded:

> I have here, I allow, not a little to foreshorten—have to skip sundry
> particulars, certain of the steps by which I came to think of my rela-
> tion to my injury as a *modus vivendi* workable for the time. (*HJA* 416)

Unquestionably, with that 'workable for the time' such a prominent
part of his analysis, James can be seen here as subscribing to the
view that 'the past is always still in flux, in the midst of being pulled
together in new configurations in response to the changing exigencies
of later moments' (Brodhead 4).[45] 'The Gettysburg Sunday,' James wrote

to Thomas Sergeant Perry after seeking some clarification about dates at the time of writing *Notes of a Son and Brother*,

> is happily a moveable feast—but how strangely one's associations with the far-off times & things get themselves twisted & turned. (Hoffmann 548)

Wilky assists not only in the act of re-membering in *Notes of a Son and Brother*, but also in the production of a prosthetic memory.[46] It is more than curious, much more, that James should select the word 'perpetrate', with its transgressive connotations, when characterizing his autobiographical activities present and prospective to his nephew Harry in 1914:

> If I am myself able to live on and work a while longer I probably shall perpetrate a certain number more passages of retrospect and reminiscence. (Letter to Henry James III, 7 April 1914: 4: 806)

(iv) 'Oranges and peppermints'

We can now return to Aldershot and the question of why James was carousing there with a 'tipsy' young soldier. 'The British Soldier', when refracted through the lens of the Civil War tales, offers much more than salacious evidence for James's genital orientation. To be a soldier is no more than, or involves as much as, playing at being a soldier; and where there is play, inversions and perversions abound. For a writer pre-occupied from the beginning with the limits of language, the quiddity of gender, and the boundless reach of performance at all levels, the soldier was a necessary object of attention. What matters in James is less that an army camp or battlefield is a bastion of essential masculinity, more that a realm of such intense essentialism easily transposes, through the trials of manhood in ritual training, regimentation, parade, and battle, into liminal zones governed by a discourse of performance by which, in any event, it has always been constituted.[47] Without a knowledge of essentializing processes and a sense of how fabricated the reality-effects of language are, there could be no art for James; and such processes become visible only in forums of strenuous essentialism. Like Ford at the outset of 'The Story of a Year', these soldiers are in dress uniform and on parade; and exhibiting themselves, they become exhibitionists.

More is involved here than 'erotic pleasure' and 'intellectual satisfaction' in James's construction of 'subject positions no longer tied to strict gender and sexual binaries' (Rowe, *The Other Henry James* 29). As parade slips into play, and the gaze becomes ever more theatrical and homoerotic, only James as an artist can exert any essential mastery. In a supreme reversal, it is only from the apparently passive position of the observer that active domination at an epistemological and aesthetic level is possible. Tellingly, General Grant's letters serve only to remind James 'not so much of what is required as of what is left out to make a man of action' (*American Letters*, 16 April 1898: 661); and in 'Pierre Loti', the contrast between the soldier as 'the man of action and the man of observation' leads to the conclusion that it is the 'poor sedentary folk' who can write about 'great things' (490). More curiously, Gabriele D'Annunzio, James believed, 'would have kept his bottom sound, so to speak, had he not remained so long at sea' ('Gabriele D'Annunzio' 936). Manhood 'functions to...transform fears of vulnerability or inadequacy into a desire for dominance', Leverenz argues (73), and 'feminization represents just another strategy for humiliating men of power' (243–4). Critical here, though, rather than simply the humiliation and feminization, are forms of 'representation' and 'transformation' so radical, because tested and developed on a site of indefatigable resistance, that when combined with the disfiguring effects of a homoerotic gaze reveal how tenuous a hold there is on the real even (and especially) in one of its most hallowed sanctuaries.

As James recollects the 'remarkably good-looking' Edward Ferrero much admired by 'mothers' in *Notes of a Son and Brother*, he recounts his 'bounding into the military saddle' only to conclude that he 'had all the felicity, and only wanted the pink fleshings, of the circus' (*HJA* 136). Similarly, Gus Barker 'threw himself into the fray, that is into the cavalry saddle, as he might into a match at baseball' (*HJA* 307). 'There hung about all young appearances at that period', wrote James with the exception of his own fiction to hand, 'something ever so finely derivative' (*HJA* 450). The desirability of the British soldier has to be set alongside this emphasis on the theatrical and the performative familiar not only from the Civil War tales, but also from William James's excursions into the military world. Soldiers are 'actually ornamental' but only 'potentially useful' ('The British Soldier' 3), and when 'armed and mounted', they are most 'picturesque'.[48] The 'rattling, flashing,[49] prancing cavalcade of the long detachment of the Household troops' strikes James as 'the official expression of a thoroughly well-equipped society', but he reserves his particular admiration for the 'tight, dark-blue tunics' of the Hussars' 'yellow braid' embroidery (9). As for the 'Rifle Brigade'

> there is a kind of severe gentlemanliness about this costume which, when it is worn by a tall, slim, neat-waisted young Englishman with a fresh complexion, a candid eye and a yellow moustache, is of quite irresistible effect. (10)

James is overwhelmed, in an emphasis acutely relevant to an over-dressed and cross-dressed Lieutenant Ford in 'The Story of a Year', by the 'brilliant fancy dress' (10–11) of the soldiers he encounters. They are 'cushioned and curtained' in 'huts' that resemble 'pretty' houses (perhaps of ill-repute) in 'Mayfair' (12). 'On this occasion at Aldershot', in an atmosphere 'more theatrical than military'—'the place looked like a "side-scene" in a comic opera'—and amidst 'such a delightful entertainment', James felt as if he were 'at the Hippodrome' (13). Inside the theatre itself, James can subject soldiers as the victims of an illusion, and now appearing as an illusion of an illusion, to even greater ridicule and ribaldry. In a performance of *Henry V*, he delights in 'the grotesqueness of the hobby-horses on the field of Agincourt' as he focuses through his 'opera-glass' on the 'uncovered rear of King Harry's troops' ('Notes on the Theatres' 60–1).

Contrary, perhaps, to popular and conventional opinion, carnival, all forms of misrule, cross-dressing, passing, and gender-bending in general thrive in war. Elizabeth Young has argued that in Louisa M. Alcott's Civil War *Hospital Sketches, and Camp and Fireside Stories* (1869), 'the vocabulary of carnivalesque gender confusion represents an embattled form of access to masculine agency' (71). Young further explores the prevalence of the image of the 'cross-dressed woman soldier' in the 'journalism, memoirs, and fiction about the war' (149). These women 'capitalized on their resemblance to the image of the soldier as a beard-less, adolescent boy' which functions 'as a figure of rhetorical excess' (149–50). Once masculinity, partly by virtue of this rhetorical excess, is perceived as an object of performance, gender boundaries become less, rather than more, stable in the vicinity of war. War has often been interpreted, in a belief that reaches back to William James, Theodore Roosevelt, and beyond, as a regenerator of 'normative maleness' (Gutterman 227).[50] These are the terms, of course, on which James has been indicted for his 'obscure hurt' and the further obscurities it generated. But as Gutterman contends, war is more effective as the supplier of 'places of slippage where the standards of gender are undermined or contested' (227).

Lizzie's desire to 'play the soldier' in 'The Story of a Year' (36) became a reality for a number of women in the American Civil War. Women who so easily disguised themselves as men, in effects not dissimilar to those identifiable in James's prose essays and prose fiction, made 'transparent those fixed and immutable barriers between the sexes', blurred 'distinctions', and raised 'questions about how they are maintained' (Wheelwright 28). For a 'male soldier', the 'homosocial world of the military afforded new opportunities for the expression and representation of homoerotic desire' (Young 169). In 1864, at an army ball in Massachusetts, 'young soldiers cross-dressed as prostitutes'. 'We had some little Drummer boys dressed up', one participant wrote to his wife,

> and I'll bet you could not tell them from girls if you did not know them...some of them almost looked good enough to *lay* with and I guess some of them did get laid with. (Young 184)[51]

The carnival of war, and the contingencies it releases, surface in James's Civil War tales and essays, then, in two distinct manoeuvres that cohabit intensely: one involves the projection of soldiers as objects of homoerotic desire, compromising a masculinity their military credentials fail to shore up; and the other represents them as occupying the feminine-gendered position of victim. Both exploit the 'multiple contradictions... found at this supposed core of masculine experience' (Morgan 176–7).

In his First World War essays, it is the soldier overthrown and unmanned that interests James. Lizzie becomes a soldier of a kind by refusing to knit any more socks ('The Story of a Year' 36), and nearly half a century later, socks still figure in James's registration of the extent to which war reveals just how mobile gender identity is in a world constituted by the mere superficies of discursive performance. He writes of 'the strong young men (no men are familiarly stronger)' who are 'mutilated, amputated, dismembered in penalty for their defense of their soil against the horde and now engaged...in the making of handloom socks' and 'to whom I pay an occasional visit much for my own cheer' ('Refugees in England' 166). There is neither squeamishness nor abjection here in the presence of what might have been regarded as incriminating stigmata. The 'obscure hurt' and the discourse of obscurity it liberates have resulted not in an abusive past that must be entombed, but in an abuse of the past that has become an art of fiction and the framework of an autobiography. This is a fragile position, however, as we shall see in Chapter 4, and James is unable to extend it much beyond *Notes of a Son and Brother*.

In the meantime, the distance travelled by James since the end of the Civil War can be measured by considering the shift in his attitude towards Walt Whitman. If the bitterness of the early *Drum-Taps* review (1865) gives way to a qualified sweetness in an 1898 essay where Whitman is praised for an 'original gift of sympathy' and a 'homely, racy, yet extraordinarily delicate personal devotion' ('American Literature: 7 May 1898: 671), then 'dear old Walt' (*HJA* 424) has to ingest saccharine at toxic levels in *Notes of a Son and Brother*. Whitman's soldierly aspirations are still treated with contempt, but now the masterly weapon is superfine irony mingled with comedy, rather than crude invective. James invokes Whitman as he recollects his own visit to wounded soldiers at Portsmouth Grove. It is in the immediate aftermath of this visit that James felt able to blur the distinction between his injury and the wounds of battle, and develop that useful analogy between war and writing. The image James conjures up of the soldiers he meets, in an elevated language designed for the extra height it gives him, is as aloof, absurd, and vindictive as any he produced. He drew from each soldier

> his troubled tale, listened to his plaint on his special hard case—taking form, this, in what seemed to me the very poetry of the esoteric vernacular—and sealed the beautiful tie, the responsive sympathy, by an earnest offer, in no instance waved away, of such pecuniary solace as I might at brief notice draw on my poor pocket for. Yet again, as I indulge this memory, do I feel that I might if pushed a little rejoice in having to such an extent coincided with, not to say perhaps positively anticipated, dear old Walt—even if I hadn't come armed like him with oranges and peppermints. (*HJA* 424)

If the Civil War has its apotheosis in *Notes of a Son and Brother*, then the final indignity for the 'American soldier in his multitude' is to become there 'the most attaching and effecting and withal the most amusing figure of romance conceivable'.[52] Yet the spectre is still that of confusion, obscurity, and what cannot be said:

> the great sense of my vision being thus that, as the afternoon light of the place and time lingered upon him, both to the seeming enhancement of his quality and of its own, romance of a more confused kind than I shall now attempt words for attended his very movement. (*HJA* 424)

3
Shakespeare and the 'Long Arras'

For presence is better than absence, if you love excess.

(Frank O'Hara)

(i) Delia Bacon and the American abuse of Shakespeare

In his preface to Rupert Brooke's *Letters from America*, James lingers over the spectre of a dead poet he casts as 'young, happy, radiant, extraordinarily endowed and irresistibly attaching', 'virtually'[1] meeting 'a soldier's death...in the stress of action and the all but immediate presence of the enemy'.[2] Transformed by death into an image, the beatified corpse of the poet seems no longer susceptible to the 'erosion of time', or available for that 'reference' whose pressure is resisted at Concord (*The American Scene* 571):

> but he is before us as a new, a confounding and superseding example altogether, an unprecedented image, formed to resist erosion by time or vulgarisation by reference, of quickened possibilities, finer ones than ever before, in the stuff poets may be noted as made of.
> (Preface, *Letters from America* 749)

The allusion to *The Tempest*—'the stuff poets may be noted as made of''[3]—like those to *The Merchant of Venice* in the musings on the American War of Independence (*The American Scene* 570), are part of a general tendency James developed for recruiting Shakespeare in the proximity of the unutterable. What James construed as the unassailable enigma of Shakespeare's life and work evolved into a necessary constituent of the grammar of obscurity and secrecy that generated his fiction and shaped his personal anxieties about the possibility of present and posthumous forms of exposure. James's eagerness to suspend Brooke as a biographical subject has affinities with the process whereby Shakespeare's position in a paradigm of imponderability is utilized: paradoxically, generations of prying scribblers seem to have protected rather than penetrated the apparent mysteries of his life. Questions of what can be covered or discovered, exposed or concealed, and published or kept private, are at the centre of an aesthetic whose deep structure is always a binary of absence and presence, of silence and utterance.

Delia Bacon's *The Philosophy of the Plays of Shakspere Unfolded*, published in 1857 with a preface by Nathaniel Hawthorne, was at the centre of nineteenth-century attempts to contest the authorship of Shakespeare's plays.[4] Delia Bacon saw irreconcilable disparities between Shakespeare's life, and the very fact that so little was known about it, and the power and originality of the plays. 'In essence', argues Budd:

> the Baconian theory was an illogical extension of the worship of Shakespeare as a moral philosopher. It was made possible by the dearth of knowledge about Shakespeare's life and by the misty claims of popular biographies. It further fed on the many uncertainties concerning the plays' texts. (359)[5]

If an obscure writer can produce great writing, however, then a logical move for James, with the careful trappings of his obscure hurt to hand, was to assume that such obscurity was indispensable to it. James dismissed Delia Bacon's hypothesis, more or less, yet he shared a fascination for the conundrum she helped to construct. To Violet Hunt he wrote:

> Also came the Shakespeare-book back with your accompanying letter—for which also thanks....You rebound lightly, I judge, from any pressure exerted on you by the author—but *I* don't rebound: I am 'a sort' of haunted by the conviction that the divine William is the biggest and most successful fraud ever practised on a patient world. The more I turn him round and round the more he so affects me. But that is all—I am not pretending to treat the question or to carry it any further. It bristles with difficulties, and I can only express my general sense by saying that I find it *almost* as impossible to conceive that Bacon wrote the plays as to conceive that the man from Stratford, as we know the man from Stratford, did. (26 August 1903: 432)

What connects James with Shakespeare at one level is 'fraud', a necessary activity when attempting to retrieve a past otherwise useless. Deception and art are happy conspirators in this anti-Stratfordian context, and the creative and self-creative processes of 'Shakespeare' seem to depend on a real or imagined obscurity both congenial and troublesome to James.

The use and abuse of 'Shakespeare' in the construction of a national canon of literature was well established before he became a focus of debates about American cultural independence and specificity. By the end of the eighteenth century, Shakespeare had become the 'quintessential "English" author' (Gorak 63) in a 'paradoxical' manoeuvre whereby 'modernity generates tradition' (Kramnick 1). Such a canon provides (in ways akin to the strategies of James' autobiographical writings) a 'retrospective pattern that becomes a "usable past" and a simultaneous order', playing a 'part in campaigns of cultural nationalism' (Gorak 87–8).[6] Aspects of Shakespeare's nineteenth-century American reception are fundamental to an understanding of the theories of history and biography underpinning Delia Bacon's *The Philosophy of the Plays of Shakspere Unfolded* and James's engagement with problems of bio-critical fact and fiction in 'The Birthplace' and elsewhere.

Shakespeare was a momentous challenge to early republicans. Writers like Orestes A. Brownson, George Wilkes, Melville, and Whitman later, were unwilling to share in a rebarbative adoration for a Shakespeare whom they saw as representing the Old World and its aristocratic rigidities. Shakespeare, argued Brownson, is 'not exactly the literature for young republicans', and the 'constant and exclusive study' of it 'cannot fail to be deeply prejudicial to republican simplicity of thought and taste' ('Specimens of Foreign Standard Literature' 72–3). What detained George Wilkes, making it more likely for him that Francis Bacon wrote the plays, was the 'singular anomaly...of a genius...who was born in comparative humbleness' and yet never revealed 'one emotion' for 'the down-trodden classes' (11).

Melville's admiration of Shakespeare, whose radical influence on him can hardly be disputed, was far from unequivocal.[7] He found the melodramatic Shakespeare of the early American stage contemptible, dwelling instead (and unforgettably) on

> those deep far-away things in him; those occasional flashings-forth of the intuitive Truth in him; those short, quick probings at the very axis of reality. (163)

Nevertheless, 'let us away with this Bostonian leaven of literary flunkey-ism towards England' (167), he exhorts, and looks forward to the day 'when you shall say who reads a book by an Englishman that is a modern?' (165).[8] Whitman sacrificed his recognition of Shakespeare's stature on a demotic and democratic altar: 'The great poems, Shakspere included, are poisonous to the idea of pride and dignity of the common people, the life-blood of democracy' (*Democratic Vistas* 282). His later quixotic move, however, and an index of the cultural turbulence provoked by Shakespeare at the time, was to announce the postponement of democracy as he harried over the 'rude, coarse, tussling facts' of 'lives' needing

> just that precipitation and tincture of this entirely different fancy world of lulling, contrasting, even feudalistic, anti-republican poetry and romance. On the enormous outgrowth of our unloos'd individualities, and the rank self-assertion of humanity here, may well fall these grace-persuading, *recherché* influences. ('Poetry Today in America—Shakspere—The Future' 321)

Within this context, it is Emerson's 'Shakespeare; or, the Poet' (1844), together with Jones Very's 'Shakespeare' (1839), that sets the stage for America's later expropriation of Shakespeare by offering a theory of personality and the artist that privileges obscurity and proscribes attention to the particular lives of individual writers.[9] Emerson and Bacon, in quite different ways, can be seen as vital determinants of James's anxious, and ambivalent, use of Shakespearean obscurity.

Preoccupations with America's belatedness and its cultural dependence on the Old World were twin-born, of course, with its political independence. In Emerson's 'The American Scholar', 'over-influence' is the 'enemy of genius', and the 'English dramatic poets' are charged with having 'Shakespearised now for two hundred years' (298). But Emerson's real objection is to the adulation of a localized, individual, non-representative Shakespeare, a Shakespeare susceptible to possessive and unyielding scholarly investigation. The vulgar imitation of Shakespeare practised by English dramatists, and subsequent American imitations of that imitation, had failed to penetrate beyond his material and bodily irrelevance, beyond that local and historical specificity out of whose lack in the infant republic of America Emerson makes a virtue.

The historical Shakespeare, however problematic the history, was a huge obstacle for burgeoning American writers in search of cultural distinctiveness. The solution for Emerson and his fellow-travelling transcendentalists was to seize on the Shakespeare mystery, on the opaqueness of his origins and life, and the apparent chasm between what little was known of these and the plays he wrote and produced, in order to evacuate the history. Crucial to this is Emerson's definition of a great man as one who can 'abolish himself, and all heroes, by letting in' the 'element of reason, irrespective of person; this subtiliser, and irresistible upward force' that destroys 'individualism' ('Uses of Great Men' 167). 'Of the universal mind', wrote Emerson in 'History', 'each individual man is one more incarnation'; Shakespeare cannot be interesting and significant in himself, for it is 'this universal nature which gives worth to particular men and things' (8). Even the plays themselves are an eventual irrelevance given that the 'true poem is the poet's mind' (16) and that 'universal nature, too strong for the petty nature of the bard, sits on his neck and writes through his hand' (25).

Delia Bacon's obsession with the question of attribution would have been scorned as ephemeral and sublunary by Emerson: he, along with Jones Very, sought to promote Shakespeare as a supreme example of a dispersed and attenuated self ventriloquized by the spiritual and divine. Far from being perplexed by the puzzle of how Shakespeare could have written such sublime and erudite plays, Emerson exploited it to demonstrate the representative, universal, and spiritual (rather than material) essence of greatness: Shakespeare is 'the farthest reach of subtlety compatible with an individual self' ('Shakespeare; or, The Poet' 121).

Predictably, Emerson saw little value in attempts to excavate facts about Shakespeare's life and expresses an abhorrence of any historical remains. The 'Shakespeare Society' (116), 'elated with success, and piqued by the growing interest of the problem', has

> left no book-stall unsearched, no chest in a garret unopened, no file of old yellow accounts to decompose in damp and worms, so keen was the hope to discover whether the boy Shakespeare poached or not, whether he held horses at the theatre door, whether he kept school, and why he left in his will only his second-best bed to Ann Hathaway, his wife. (117)[10]

Such 'gleaned...facts' can 'shed no light upon that infinite invention which is the concealed magnet of his attraction for us' (118). 'Shakespeare...the only biographer of Shakespeare' is released from corporeal and cultural bondage by a simultaneous erasing of the category of individualism and that incubus of nascent America, history:

> It is the essence of poetry to spring, like the rainbow daughter of Wonder, from the invisible, to abolish the past, and refuse all history. (119)

Established here are consanguinities between an America of wonder, spontaneity, and the natural, and a Shakespeare similarly unencumbered. For Emerson, Shakespeare is indeed 'such stuff as dreams are made on'.

Jones Very's 'Shakespeare', which anticipates 'Shakespeare; or, The Poet' by five or six years, again concentrates on the elusiveness of 'Shakespeare's self' (77). In strains similar to Emerson's, Very unearths for Shakespeare ethereal realms and disembodies the individual poet. His life was 'as various and all-embracing as nature's' (77). As an individual, he

> seemed lost and blended with the universal. In him we have a gift not of a world of matter but one of mind; a spirit to whom time and place seemed not to adhere. (77–8)

Shakespeare is the paradigm of a 'genius' that is nothing but the

> natural action of the mind rendering obedient to itself by a higher principle those objects to whose power it might otherwise have been subjected. (88)

His mind, affiliable to God's, is 'phenomenal and unconscious, and almost as much a passive instrument as the material world' (78). In an interpretation which Delia Bacon would have rejected but to which James was ambivalently attracted, or to versions of it at least, Shakespeare's thinly documented life, with its cryptic penumbra, arises from his genius and what defines it. His was a transcendental access to the divine enabled by ecstatic self-renunciation, an achievement open to anyone whose mind could be liberated from material distraction: 'universality is not a gift of Shakespeare alone, but natural to the mind of man' (84). In Very, far more so than in Emerson, Shakespeare is a conduit of the heavenly:

> In Shakespeare's works, I see but the ordinary power of the Deity acting in mind, as I see it around me moulding to its purpose the forms of matter. (97)

Emerson is aware that both the 'Shakespeare' with whom he is dealing and the transcendent genius to which he is allied are products, in the main, of German idealism; although he does not reach out for the retrospective paternity available to his analysis, whereby 'the child is father of the man'.[11] Until the German reappraisal of Shakespeare, the 'poet's mask was impenetrable':

It was not possible to write the history of Shakespeare...for he is the father of German literature: it was on the introduction of Shakespeare into German, by Lessing, and the translation of his works by Wieland and Schlegel, that the rapid burst of German literature was most intimately connected. It was not until the nineteenth century, whose speculative genius is a sort of living Hamlet, that the tragedy of 'Hamlet' could find such wondering readers. ('Shakespeare; or, The Poet' 118)

In his *The Authorship of Shakespeare*, written under the influence of Delia Bacon and at a time when Baconianism, and not just disputed attribution, was becoming highly fashionable, Nathaniel Holmes argued that

for the most part, all that has been seen in Shakespeare has been considered as the product of some kind of spontaneous inspiration. The reason has been merely this, that since Bacon...England, or the English language, has never had a philosophy at all. (248–9)

Since Bacon's philosophy was 'still-born', its presence in Shakespeare was 'not grasped' (249). German thinkers, as Emerson had correctly identified, had defined 'genius' as a transcendental category, in the wake of Kant, and allocated it to Shakespeare. But 'in truth', Holmes would have his readers believe:

these new wonders of Shakespeare are precisely the parts, qualities, and characteristics of him, wherein the higher philosophy of Bacon is displayed....All that gives peculiarity and pre-eminence to these plays is to be found in Bacon.

This is because Shakespeare was none other than Francis Bacon himself (254).

Holmes, together with Delia Bacon and her compatriots, saw their displacing of Shakespeare as a vanquishing of 'wonder' by the methods of a modern empiricism rooted in Francis Bacon. Throughout her book, Delia Bacon positions Bacon as the inaugurator of that 'practical philosophy from which the scientific arts of the Modern Ages proceed'. This 'Wisdom of the *Moderns*' arises in opposition to the Tudor Court and the aristocratic mystification it symbolizes (*The Philosophy of the Plays of Shakspere Unfolded* 207). Delia Bacon's strategy aligns America with the modern and attempts to replicate what she inferred as being Bacon's anti-authoritarian and secular celebration of individual enquiry.[12] This was a defeat of the old by the new, and a subjugation by scientific methods more appropriate to republican America of those English and European formations of Shakespeare that had contaminated Emerson and Very. Available here are collisions and collusions between the romantic and the real, idealism and empiricism, and tradition and history that are at the dramatic centre of James's 'The Birthplace', and its connections with that fire at Newport, and which invite a reading of Delia Bacon's work other than as the ramblings of a woman half-crazed, or more.

Delia Bacon was born in 1811 and died in 1859 within two years of the publication of her *The Philosophy of the Plays of Shakespere Unfolded*. After running private schools and failing to achieve renown as a public lecturer in Boston and New York, she turned her energies towards unearthing the mystery of Shakespeare,[13] having convinced herself that he was not the author of the plays bearing his name. Subsidized in the enterprise by the New York banker and philanthropist, Charles Butler, Bacon was able to sail for Liverpool on 13 May 1853, carrying 'a letter of introduction to Emerson's friend Thomas Carlyle' (Schoenbaum 387). Thomas Carlyle was astounded by her claims, although he supplied a further letter of introduction and contacted various publishers on her behalf.[14] After spending ten months in St. Albans in the proximity of Bacon's tomb and failing to persuade the beadle to open the sepulchre or to get permission for such a sacrilege from Bacon's descendant, Lord Verulam, she eventually moved on to Stratford. She laid siege to Shakespeare's gravestone believing that a will and other relics were hidden there. This aspect of her researches is the subject of Nathaniel Hawthorne's 'Recollections of a Gifted Woman'. As Hawthorne transposes there her scientific proclivities into the irrational and mysterious, Delia Bacon becomes a character in a lurid romance redolent of all the sombre hues of one of his tales, complete with a graveyard, a vicar and, soon enough, rampant insanity. On the brink of discovering the necessary evidence, 'her own convictions began to falter', Hawthorne suggests:

> A doubt stole into her mind whether she might not have mistaken the depository and mode of concealment of those historic treasures; and after once admitting the doubt, she was afraid to hazard the shock of uplifting the stone and finding nothing. (230)

Hawthorne encountered Delia Bacon in his capacity as the American consul in Liverpool. He asked a friend to edit her manuscript, he dealt with the printers, he read proofs; most important, he footed the publication bills, of which she was kept ignorant. (Schoenbaum 391)

He was nevertheless quick to disentangle himself from the project:

> I believe that it has been the fate of this remarkable book never to have had more than a single reader. I myself am acquainted with it only in insulated chapters and scattered pages and paragraphs. ('Recollections of a Gifted Woman' 234)

He found Delia Bacon 'remarkably suggestive' and 'alluring', and her 'deep and powerful under-current of earnestness' could not fail to produce in his 'mind, something like a temporary faith in what she herself believed so fervently' (229). Judging from the conclusion to his preface, however, that faith was temporary in the extreme. Hawthorne sees the unintended consequence of her attack as one of magnifying Shakespeare's power by emphasizing its inexplicability:

> In the worst event, if she has failed, her failure will be more honourable than most people's triumphs; since it must fling upon the old tombstone, at Stratford-on-Avon, the noblest tributary wreath that has ever lain there. (Preface, *The Philosophy of the Plays of Shakspere Unfolded* 206)[15]

These attempts to deface Shakespeare and maraud the site of his grave, metaphorically and actually, were to have a reverse effect fully anticipated by Hawthorne. The ingenuity of her cryptology (in ways congenial to James), far from bringing any truth to light, simply demonstrated that the bard has 'surface beneath surface, to an immeasurable depth, adapted to the plummet-line of every reader':

> There is no exhausting the various interpretations of his symbols, and a thousand years hence, a world of new readers will possess a whole library of new books, as we ourselves do, in these volumes old already. ('Recollections of a Gifted Woman' 227)

Delia Bacon's book—or rather, a hearsay acquaintance with the vague drift of its argument—created a storm in England that continued to rage until Henry James's 'The Birthplace' in 1903 and beyond.[16] Baconianism from across the Atlantic was dramatized, especially by 'the hack-critics of the minor periodical press in London' (Hawthorne, 'Recollections of a Gifted Woman' 233), as a specifically American assault on a monumentally English Shakespeare. The flaws in Bacon's argument, and the primitive nature of its logic, are exasperating. Consternating is the coalescence of what appear to be a detailed knowledge of the material examined yet a repudiation of any kind of historical method or sense.

In her 1856 article, 'William Shakespeare and His Plays', which abounds in feral rhetoric, ill-considered ridicule and invective, Bacon is always struggling for control as she drifts from time to time into seeing herself as one of Shakespeare's contemporaries. The article appeared in *Putnam's Magazine* and Richard Grant White, a formidable American Shakespeare critic, received a request for an introduction from the publishers which he declined.

> After reading it carefully and without prejudice...I returned the article to Mr. Putnam, declining the proposed honor of introducing it to the public, and adding that, as the writer was plainly neither a fool nor an ignoramus, she must be insane. (521)

As Schoenbaum has it: 'great tides of rhetoric—incantatory, brilliant, inchoate—swirl over the seaweed and scattered pebbles of thought' (389). A harangue over the 'lost' manuscripts, for example, shifts into a second-person address to a Shakespeare resurrected rather than entombed:

> He had those manuscripts! In the name of that sovereign reason, whose name he dares to take upon his lips so often, what did he do with them? Did he wantonly destroy them? No! Ah, no! he did not care enough for them to take that trouble. No, he did not do that! That would not have been in keeping with the character of this most respectable impersonation of the Genius of the British Isle, as it stands set up for us at present to worship....No! Traitor and miscreant! No! What did you do with them? You have skulked this question long enough. You will have to account for them. (178–9)

This article in particular, however, is significant for all kinds of accidental reasons. It tests to the point of destruction the universalist hypothesis with which Emerson and Very oppose empirical assumptions and procedures; and it reveals the degree to which a scientific historical methodology would not accommodate without substantial modification the Shakespeare of transcendent genius offered by German idealism. Bacon seems aware of the extent to which the projection of a wondrous Shakespeare universal and on the threshold of the divine, could be deployed for a variety of cultural purposes, not least that of deferring ruinous investigations.

In reaching back to Emerson, Delia Bacon also looks forward to Henry James and to later senses of cultural and ideological construction in her excavation of Shakespeare as constituted by ignorance, silence, and the inexplicable. The impression produced by these plays has been so 'profound and extraordinary' as 'to give to all the circumstances of their attributed origin a blaze of notoriety', this

> covering, beforehand, the whole ground of attack. The wonderful origin of these works was, from the first, the predominant point in the impression they made—the prominent marvels, around which all the new wonders, that the later criticism evolved, still continued to arrange themselves. ('William Shakespeare and His Plays' 172)

A Shakespeare disembodied and detached from history—the Shakespeare of the Germans and of Emerson, perhaps—can not only be integrated into otherwise alien (American) national cultural formations, but also retrieved, perpetuated, and protected, rather than displaced and erased, by an endlessly circulating discourse of the eternally ethereal and impalpable.

The continuing mystery on which Shakespeare thrives, Delia Bacon and Henry James might have agreed, although reacting quite differently to the consequences, is a function of impenetrability and a corresponding return on sustained investments in protecting what can be known from the forensic gaze. Shakespeare's critics may see the playwright as Protean, but for Bacon he is a veritable Proteus, or even a composite Ariel and Prospero, who can extend himself infinitely to avoid her grasp:

> And are not the obscurities that involve his life, so impenetrably, in fact, the true Shakespearean element? In the boundless sea of negations which surrounds that play-house centre, surely he can unroll himself to any length, or gather himself into any shape or attitude, which the criticism in hand may call for? ('William Shakespeare and His Plays' 175)

By the 1850s, an expanding American cultural, embryonic mass-cultural, and academic industry had a large and growing stake in Shakespearean wonders past, present, and in prospect.[17] This group is given a collective voice by Delia Bacon as it rises to his defence and strives to preserve the spectral inscrutability of a Shakespeare whose continuing significance depends on his remaining untouched. Acknowledged by implication is the risk of a counter-productive dissolution which would necessarily involve Delia Bacon's own work should the Shakespeare myth succumb to the empirical forces of a modern, scientific age:

> Is it wonderful? And is not that what we like in it? Would you make a man of him? With this miraculous inspiration of his, would you ask anything else of him? Do you not see that you touch the Shakespearean essence, with a question as to motives, and possibilities? Would he be Shakespeare still, if he should permit you to hamper him with conditions? What is the meaning of that word, then? And will you not leave him to us? Shall we have no Shakespeare? Have we not scholars enough, and wits enough, and men, of every other kind of genius, enough—but have we many Shakespeares?—that you should wish to run this one through with your questions, this one, great, glorious, infinite impossibility, that has had us in its arms, all our lives from the beginning. If you dissolve him do you not dissolve us with him? If you take him to pieces, do you not undo us also? ('William Shakespeare and His Plays' 175–6)

Delia Bacon was in danger of pursuing the logic of her argument to the point of destroying the wonder and interest generated by Shakespeare. Shakespeare, if he was to be of use in a rational age committed to scientific standards of evidence, had to be brought down from his transcendental heights; but Bacon seems to recognize, even in the act of welcoming it, that this descent would be a murderous experience under the auspices of the empirical school. Implicit, though, is the extent to which her 'running through', might have redeeming features: sacrificial penetration, or disputes about the credibility of such penetrations, inflating the value of any after-life.[18] Increasingly available was a form of secularization preserving more than a semblance of profitable mystery, however much an affair of nudges and winks: the American production of a Shakespeare tradition, not least on the site of Stratford-upon-Avon.[19]

(ii) 'Such places as this': accommodating Shakespeare in 'The Birthplace'

When the house traditionally[20] regarded as Shakespeare's birthplace came up for auction on 16 September 1847 there were reports that it was about to be shipped across the Atlantic. A flurry of letters to

The Times (of London) expressed in overtly chauvinistic terms fears for the future of what was nominated by the auctioneers as the 'most unique relic amongst England's treasures' and 'the most honoured monument of the greatest genius that ever lived' (Fox, *In Honour of Shakespeare* 6). This house, wrote one correspondent,

> belongs to the greatest intellectual glory not only of our nation, but of our race. And this, Sir, is the house which is to be brought to the hammer! to be sold by some prattling auctioneer, to whoever chooses to speculate in these universal associations!—perhaps to be plundered for the curiosity shops, or even transported to the United States. (Letter to the Editor, *The Times*, 10 April 1847: 7)

The dread was that some dire, peripatetic fate awaited the house:

> one or two enthusiastic Jonathans have already arrived from America, determined to see what dollars can do in taking it away. The timbers, it is said, are all sound, and it would be no very difficult matter to set it on wheels and make an exhibition of it. We hope and trust that no such desecration awaits it. (Letter to the Editor, *The Times*, 15 June 1847: 7)

According to Fox, it was 'the rumour that a plan was on foot to remove the Birthplace to America' that 'seems to have produced immediate action':

> Committees were set up in London and Stratford to raise funds to purchase the property. An appeal for contributions was circulated widely and special dramatic performances and concerts were staged in London and the provinces to assist the cause. (*Shakespeare's Birthplace* 5)

In the event, on the day of the auction, the house was purchased from public subscriptions by the Shakespeare Birthplace Trust on behalf of the British nation.[21]

Phineas T. Barnum, the American showman and entrepreneur of the spectacular and unbelievable, writes in his *The Life of P. T. Barnum* that he had 'the refusal of the house in which Shakespeare was born, designing to remove it in sections' to his 'museum in New York':

> but the project leaked out, British pride was touched, and several English gentlemen interfered and purchased the premises for a

Shakesperian Association. Had they slept a few days longer, I should have made a rare speculation, for I was subsequently assured that the British people, rather than suffer that house to be removed to America, would have bought me off with twenty thousand pounds. (344)

In his *Following the Equator: A Journey Around the World*, Mark Twain claims to have heard a more extravagant version of this event from a 'Second-class passenger' he came across on his travels, Barnum's designs on the house being turned into an improbable stratagem for purchasing Jumbo the Elephant from London Zoo. Arranged thereby, for Twain the enthusiastic anti-Stratfordian, was a debunking of Shakespeare by aligning the glories of his remains with elephants and circuses.[22]

Charles Jamrach (1815–55), the animal dealer and 'naturalist', was engaged by Barnum as an agent in the scheme, but was told that 'Jumbo couldn't be had; the Zoo wouldn't part with that elephant':

all England would be outraged at the idea; Jumbo was an English institution; he was part of the national glory; one might as well think of buying the Nelson monument. Barnum spoke up with vivacity and said:
'It's a first-rate idea. *I'll buy the monument*'. (*Following the Equator* 403)

Nelson's monument not being for sale, Barnum seized eagerly on newspaper accounts of the ruin into which Shakespeare's birthplace had fallen:

I'll buy Shakespeare's house. I'll set it up in my museum in New York and put a glass case around it and make a sacred thing of it; and you'll see all America flock there to worship; yes, and pilgrims from the whole earth; and I'll make them take their hats off, too.

'In America', Twain has him continue, with all puns on 'value' doubtless intended, 'we know how to value anything that Shakespeare's truth has made holy'. 'England rose in her indignation' at the scheme, and Barnum, having purchased the house in Twain's account, 'was glad to relinquish his prize and offer apologies' (404).

However, he stood out for compromise; he claimed a concession— England must let him have Jumbo. And England consented, but not cheerfully. (404–5)

In 'clarifying' his fellow-passenger's account, Twain mischievously adds, as he embellishes Barnum's own recollections, and with the whole Shakespeare mythology in his sights, that 'it shows how, by help of time, a story can grow'.

> Mr. Barnum told me the story himself, years ago. He said that the permission to buy Jumbo was not a concession; the purchase was made and the animal was delivered before the public knew anything about it.

One of the significant reverberations of this story, however tall, for James's 'The Birthplace', is in Twain's drawing out the irony that Americans, here in the unlikely shape of Barnum, were the true custodians of Shakespeare's Birthplace:

> He handed the house back, but took only the sum which it had cost him—but on the condition that an endowment sufficient for the future safeguarding and maintenance of the sacred relic should be raised. This condition was fulfilled. (405)

In *A Small Boy and Others*, James intersperses his recollections of visiting 'Barnum's great American Museum by the City Hall' in New York (*HJA* 38), with its 'dusty halls of humbug, amid bottled mermaids', and 'bearded ladies' (89), with accounts of early and frequent visits to the theatre to see Shakespeare's plays (*HJA* 56ff., 91). He recollects an 'old rickety bill-board in Fifth Avenue', the 'main source of its spell' being the 'rich appeal of Mr. Barnum', (*HJA* 89) and partly traces his obsession with the theatre and the 'scenic' to early sightings of the 'Barnum announcements':

> These announcements must have been in their way marvels of attractive composition, the placard bristling from top to toe with its analytic 'synopsis of scenery and incidents'. (*HJA* 90)

Barnum and Shakespeare have a persistent bearing on the forms in which James implies his autobiographical angst and nervous avariciousness for obscurity. However incredible—or rather, precisely because of the incredibility of its details when it comes to the business of actual acquisition and exchange—Barnum's vaunting of the purchase, and Mark Twain's later account of it, allow a conjectural elucidation of Delia Bacon's Shakespeare project and an interpretative entry into James's 'The Birthplace' and its anti-Stratfordian associations.

More than tangentially, Barnum can be connected with Delia Bacon and what had become a peculiarly American interrogation of the ramifying conflicts between wonder and cynicism, and a reverence for tradition and the contemporary spirit of profitable amusement.

  Barnum's exhibitions frequently challenged the spectator to test the limits of what could be observed and believed, offering examples at the threshold of the real and the fantastic, of the credible and incredible. As Neal Harris has argued, Barnum arranged his 'hoaxes and exhibits to encourage debate about which processes were real' (82). He

> accepted...that perfection and absolute conviction in exhibits made them less valuable. Spectators required some hint of a problem, some suggestion of difficulty. (89)[23]

The Baconians, and the anti-Stratfordians in general, can be seen as a part of the means by which Shakespeare, especially on the site of Stratford-upon-Avon, was popularized as an exhibit of a Barnum-like variety: doubt, a destructive element in Delia Bacon, filled the coffers with American dollars at the Birthplace.[24] Significantly, Shakespeare is identified with Barnum at one point in Bacon's 'William Shakespeare and His Plays' as 'New Place' at Stratford-upon-Avon is displaced by Barnum's 'stately' home in Connecticut, the implication being that Shakespeare's claims to authorship are tantamount to a hoax worthy of the celebrated American showman himself. Reciprocities between the two surface in terms of a common dependence on rewarding deceptions; Shakespeare and Barnum alike being responsible for a lucrative trade in 'literary conveniences':

> If the prince of showmen in our day, in that stately oriental retreat of his, in Connecticut, rivaling even the New Place at Stratford in literary conveniences, should begin now to conceive of something of this sort, as his crowning speculation, and should determine to undertake its execution in person, who would dare to question his ability? (187–8)

After its 1847 purchase, Shakespeare's birthplace could be displayed on an industrial scale. But such a site, as Barnum had discovered in related arenas, could only prosper if hostilities between tradition and the verifiable facts, and between credulousness and unbelief, could be contained and utilized. In Henry James's 'The Birthplace', transcendental maunderings on Shakespeare, Delia Bacon's tortured ramblings on authorship, and the discourse of exhibitionism (presided over by Barnum) converge and collide. Ignored or unknown, apparently, to the critics of Henry James's 'The Birthplace' is the immediate context of the tale.[25] 1903 saw the culmination of Marie Corelli's unsuccessful campaign to prevent the demolition of sixteenth-century buildings close to the Henley Street house, the purpose of the demolition being to make way for one of the Scottish-American steel millionaire Andrew Carnegie's public libraries.[26] Raised yet again was the spectre of the American plunder of Shakespeare as fiery debates about the authenticity of the birthplace, and of the provenance of Shakespeare's authorship, were re-ignited.

In an allusion to Delia Bacon's escapades in Stratford-upon-Avon, Corelli likened this latest American attack on Shakespeare to the activity of 'digging up...dead bodies for dissection in surgical laboratories' (55). Shakespeare now furnished 'a whole larder of feasting for the tribe of body-snatchers and soul-killers', and Carnegie's library would result in a street smelling 'to Heaven of most unpoetic millions' (59). Corelli saw a direct connection between such a threat, a symbol of American financial and economic intimidation on the very site of England's cultural emblem, and those earlier Baconian manoeuvres:

> Any lie will serve them in their ghoulish work of rending asunder a noble and gifted life piecemeal, and exposing the morsels to the public gaze, labelled side by side with their own paltry names. When they cannot do it in books written to deny the genius of the man they envy and vilify, they try it on in assertive buildings, which in the way of 'beneficence' they stamp with the great name and their own together, linking the two in the same laurel-wreathed scroll. (60)

Furthermore,

> if English literary men thought less of themselves, and more of the honour of their greatest master and leader, whose brains every scribbler, great and small, has sucked at for over three hundred years, they would never find space in any magazine or newspaper for so much as a comment on the idiotic 'Bacon theory'. (56)

Bemoaning the generally ineffectual way in which 'literary England' had 'defended her greatest literary possession', Corelli looked back to the sale of the Birthplace in 1847 and to the uncertainty about whether it would be acquired by the English or the Americans. England's 'grand-motherly hesitation' in defending Shakespeare in 1847 and now in 1903 is starkly contrasted with America's 'eagle "scream"'. 'If you do not value your most priceless possession', Corelli hears America crying 'across the roaring waters of the Atlantic, "I will take it from you...and I will build the treasure of the Old World up again in the New!"' (60) But what Barnum recognized and Corelli does not is that publicizing the dubiety of a cultural artefact or state, or arranging and exploiting as James had done an obscurity about his past and its accessibility, and dramatizing the extent to which it is under suspicion, can increase rather than dimin-ish its value. Whereas Corelli and Halliwell-Phillips, among others, saw incredulity only in negative terms, as part of an attack to be fended off, the Barnum school welcomed it as enhancing the spectacle.[27]

In keeping with the 'boundless sea of negations' Delia Bacon regard-ed as defining Shakespeare (*The Philosophy of the Plays of Shakspere Unfolded* 175), the 'Him, *him*, HIM!' ('The Birthplace' 445) of 'The Birthplace' is never identified.[28] The reader may infer that as this is the nominal 'Birthplace' of the 'supreme poet, the Mecca of the English-speaking race' (443), Shakespeare must be at the absent centre of the tale, especially given the mischievous allusions to his plays throughout; but in withholding the name, James intensifies the impalpability he dramatizes.[29]

Similarly, 'Shakespeare' is all but absent from James's 1877 account of his visit to Warwickshire. James twice announces that he has 'no inten-tion of talking about the celebrated curiosities in which this region abounds' ('In Warwickshire' 166); and on the second occasion, the belated appearance of 'Shakespeare' is practically elided by ponderous negatives and suspended by an evasive subjunctive:

> It was, however, no part of my design in these remarks to pause before so thickly besieged a shrine as this; and if I were to allude to Stratford it would not be in connection with the fact that Shakespeare planted there, to grow for ever, the torment of his unguessed riddle. (175)

When at the churchyard in what is described as 'the heart of England', James focuses not on Shakespeare's tomb (which goes unnoticed), but on a 'poor little girl, who seemed deformed' (168). If 'the American tourist usually comes straight to this corner of England—chiefly for the purpose of paying his respects to the birthplace of Shakespeare', James swiftly departs for Warwick where he can linger over some 'old hospi-

tallers' housed in an 'odd little theatrical-looking refuge for superannu-
ated warriors' (174).

In a process that connects the Newport of James's 'obscure hurt' with
the Birthplace and the 'Birthplace', uncertainties about Shakespeare
are a perpetuating element of his life and work. The 'fatal futility' of
facts (*PSP* 1140) in this tale is what makes them profitable within the
scheme of the story at large, and intricately useful for a James acutely
interested in the complex and often perilous connections he perceives
between the past and its fabrications, and the life, biography, and work
of a writer. If 'The Aspern Papers' relishes the failure of a narrator
unable to possess the relics of the past he seeks, and to realize the utter
vacuity of his pursuit, the concern in 'The Birthplace' is with the potential yield from the processes of commodification and memorialization
it also satirizes. Exploring the curious relation between facts, invented
facts, and fiction, 'The Birthplace' is much more than 'The Aspern
Papers' 'brought down to date' (James, 'Edmond Rostand' 524).

Maurice Gedge and his wife Isabel are troubled relentlessly by the
boundary between fact and fancy and the pecuniary consequences of
straddling it ineffectually. Struck at the beginning of the tale is a note
that continues to sound: Gedge 'had tried several things, he had tried
many, but the final appearance was of their having tried him not less',
and now he is 'in charge of the grey town-library of Blackport-on-
Dwindle, all granite, fog and female fiction' (442). At the height of his
crisis over whether to capitulate to the demand from his Barnum-like
employers not to 'give away the Show', the 'Biggest on Earth' (478), his
wife recoils in horror from 'the night of early winter on the other side
of the pane' and the possibility of their being evicted into 'the small flat
town, intrinsically dull' (479) with its 'stupid little street' (472). This is
a bleakly industrial, utilitarian terrain, from which Gedge is protected
by a 'short moreen curtain artfully chosen by Isabel' (478). At one level,
fiction and the necessary consolations of a world of illusion are
gendered powerfully feminine, whereas Gedge's view of the Birthplace
and its relics as no more than 'extraneous, preposterous stuffing' (457)
is impotently masculine. As always in James, however, the geometry is
more intricate than this scheme suggests. The prospect as Isabel Gedge
views it—'we shall live as in a fairy tale'—is of the 'vaguest' (443).

Much more important for Mrs. Gedge than what she and her husband know, or what can be known, is the keeping up of appearances in
a performance for the benefit of the Birthplace visitors of what she
thinks they are; and this liberates them, she believes, from the demean-
ing requirements of truth. Isabel thinks she can discriminate between

the real and the vulgar at the social level, but is unwilling, or unable, to pay the cost of extending her analysis to the domain of the Birthplace itself:

> We've no social position, but we don't *mind* that we haven't, do we? a bit; which is because we know the difference between realities and shams. We hold to reality, and that gives us common sense, which the vulgar have less than anything. (444)

By 'holding to reality', Mrs Gedge disqualifies herself as an artist, at least in James's world. As the narrator has it in 'The Real Thing' (1892):

> I liked things that appeared; then one was sure. Whether they *were* or not was a subordinate and almost always a profitless question. (38–9)

The Monarchs, in that tale, are the real thing, but they cannot 'appear' and are useless, therefore, for the purposes of representation; as in 'The Birthplace', the myth of the real is valuable only as a pretext for the appearance of fiction.[30]

Gedge, by contrast with his wife, is at first naïvely oppressed by those 'discoveries' and 'facts' eschewed by Emerson, and he makes a move whose facetious tone suggests that he will be protected from the failure and misery experienced by characters elsewhere in James who settle seriously on a similar trajectory: '"ah", he said as if it were a question of honour, "*we* must know everything"' (446).[31] From the perspective of the initially stifling role that awaits him, Gedge's early preparations are singularly inappropriate: he absorbs himself in the plays with his wife, and 'they declaimed, they almost performed, their beneficent author' (447). This deepens his sense of how little he can offer to visitors who care only for the 'empty shell' of the Birthplace (457):

> 'It's absurd', he didn't hesitate to say, 'to talk of our not "knowing". So far as we don't it's because we're donkeys. He's *in* the thing, over His ears, and the more we get into it the more we're with Him. I seem to myself at any rate', he declared, 'to *see* Him in it as if He were painted on the wall'. (447)

James conjures up *A Midsummer Night's Dream* here with Gedge as Bottom-the-ass.[32] But if Gedge is asinine, he is also the means by which the necessary dependence of reality on illusion explored in that play is recuperated by the end of this tale.

The story moves through four distinct phases. Firstly, there is a reluctant acquiescence by Gedge in his task; he veils his beliefs from the public at large, but bleeds 'under his coat' as he overhears his wife's voluminous fictions. Gedge is an Antonio for whom there is no Portia to plead for mercy as the usurious Shylock-like hordes daily carve from him their 'pound of flesh' (465); but Antonio, rather than Shylock, of course, is the merchant of Venice, and Gedge is not without his own appreciable interest in the Birthplace by the end of the tale. From the 'first evening, after closing-hour, when the last blank pilgrim had gone', Gedge has daily undergone a transposition into the releasing solitude of 'the mere spell, the mystic presence' (448). His uneasy compromise of searching in the dark for the author's spirit and trading by day with his dubious remains encodes a form of schizophrenia familiar to James. Gedge

> was on his way to become[33] two quite different persons, the public and the private, and yet that it would somehow have to be managed that these persons should live together. He was splitting into halves....One of the halves...was the keeper, the showman, the priest of the idol; the other piece was the poor unsuccessful honest man he had always been. (460)

Everywhere in James, and not least in this story, there is 'the roar of the market and the silence of the tomb' (James, 'Dumas the Younger' 291), together with disturbing yet productive realizations that, in reality, these sites are intercalated.[34]

In the second phase, Gedge is unable to sustain his precarious double life after the first of two visits—and the 'young man' had also visited Stratford 'four years ago' (468)—from a New York couple. They arrive when Gedge's divided self is at its most vulnerable: at the 'fall of the day' but 'before the hour of closing' (465). In this liminal zone between the public and the private, Gedge is lured by his sense of their Emersonian 'transcendent freedom' (467) and independence into revealing indiscretions they admire about the stupendous incredibility of it all. 'There has been a great deal said' about the house, but

> 'Much of it, in such places as this', he heard himself adding, 'is of course said very irresponsibly'. *Such places as this!*—he winced at the words as soon as he had uttered them. (468)

Henceforth, in phase three—given that this is a Barnum-like show to an exquisite fault and that, as he later says, 'the look of it...is what I give' (491)—Gedge carries on with his duties but 'looked so perpetually as if something had disagreed with him' (475) that word reaches the menacing Grant-Jackson. The secretary of the Birthplace Committee arrives like the ghost of Hamlet's father at the same testing twilight time, now the 'horrid hour' (491), as the New York Hayes couple to threaten Gedge with the 'sack' (479) unless he can put a better face on things. Gedge is mesmerizingly eloquent in the final phase, for 'they wouldn't let you off with silence' (465), and the longer the yarns he spins, the greater the number of tickets he sells. He seems, at this point, to have become a writer, gendered feminine by his garrulity and popularity, of those very novels he lent out so industriously in Blackport-on-Dwindle (442). Gedge discovers, however, like Hamlet, that there is more than one way to secure revenge if 'the rest is silence',[35] and that such a state is not necessarily at odds with incontinent utterances of a kind.[36]

The Gedges lack a social position, but 'you're a gentleman', Isabel Gedge reassures Maurice as she urges him, in effect, to 'screw' his 'courage to the sticking place'.[37] If Macbeth and Lady Macbeth are brought to mind here, then Isabel, as one who 'should have died here-after',[38] is excluded from an understanding of, certainly from a sympathy for, the strategy by which Gedge is ultimately able to exploit the Birthplace by undermining it, James himself being the main beneficiary of these tactics. When Grant-Jackson forces Gedge to surrender, he delivers 'only two words' (478): in effect, 'remember me'.[39] The injunction 'remember me' silently appropriates from *Hamlet*, for the actual words are not uttered, strategies of dissemblance and masking, of indirection and irony, which are essential to an understanding of the New York couple's second trip to the Birthplace. Also invoked are urgent needs in the present to find ways of accommodating a past whose pressures can otherwise be unbearable.

Critical distance in this tale, as elsewhere in James, takes the form of complex ironies which recruit knowing readers into a community and establish a hieratic communion from which women, frequently, and undiscriminating readers in general are excluded. Lost in reverie before the paintings of John Singer Sargent at Burlington House in 1897, these are the readers James imagined as his thoughts wandered to a recent reading of Anatole France's *L'Orme du Mail*. Reflecting on France and his readers, James's concern was not with the 'particular multitude depended upon, in the artist's thought to admire and to buy', but with 'the public involved or implied, the public addressed and aimed at, wooed, whether won or not' (509). In characterizing his sense of France's implied readership, he fantasizes about his own:

Oh, the adorable people; the intelligent, exquisite, delicious people; oh, the people to commune with, to live with, to work for!...Does any public so particular exist?—is any such appeal to be conceived as being really met? ('London': 5 June 1897: 509–10)

James has Gedge organize a compromise: he tells tales to satisfy popular demand but seeks his consolations in forms of irony signalled to the cognoscenti. Mr. Hayes, rather than his wife, is an observer of Gedge's developing artistry. Under-statement and scrupulousness are replaced by forms of irony-transmitting excessiveness in self-protective, subtly disclaiming, presentations. The public at large 'wanted...to feel that everything was "just as it was"' (461), but what this amounts to is a refusal to permit Gedge to depart from the received script: 'They show *me*. It's all in their little books' (471). Captured here is part of the dynamic of Barnum's hoaxes whereby unstable disparities between what was, is, or could be, act to stimulate curiosity, but always within a narrative framework that to remain infinitely enigmatic must not be dispelled. The vulgarity exploited by Barnum, and James in this story, has its sophistications. If the 'American imagination', at least in the manifestation of it under scrutiny in Barnum and 'The Birthplace', 'demands the real thing and, to obtain it, must fabricate the absolute fake' (Eco 8), there is also the question of a patronization of the past which is 'always... in a spirit of gluttony and bricolage' (Eco 31).

As part of their induction, the Gedges receive 'various little guides, handbooks, travellers' tributes, literary memorials, and other catch-penny publications', but these are for the moment 'swallowed up in the interesting episode' of their 'induction or initiation' (448) by Miss Putchin, 'one of the ladies who had for so many years borne the brunt' (449). Vulgarity and irony, within a context of gender, come into immediate collision. 'And are They always, as one might say', Gedge asks of Miss Putchin, 'stupid?'

'Stupid!' She stared, looking as if no one *could* be such a thing in such a connection. No one had ever been anything but neat and cheerful and fluent, except to be attentive and unobjectionable and, so far as was possible, American.

'What I mean is', he explained, 'is there any perceptible proportion that take an interest in Him?'

His wife stepped on his toe; she deprecated irony. (451)

Miss Putchin's resort is always to 'the facts' and the '*one* way' of dealing with them. Gedge

> repeated it, after this conversation, at odd moments, several times over to his wife. 'There can only be one way, one way', he continued to remark—though indeed much as if it were a joke; till she asked him how many more he supposed she wanted. (453)

Whereas Mrs. Gedge deprecates irony, which is much the same thing in this context as being unwilling to understand how indispensable it is to Gedge's duplicities, it operates as a rarefied *lingua franca* for Mr. Hayes—rather than his wife, again—and a Gedge who deploys it as a more or less secret mode for negotiating the two 'halves' into which he has split. By the time of the Hayes's second visit, the mere show-man has become a consummate performer whose art depends in self-corrosive ways on the material he scorns.

What distinguishes the American couple, in a tale where so much is revealed in the dying embers of the day, is the late hour of their visit: desiring to escape 'the crowd', they 'almost' treat it 'as personal and private' (466). This allies the couple with Henry James, who in his own travel writing never ceases to stress the value of arriving after hours to visit country houses and the like. He visits, for instance, Haddon Hall in the 'twilight hour':

> Haddon Hall lies among Derbyshire hills, in a region infested, I was about to write, by Americans. But I achieved my own shy pilgrimage in perfect solitude. ('Lichfield and Warwick' 73–4)

Detecting 'a pleasant irony...in the air—he who had not yet felt free to taste his own' (468), 'Gedge had suddenly, thrillingly, let himself go' (467). Released from the show, he takes them up 'without words, without the usual showman's song', and from this silence Mr. Hayes guesses the 'travail of his spirit' and catches 'the gleam of his inner commentary' (468). The real 'interest', in all its immensity, of the Birthplace, Gedge voicing positions held by James in his introduction to *The Tempest*, is 'the fact of the abysmally little that, in proportion, we know': 'He escapes us like a thief at night, carrying off—well, carrying off everything' (469). Hayes's wife reaches for an American solution, certainly, at least, that of Emerson and Very: 'Why not say, beautifully...that, like the wind, He's everywhere?' 'What's the use' she asks, 'if you say it *wasn't* in this room He was born?' It is Mr. Hayes who defines 'use' in terms other than crude gain and implies an alternative for Gedge to torrential inanities on the one hand, and a taciturnity, on the other that invokes the threatening spectre of Grant-Jackson:

> What's the use of what? her husband asked. 'The use, you mean, of our coming here? Why, the place is charming in itself. And it's also interesting', he added to Gedge, 'to know how you get on'. (470)

An 'increase of communion' between the two not unrelated to the exchange of a sovereign, has resulted in a shift in attention from Shakespeare to Gedge himself, and to the potential for art and artfulness in the presence of an 'historic void' (472).[40] Crucially, Mr. Hayes now descries in Gedge's performance 'an intention beyond a joke' (483), although the ambiguity of the expression allows James to undercut the endorsement. Gedge, like James, supremely, and unlike Mrs. Hayes, thrives when surveying 'all there wasn't to be seen' (472). 'The "play's the thing". Let the author alone', asserts Mr. Hayes (472).[41] For most of the story, Gedge is a Hamlet-*manqué* deliberating over whether 'to be, or not to be'.[42] What the Hayes couple provide, like the visiting players in *Hamlet*, is a play-within-the-play that offers transforming encounters and reflections. 'The play's the thing', in the sense of a superior form of playfulness Gedge is released into deploying; but the 'play's the thing', also, 'wherein' the 'conscience of the King' is caught; and 'caught', in all its senses, is James when it comes to his way with truth and the past for the purposes of his art.

That James has filled the void with his own fiction, mastering a Shakespeare he puts to profitable use, up-staging Barnum and dwarfing Gedge in the process, emerges on the second visit of the New Yorkers. Shakespeare's Birthplace becomes Gedge's cradle as an artist but, above all, the site of a story, James's 'The Birthplace', that displaces both. 'The evening was now a mild April-end'—the traditional date of birth for Shakespeare, of course, is 23 April—'and this was the second spring' as 'history' repeats 'itself' (480). The morose silence and fractured ruminations of the first visit have given away on the second to an eloquent fiction whose distance from Mrs. Gedge's 'feminine' incontinence and its proximity to James's art is in its irony:

> Across that threshold He habitually passed; through those low windows, in child-hood, He peered out into the world that He was

to make so much happier by the gift to it of His genius; over the
boards of this floor—that is over *some* of them, for we mustn't be
carried away!—his little feet often pattered. (482)

The chasm has widened between Gedge and his wife in ways that impli-
cate women and women's fiction in the tawdry coarseness of it all:[43]

The morality of women was special—he was getting lights on that.
Isabel's conception of her office was to cherish and enrich the
legend. (462)

If Mrs. Gedge is anxious about her husband's going too far in the
indulgence of an irony she fails to value, then Mrs. Hayes is
excommunicated as an unregenerate *ingénue*: 'Don't They want then
any truth?' she asks, to which the 'young husband' replies 'with an "Ah,
wives are terrible!"' (491). Whereas Mr. Hayes isolates Gedge's artistry,
'you conceal your art', he tells him (488), his wife acclaims his 'genius'
and brings news of his American notoriety 'in the papers' (487). Gedge
fears that 'there would be more than one fashion of giving away the
show, and wasn't *this* perhaps a question of giving it away by excess?'
(484); but 'the receipts' are 'proof positive that the winds were now at
rest' (485). Gedge is cast in the role of a Prospero taken by James in his
Tempest introduction to be Shakespeare's surrogate; but like Prospero's,
his temporary magical powers are on loan. He is left suspended, his
'charms...all o'erthrown', by an author who begs an indulgence,
obliquely, for the necessary iniquities of art:

> As you from crimes would pardon'd be,
> Let your indulgence set me free.

(Epilogue, *The Tempest* 19–20)

Gedge's control of the irony can only be partial, as he, in turn, is
ironized by a James who consigns the evaluation of his success to
the press, a medium whose squalors it is now in Gedge's interests to
overlook. Gedge is compromised by a craving for publicity whose
renunciation first gave rise to the very fictional and counter-fictional
manoeuvres that have become the object of gross celebration. He has
'found a vocation much older, evidently, than he had at first been prepared to recognise' (485). James mobilizes equivalences from which he
cannot be detached between Eve's first lie in the Garden of Eden, prostitution (traditionally the 'oldest profession'), and the art of fiction, but

he allocates Gedge a recognition, an awareness, that separates him from the women of the tale, and from their fiction.

Although from the New York of Barnum's most successful exhibitions and hoaxes, the Hayes couple are connected by the narrator, in a 'heavenly mingle'[44] of vulgar spectacle and aesthetic discrimination again subjected to irony by James, to those supreme arbiters of taste, the Bostonians:

> Mr. and Mrs. Hayes were from New York, but it was like singing, as he had heard one of his Americans once say about something, to a Bostonian audience. (485)

It is less, in this tale, that Shakespeare is that measure of American culture feared by early republicans, more that America has become his custodian as the developers of just the right mixture of interrogation and awe necessary for his modern-day accommodation. What the Hayes participate in is a form of branding: with corporate and incorporating resonances abounding, they are entered in the 'public register' as 'Mr. and Mrs. B. D. Hayes, New York':

> one of those American labels that were just like every other American label and that were, precisely, the most remarkable thing about people reduced to achieving an identity in such other ways.

For Gedge, Mr. and Mrs. Hayes seek to occupy a space beyond their label, and it is in this way that they assist in the identification of the Henley Street house as a commodity fit for aesthetic use. If the story begins with pathological doubleness, it ends with a productive, if not a creative, duplicity:

> They could be Mr. and Mrs. B. D. Hayes and yet they could be, with all presumptions missing—well, what these callers were. (481)

'The Birthplace' exploits the Birthplace by subjecting it to the main constituents of its value: irony and scepticism. Thereby, as in his introduction to *The Tempest*, James holds himself aloof from processes he is nevertheless unable to resist.

The auctioneer of the Henley Street house in 1847 was asked to vouch for its authenticity. He replied that 'tradition pointed out this house as that of Shakespeare's birth', a tradition endorsed by upwards of seven thousand visitors a year, 'a good proportion of whom were Americans' (Brown and Fearon 49–50). Irrespective of the facts of the Barnum episode, the claims of the New World on Shakespeare, and even on the domain of Stratford-upon-Avon, had long been secure in terms of a lease by association. Washington Irving, Nathaniel Hawthorne, and Henry James are among the many American writers who helped constitute the traditions of the Birthplace by writing accounts (highly popular in the case of Irving) of their visits. 'American travellers clung, for the most part', as Gordon tells us, 'to their copies of Hawthorne and Washington Irving' (126). Gedge's roots are in a tradition of American writing about Shakespeare whose main characteristics are unstable irony of a comic variety and that knowing suspension of disbelief on which Barnum was to capitalize.

That Irving established the paradigm within which Americans were to visit Stratford-upon-Avon is evident from Barnum's *The Life of P. T. Barnum*. When visiting Stratford, Barnum 'called for a guide-book', and the waiter fetched what he said was 'the best description extant of the birth and burial-place of Shakspeare':

> I was not a little proud to find this volume to be no other than the 'Sketch-Book' of our illustrious countryman, Washington Irving; and in glancing over his humorous description of the place, I discovered that he had stopped at the same hotel where we were then awaiting breakfast. (275)

More specifically, Miss Putchin and the Gedges have models in both Irving and Hawthorne,[45] and in the kind of exchange (recorded in Barnum's *Life*) where Barnum, the expert in such affairs, proposes with some irony to the 'old porter' at Warwick Castle:

> 'I suppose', I continued, 'that you have told these marvellous stories so often, that you almost believe them yourself'.
>   '*Almost!*' replied the porter, with a grin of satisfaction that showed he was 'up to snuff', and had really earned two shillings. (277)

Irving was shown around the Birthplace by a 'garrulous old lady' who was

> peculiarly assiduous in exhibiting the relics with which this, like all other celebrated shrines, abounds....There was an ample supply also

of Shakespeare's mulberry tree, which seems to have as extraordinary powers of self-multiplication as the wood of the true cross; of which there is enough extant to build a ship of the line. ('Stratford-on-Avon' 43)

The curator's rival is the sexton, who envies her more frequent visitors, and peddles doubts about the authenticity of the Henley Street house.

Richard Grant White lamented the 'inflated nonsense', 'pompous platitude', and 'misleading speculation...uttered upon Shakespeare' ('The Anatomization of William Shakespeare' 332). Like Delia Bacon, White argues that because Shakespeare, unlike other 'subjects which are of general interest', is 'the most remote from reason', he spawned 'high-priests' who 'prophesy' and 'utter fine sayings...apocalyptically, by way of revelation' (332–3). Irving's curators, like Maurice Gedge in his final manifestation, are weak versions of White's high-priests; but in an effect similar to that on which Barnum prospers and which is dramatized in 'The Birthplace', and a possible engenderer of it, the traditions are strengthened rather than weakened by the doubtfulness of it all:

> I am always of easy faith in such matters, and am ever willing to be deceived, where the deceit is pleasant, and costs nothing. I am therefore a ready believer in relics, legends, and local anecdotes of goblins and great men; and would advise all travellers who travel for their gratification to be the same. What is it to us whether these stories be true or false, so long as we can persuade ourselves into the belief of them, and enjoy all the charm of the reality? ('Stratford-on-Avon' 44)

Irving embraces Shakespeare and his traditions and tacitly repudiates counter-productive scruples. Shakespeare occupies, as in 'The Birthplace', a position beyond ascertainable and verifiable facts and, in the end, beyond the reach of fiction. Mr. Hayes and Gedge, under the tutelage of irony and previous constructions of the curator's role, are part of a process whereby the enigma of Shakespeare is sustained. There are manoeuvres similar to those in 'Stratford-on-Avon' in Irving's 'The Boar's Head Tavern, East Cheap: A Shakesperian Research', where the issue is even more conspicuous. Irving detects in Shakespeare's plays a merging of imaginary characters and events with the 'facts and personages of real life'; licensed by this, he surrenders his historical researches to the 'illusions of poetry' (33). This is very much the mode of treating Shakespeare and Stratford-upon-Avon that James adopts, however ironically, for 'In Warwickshire':

> I looked about for the village stocks; I was ready to take the modern vagrants for Shakespearean clowns; and I was on the point of going into one of the ale-houses to ask Mrs. Quickly for a cup of sack. (166)

Irving relates his work to a Shakespeare industry then in its early stages and whose later debt to the tradition his writing is fostering will be heavy indeed:

> Thus have I given a 'tedious brief' account of this interesting research, for which, if it prove too short and unsatisfactory, I can only plead my inexperience in this branch of literature so deservedly popular at the present day. I am aware that a more skillful illustrator of the immortal bard would have swelled the materials I have touched upon, to a good merchantable bulk....All this I leave as a rich mine to be worked by future commentators. (41)

James and Irving, then, share a scepticism about the facts of Shakespeare, and in 'The Birthplace' James explores, in the tradition of Irving and Barnum, with Delia Bacon as an unlikely mediator, how such scepticism can be put to use within the context of an American commodification of the bard. But James's contempt for facts, his deep suspicion of all forms of utterance and representation, and his anxieties about the penetrability of his own life, make Gedge's compromise, constantly undermined by ironies beyond him, ultimately seem tenuous and unconvincing.[46] Gedge is confined to the emptiness of interminable stories, whereas James reserves eloquent silence, from time to time, for himself.

(iii) 'Unabashed duplicity': 'The Papers' and 'The Private Life'

What James called the 'paraphernalia of concealment—the drama of alarm and exposure' ('The Present Literary Situation in France' 120), or '*enclosure* and...disclosure' (*N* 235), together with doubleness, duplicity, and the uses of obscurity, are at the centre of both 'The Papers' and 'The Private Life'; and both tales involve complex deployments of Shakespeare the partial key to which is in the introduction to *The Tempest*. The focus of 'The Papers' is on the 'museum' of 'publicity', 'the prize object, the high rare specimen' of which is 'Sir A. B. C. Beadel-Muffet K.C.B., M.P'. Like Shakespeare, and the James of Newport as an object of his own critical attention and that of others, Beadel-Muffet specializes in becoming a subject of 'fallacious report, one half of his chronicle' appearing 'to consist of' an 'official contradiction of the other half'. (546) He is consummately adept at recruiting Barnum's strategies for constructing celebrity by arousing public curiosity. The story demonstrates the extent to which if 'fame' arose in the past from public actions for the 'good of the state', by the early 1900s 'the conditions of modern celebrity' had made it a goal in itself (Braudy 488); or as Bennett, writing in 1901, expressed it: 'not only is art a factor in life; it is a factor in all lives....Everyone is an artist, more or less' (3). In Beadel-Muffet's 'artful...imitation of the voice of fame', James's satirizes decadent appropriations of a once classical ideal:

> The fame was *all* voice....the items that made the sum were individually of the last vulgarity, but the accumulation was a triumph...of industry and vigilance. It was after all not true that a man had done nothing who for ten years had so fed, so dyked and directed and distributed the fitful sources of publicity. (547)

'The Papers' revolves around two hack-journalists, Howard Bight and Maud Blandy. Maud is less successful than Bight, envying yet also fearing his ability to capitalize on trivial information about essentially mediocre and mendacious public figures in the form of lucrative articles. The 'young pair'

> knew...as they considered, many secrets, but they liked to think that they knew none quite so scandalous as the way that, to put it roughly, this distinguished person maintained his distinction. (546)

It seems, and Maud spends much of the story speculating about this as her marriage to Bight is one of its contingencies, that Howard's predatory interest, and worse, in Beadel-Muffet, has driven him into disappearance and suicide given that a wealthy widow, Mrs. Chorner, refuses to marry the politician unless he can find a way of quelling the publicity on which he thrives. Beadel-Muffet's disappearance— designed to achieve this purpose, in a tale whose exploration of the metaphysics of absence and presence, and silence and utterance, as imbricated in its own fiction, is intense—results, paradoxically, in a fervour of publicity over which neither he (or can he?), hence his apparent suicide, or the journalists can exercise any control. Bight protests, after puzzling over how 'one' is 'to mention that he wants *not* to be mentioned' (560), about a dynamic familiar enough in James: 'We've all in fact been turned on—to turn everything off, and that's exactly the job that makes the biggest noise'. 'It appears everywhere' that Beadel-Muffet

> desires to cease to appear *anywhere*; and then it appears that his desiring to cease to appear is observed to conduce directly to his more tremendously appearing, or certainly, and in the most striking manner, to his not in the least *dis*appearing. The workshop of silence roars like the Zoo at dinner-time. (581)

Mortimer Marshall, an ignored (and ignorable) playwright, is desperate for publicity and acts as a failed double of Beadel-Muffet. If Beadel-Muffet—allied in unutterable, certainly barely uttered, ways with Bight—has disappeared only to return in a blaze of publicity (drawing on the Duke's strategy in *Measure for Measure* and its more subtle manifestation in the Prospero of *The Tempest* who also fails to return), then his suicide is inexplicable. Mischievously, Bight proposes that Mortimer might take advantage of this botched plot to arrange a more successful show. Mingling here are menace and desire, with Maud between the men, as Bight the 'cruel creature' (568) fixes Marshall, a man with nine 'machines for stretching his trousers' (580) and designs on Maud, 'in a manner that might have been taken for the fascination of deference' (568). Maud has remained unpublished until Bight, out-manoeuvring her, initiates a receptive environment for Marshall by writing up their uneventful lunch together in 'journalism of the intensest essence; a column concocted of nothing' (576). Maud is left 'lost in the wonder' at how 'without matter, without thought, without an excuse, without a fact', he 'had managed to be as resonant as if he had beaten a drum on the platform of a booth' (577).

As the story progresses, Maud and Bight move along a trajectory the unstable and indefinite elements of which are connected in shifting and complex ways. They begin by attempting to report facts invented, distorted, or shaped for the purposes of a press at least as much involved in constituting them as the agents involved, but fact and fiction tend to merge in a story that becomes increasingly reflexive and metafictional. Bight seizes on Maud's reference to 'facts' after Beadel-Muffet's death is reported:

> 'Do you call them facts?' the young man asked.
> 'I mean the Astounding Disclosures'. (628)

In this process, questions about who knows what, what it is that can be known, and even whether there is anything to be known, mesmerize Maud in particular and increasingly, in self-protective ways, perhaps, Bight.

Hugh Stevens has argued that 'The Papers' can be situated in the homosexual panic resulting from Oscar Wilde's trials, and from the 'Cleveland Street Scandal of 1889–90', although it seems a little late for that, 'involving liaisons between members of the aristocracy and a number of telegraph boys' (147). Curiously, he seems to overlook the fact that Maud and Bight are journalists, mistaking them as rivals for Beadel-Muffet's publicity: 'The Papers' describes the efforts of...Maud Blandy' and 'Howard Bight to get themselves mentioned in 'the Papers', yet 'the Papers are only interested in...Beadel-Muffet' (148). In large measure, however, Bight is the creator of Beadel-Muffet, a monster, with himself as Frankenstein, over which he loses control. Speculating about the likely outcome of the relation between Beadel-Muffet and Bight, Maud envisions him as

> having for some reason, very imperative, to seek retirement, lie low, to hide, in fact, like a man 'wanted', but pursued all the while by the lurid glare that he has himself so started and kept up, and at last literally devoured (like 'Frankenstein', of course!) by the monster he has created. (552)

'We may have been great fools', James speculated in 1898,

> to develop the post office, to invent the newspaper and the railway; but the harm is done—it will be our children who will see it; we have created a Frankenstein monster at whom our simplicity can only gape' ('American Letters', 23 April 1898: 663).

The 'reason' for Beadel-Muffet's 'retirement' is the hermeneutic crux of the tale, and there are two, by no means antithetical, ways of dealing with it. First of all, Bight and Beadel-Muffet can be seen as having, or as having had, a scandalous, luridly vague, relationship involving sex and many of its cognates, including publicity, exposure, the production of sensationalism, money, politics as a form of prostitution, and the use of women as a conduit for their activities.[47] Secondly, Beadel-Muffet, as a skilful manipulator of the press and his relationship with Bight, is a James surrogate who, like the Shakespeare of the popular and commercial imagination and the Master himself, has discovered the endless rewards of obscurity. The reader is left considering the extent to which registered in 'The Papers' are James's fears about his vulnerability to public exposure, both during his life and after his death, and whether his interest in the production of mystery and the preservation of secrecy by Shakespeare and Beadel-Muffet is mostly just a rehearsal of those fears.

The central enigma of the tale is what it is that Bight knows about why Beadel-Muffet had fled and, further, what, if anything, Mrs. Chorner (who, Maud and Bight have concluded, plans to marry Beadel-Muffet once he is out of the glare of publicity) reveals to Maud about the situation. Bight's involvement in the complex erotic economy of 'The Papers' is signalled in its constant resort to sexual innuendo, the language of the tale supporting David Howard's contention that it is 'brilliantly obscene' (52).

'You're his man, or one of his men' Maud informs Bight, who regards that as a 'proof' of how much she sees (554), adding later:

> Well, you know you've more or less lived on him. I mean it's the kind of thing you *are* living on. (559)

Maud proposes that as a 'rising young journalist', Bight has 'egged' Beadel-Muffet on, 'Dear no,' he assures her, 'I panted in his rear' (560). 'Why shouldn't you keep it up?' Bight is asked by Maud, 'I mean lunching with Morton Marshall?' (579) Bight observes, when he is thinking of publicizing Morton Marshall now that his man is missing or dead, that he might step 'into his place', which is a 'lovely opening' (580). Marshall 'wants to be—well, where Beadel-Muffet is'; 'Oh, I hope not!' said Bight with grim amusement' (558). Abroad, Beadel-Muffet is in 'some hole', or has 'died, in the hole', 'in which the Papers wouldn't find him out' (596), or where he is free from the 'Organs of Public Opinion' (580); elsewhere, the Continental retreat is described as a 'queer box or tight place' (601). 'What have you done with poor Beadel?' (582), Maud asks Bight (Bite), and canine imagery and the animalistic structure the tale's approaches to Bight's relationship with Morton Marshall—'the poor gentleman saw a possible "leg up" in every bush' (568)—and his tracking and pursuit of Beadel (Beagle)-Muffet: Bight 'hounded' (583) him (yet Beadel-Muffet-as-beagle, a hunting hound, tellingly inverts the roles), the Strand news-boys 'howl' out information about the latest events, and there is much talk of 'muzzling', of Beadle-Muffet as a 'wild ass', (586) and of the 'zoo' (581). Bight's piece on Marshall is a 'rouser' in a story where 'something' is always coming 'up' (579). When Bight declares that he is 'spent, seedy, sore', and 'sick' of Beadel-Muffet's 'beastly funk', there is also a question of the proximity of 'funk' to 'spunk' (582).[48]

On a number of occasions, Bight looks or behaves 'queerly' (558).[49] Maud herself perceives Beadel-Muffet's predicament 'dimly and queerly' and identifies the 'grand "irony"' of his disappearance, the counterproductive unleashing of yet more publicity, as a 'queerness' (561). In contemplating whether or not she has invited Morton Marshall's attentions, and thereby engaged the interest of Bight in the playwright, Maud further reflects that 'it was a queer business...for her to ask herself if she...had produced on any sane human sense an effect of flirtation' (593). Bight wants to know whether Mrs. Chorner has named the 'queer reason' (586) why Beadel-Muffet has absconded. Stevens has drawn attention to the connotations of 'Middlesex Incurables' (575) suggesting, as he borders on anachronism, that James 'is inviting a sophisticated readership to enjoy the pleasures of queer reading' (149). Perhaps, though, it is sufficient to note that in reviewing this phrase among others, Maud is described as reading 'into them mystic meaning that she had never read before' (576).

The Mrs. Chorner sub-plot, with its stale residues of the circulating libraries, is largely an invention of the journalists, and one of its functions is to protect Bight from prurient, and even judicial, interrogations: twice Bight finds himself near a 'little quiet man with blue spectacles and an obvious wig, the greatest authority in London about the inner life of the criminal classes' (601). As Maud deliberates over Beadel-Muffet's motive for absence and silence, Bight tells her: 'if it's only bad enough...you'll want to save him', adding: 'I believe you'd really invent a way' (562–3). This element of the story entails a collision between two discourses: fiction, with its camouflaging, defensive tendencies, and a journalism whose imperatives are those of exposure and attack. Mobilized as part of this dialectic are the resources of Shakespeare.

From this point on, if not before, Maud in particular becomes a writer of fiction, a plotter and plot-anticipator, and an observer of and speculator on, in the Shakespearean tradition, the play-within-the play. Like Puck in *A Midsummer Night's Dream*, she is both 'auditor' and 'actor'.[50] To Bight, Mrs. Chorner 'seems a figure of fable' (586); and the romance constructed for her, which is eventually grounded in murky realities by her belated appetite for publicity, screens the truth, whatever that might be. Bight's relief at realizing that Mrs. Chorner does not know, or has not revealed, what is 'behind' (a word thrice repeated) Beadel-

Muffet's disappearance lends support to the view that Bight's relation-ship with the absentee is at the tale's core: 'Then she *hasn't* known...of what was behind. Behind any game of mine. Behind everything?' (630) At the close of 'The Papers', the two characters pick over the plot strands in a metafictional space; and Bight remains eager to seize on the protections afforded by Mrs. Chorner. 'There's always, remember, Mrs. Chorner', offers Maud, to which Bight replies:

> 'Oh yes, Mrs. Chorner; we luckily invented *her*'.
> 'Well, if she drove him to his death—?'
> Bight, with a laugh, caught at it. 'Is that it? *Did* she drive him?'
> It pulled her up, and, though she smiled, they stood again, a little, as on their guard. (637–8)

There are discernible erotic pressures, in the context of the tale as a whole, on an earlier exchange when Maud declares: 'His blood is on your hands'; Bight 'eyed his hands a moment. "They *are* dirty for him!"' (583). This jocularity, whatever the undertow, gives way to terror after the news-boy cries 'Death of Beadel-Muffet—Extraordinary News!' (609). Pressing for the rest of the story are Maud's two questions, the most penetrating of which (as always in James) is the second:

> Do you expect his situation won't be traced to you? Don't you suppose you'll be forced to speak? (628)

After a spasm of terror that indicates just how much Bight might have to cover up, he resorts, when considering the possible incriminations of his correspondence with Beadel-Muffet, to his powers of dissimulation and the screen of language: 'my letters are—gems of the purest ray. I'm covered' (629). Before then, however, James constructs a metropolitan melodrama of the 'roused Strand, all equipped both with mob and with constables'. 'He showed' to Maud

> at these strange moments, as blood-stained and literally hunted; the yell of the hawkers, repeated and echoing round them, was like a cry for his life. (611)

Displaced here is a horror in Frankfurt soon evoked and later revoked, revealed and secreted—for Maud's last question after Beadel-Muffet's return, 'Who was the dead man in the locked hotel room?' (636), continues to reverberate after the story ends as the great 'hole' in the tale—a horror in which Howard's blood, and therefore possible fate, mingles once more in acts of sex and death with his journalistic prey's. Lingering, too, is the spectre of blackmail, with Bight as one of Mayne's 'grasping' enemies of the uranian.[51]

> It was a fact, none the less, that she had in her eyes, all the while, and too strangely for speech, the vision of the scene in the little German city: the smashed door, the exposed horror, the wondering, insensible group, the English gentleman, in the disordered room, driven to bay among the scattered personal objects that only too floridly announced and emblazoned him....the poor English gentleman, hunted and hiding, done to death by the thing he yet, for so long, always *would* have, and stretched on the floor with his beautiful little revolver in his hand and the effusion of his blood, from a wound taken, with rare resolution, full in the face, extraordinary and dreadful. (612)

The reader is later told that Bight 'wouldn't be able not to smell of the wretched man's blood' (619).

For James, publicity and the new journalism of his time were ever consanguineous with sex; and the act of 'interviewing', the 'Personal Peeps' (576) of this story—with its unveiling discourses, or intercourses—have sexual connotations, as exhibited in the relation between Morton Marshall and Maud. Scandal, homosexuality, whatever the validity of the not so proximate Cleveland Street connection identified by Stevens, and the press were synonymous, more or less. 'The Papers' is certainly a story that explores the functions of secrecy, presence and absence, revelation and exposure, and the imperatives of all forms of delay. From these two premises, it would be straightforward enough to reach the conclusion that at issue in this story for James, in the main, is not just the importance of concealment in general, but the concealment of his homoerotic sexual proclivities. The situation is more complicated and conflicted than that, however. James railed against the press and its invasions, in the same way as he abjured the values of the market-place. Yet he craved the popularity he condemned; and in his texts, there is evidence of a profound dependence of his art (as in 'The Birthplace') on the democratic tastes and material he scorned.

Peter Conn's belief that 'The Papers' images James's 'direct dissent from the consciousness of the new century' (22) is much too simplistic in that it ignores the extent and energy of his dealings with it.[52] James and Beadel-Muffet have a grasp of the value, in *As You Like It*, of being 'news-crammed' (I ii 95), Rosamond's fears for which are countered by Celia's much more pragmatic 'all the better; we shall be more marketable' (I ii 97). These cross-currents are typified by a Maud who is attracted by and yet recoils from Bight's journalistic mastery: 'there was something in her mind that it still charmed—his mastery of the horrid art' (616). The couple renounce journalism for fiction, of a kind, in the end; the material of their art has been gathered, however, in a Fleet Street which also generates James's story, notwithstanding his ostensible condemnation of all that it represents. From Henrietta Stackpole in *The Portrait of a Lady*, through the character of Matthias Pardon in *The Bostonians*, where 'all things, with him, referred themselves to print, and print meant simply infinite reporting…abusive when necessary, or even when not' (107), to the narrator in 'Flickerbridge' (1902), who attacks the 'age of prodigious machinery, all organised to a single end' of 'publicity—a publicity as ferocious as the appetite of a cannibal' (439), James's apparent position on the evils of the press is only putatively emphatic and unambiguous.

George Flack, as Delia Dosson supposes early in *The Reverberator*, is 'connected…with literature' (13), and that connection is as advantageous to James, ultimately, as Francie Dosson's 'tell-tale character' (148). As an American reporter for the yellow press, Flack 'was not a particular person, but a sample or memento—reminding one of certain "goods" for which there is a steady popular demand' (14). But the hinge on which James's novel turns is the 'newspaper' containing the 'two horrible columns of vulgar lies and scandal' (135) about a Probert family subjected to considerable irony. Gaston Probert's 'genius' is for 'the worship of privacy and good manners', and 'a hatred of all the new familiarities and profanations' (194); for Charles Waterlow, however, he has the 'communicative despair' of a 'foreigner' (192). Gaston is 'effusive and appealing and ridiculous and graceful—natural, above all, and egotistical', but lacks 'moral independence':

> It was this weakness that excited Waterlow's secret scorn: family feeling was all very well, but to see it erected into a superstition affected him very much in the same way as the image of a blackamoor upon his knees before a fetish. (193)

Beadel-Muffet may have returned, but more important for Maud than his possible death, at one level, is the story she is contemplating: 'The Last Cab' is both a striking newspaper 'heading' and a good title for her own literary production (590). The fissures of James's entire *corpus*—in terms of an aesthetics of obscurity, doubleness, and duplicity—can be detected in the conflict between the 'sinuosities and convolutions' of style for which one anonymous reviewer berated 'The Papers' ('Books, Authors and Arts' 19), and the journalistic world on which it preys. James's repudiation of the press, like Beadel-Muffet's efforts to silence it by absenting himself, is acutely disingenuous. Much of the vigour of the tale arises from its acknowledgement of a symbiotic relation between the deep structures of journalism and fiction: their common anchorage, that is, in sensation, anecdotal experience, and the voyeuristic. But what the fiction possesses, which journalism lacks, is an aura of initiating and sustaining obscurity; and the production of this aura is ultimately what elevates Beadel-Muffet over Maud and Bight.

In different ways, 'The Birthplace' and 'The Papers' profit from the ironies involved in high culture's confrontation with mass cultural appropriations of Shakespeare and what is to be gained from the abuse of the past. In 'The Papers', James derives and adopts a plot from *As You Like It* to offer a critique of a popular press whose processes turn out, however, to have much in common with the metaphysics and aesthetics of appearance and reality that have fashioned his fiction. Thomas Strychacz maintains that 'publicity' in the story 'assumes the character of an autotelic force, functioning beyond the control of individual agents' (141), yet Beadel-Muffet's adroit manoeuvre, with its specious manipulation not just of presence and absence, but of life and death, leaves Maud and Bight musing over his ruling, 'immortal, the night' (636). His retreat has much the same structure and effect as James's failure to fight in the Civil War and Shakespeare's abandoning London for Stratford after writing *The Tempest*:[53]

> 'Well', the young man said, 'he *has* disappeared. There you are. I mean personally. He's not to be found. But nothing could make more, you see, for ubiquity. (581)

Bringing the 'obscure hurt' to mind:

> Beadel shows so tremendously what a catastrophe does for the right person. His absence, you may say, doubles, quintuples, his presence. (604)

Relevant to an assessment of Maud, the tale's ending, and a conflict between journalism and fiction more nominal than real in the story, is James's disquiet over the threat embodied by women to men, and a commitment to what he generally believed should be the masculine preserves of writing and culture considered in Chapter 2. Maud is unsuccessful as a journalist partly because she has too much 'imagination' (552), but the story blocks her rite of passage to fiction and artistry. Bight earlier interjects, on Mortimer Marshall's unsuccessful assaults on the citadel of the press, which is actually a consequence of Maud's inability or unwillingness to make an omelette 'without even the breakage' of an 'egg or two' (576): 'Oh well...if he can't manage to smash a pane of glass somewhere—!' (565). The 'practical point' of the pen Maud lacks has extensive, if uncertain, phallic reaches in this tale:

> That word of Bight's about smashing a window-pane had lingered with her; it had made her afterwards wonder...if there weren't some brittle surface in range of her own elbow. She had to fall back on the consciousness of how her elbow, in spite of her type, lacked practical point. (566)

There is a contact here with James's essay 'The Future of the Novel'. The starkly expressed fear, as James ambiguously remarks that 'there are too many reasons why newspapers must live' (104), is of 'the revolution taking place in the position and outlook of women':

> we may very well yet see the female elbow itself, kept in increasing activity by the play of the pen, smash with final resonance the window all this time most superstitiously closed...when women do obtain a free hand they will not repay their long debt to the precautionary attitude of men by unlimited consideration for the natural delicacy of the latter. (109)

James has returned to a problem posited in *The Bostonians* (1886) by Basil Ransom, a Civil War veteran of the South: 'the whole generation is womanized; the masculine tone', 'a very queer and partly very base mixture'

> is passing out of the world; it's a feminine, a nervous, hysterical, chattering, canting age...which, if we don't soon look out, will usher in the reign of mediocrity. (290)

Ransom, or aspects of his characterization at least, can easily be identified with the Henry James who remarks in his notebooks on the possibility of a 'big comprehensive subject' in the 'decadences and vulgarities' of the age, the 'feminizations—the materializations and abdications and intrusions, and Americanizations, the lost sense, the brutalized manner—the publicity, the newspapers, the general revolution, the failure of fastidiousness' (*N* 120).[54]

If James's Civil War stories, as suggested in Chapter 2, are in part perverse forms of re-masculinization, the popular press is a pretext for a regeneration of virile fictional strategies by the nature of its very threat. For G. M. Young, firmly anchored in a turn-of-the-nineteenth century discourse of degeneration to which James was far from immune, verbal incontinence, the press, and failures of masculinity are inseparable;[55] it is their inter-dependence, however, as much as their fusion, that preoccupies James in 'The Papers':

> fundamentally, what failed in the late Victorian age, and its flash Edwardian epilogue, was the Victorian public, once so alert, so masculine, and so responsible....the English mind sank towards that easily excited, easily satisfied, state of barbarism and childhood which press and politics for their own ends fostered, and on which in turn they fed. (187)[56]

In *The Bostonians*, Verena Tarrant's outpourings on the rights of women are silenced by Ransom's abducting her with a view to marriage.[57] As Olive Chancellor has earlier foreboded, 'there are gentlemen in plenty who would be glad to stop your mouth by kissing you!' (119). The allusion is to Shakespeare's *Much Ado About Nothing*, where a similarly vociferous Beatrice eventually loses her struggle against matrimonial confinement, and where the heroine of the play, Hero (gendered masculine by name) is celebrated for her almost entirely wordless state. Hero's suitor endorses 'silence' as the 'perfectest herald of joy' (II i 306), whereas Beatrice's injunction—mobilizing the alternatives for women surveyed and rejected in *The Bostonians* and 'The Papers', both of which explicitly or by implication re-gender the utterance—is to 'Speak, cousin, or (if you cannot) stop his mouth with a kiss, and let not him speak neither' (II i 310–11). In *Much Ado About Nothing* and *The Bostonians*, marriage becomes the enabling subterfuge by which men impose silence on women. A scheme of this kind is eventually adopted in 'The Papers'; it is radically re-written, however, given the acrobatic cross-genderings and queer circuits of desire in the tale.

What frames the scheme is the degree to which Maud is a great threat to Beadel-Muffet, Bight, and James, for as an imaginative woman (eventually) with powers of detection who can write, she is on the threshold of discovering and revealing what produced the fiction in the first place:

> She had moments, before shop-windows, into which she looked without seeing, when all the unuttered came over her. (595)

Journalists are defined, for Bight, by their not having the 'gift...of not seeing' (549), so Maud's blindness before the very panes of glass she will never get to smash (which would initiate her into the guild of authors), here mobilizes a quite different sense of redemption—'I want to save them' (571)—than the conventional one initially in play. Now, 'she was laying up treasure in time—as against the privations of the future' (593). She makes two discoveries that take her close to James's own 'treasure-house of details' (Rev. of *Middlemarch* 958): the first is that unless the past is complicated and obscure, then the 'proportion and relation' of the present and the 'treacherous' future (James, *Hawthorne* 427–8) on which fiction depends for its generation will be absent; secondly, she understands that it is not real obscurity that produces fiction, but the use to which the past is put and the obscurity thereby constructed: 'Only I feel how little', Maud tells Bight towards the end of the story, 'about what has been, all the while, *behind*—you tell me'. 'Nothing explains', she says, as the powerful ambiguity of the phrase becomes apparent: nothing has been explained, and there is nothing, really, hence the need for an obscurity that compels life-enabling illusions and fictions. 'Explains what?' asks Bight:

> 'Why, his act'.
> He gave a sigh of impatience. 'Isn't the explanation what I offered a moment ago to give you?'
> It came, in effect, back to her. 'For use?'
> 'For use'. (619)

There are similarities here between Beadel-Muffet's 'act' and Gedge's: whatever is, or is not, behind Gedge's manic odes, for the Hayeses they have a charm and interest of their own (470), and a speculative anteriority whose justification is in its utility-value. Like James at Newport, Beadel-Muffet organizes a 'plunge into the obscure' which creates 'rumours' and 'excitement' (589–90) and produces that disjunction between facts and utterable knowledge indispensable to fiction: Maud 'believed' Bight 'knew more than he said, though he had sworn as to what he didn't' (590), and 'it was his silence that completed the perfection of these things' (624). If homoerotic activity subjected normative conventions, at the time James was writing, to destructive pressures, then focusing on it is the sharpest way of exploring what constitutes fiction and its processes. It follows, then, that heterosexual marriage, even with the complexities James posits for it in this tale, is likely to reinscribe the conventions that silence women as writers.

It is Maud, as the two renounce the press in favour of the 'littery' (636), who can provide for Bight the protections of marriage in the atmosphere of danger in which he is enveloped; but not unambiguously so: Bight, now 'helpless and passive...let her do with him as she liked', and she draws 'his hand into her arm as if he were an invalid or as if she were a snare' (611–12). Marriage is allied with fiction and the hidden, whereas the press is an affair of pursuit and possible discovery. Bight achieves a certain mastery over the world from which he isolates himself, but his final position is also one of puzzled superiority, whereas Maud mixes failure with a refusal to compromise when success, in the form of a sensational interview with Mrs. Chorner she could publish, is within reach. Maud is described at the outset as 'a suburban young woman in a sailor hat' (542), 'a shocker, in short, in petticoats' (543), and a 'young bachelor' (544); and she later declares 'I ain't a woman....I wish I were' (562). Bight's gender also comes under scrutiny: he is 'not so fiercely or so freshly a male as to distance Maud in the show' (544), and 'he was so passive that it almost made him graceful' (545). James weaves into the fabric of 'The Papers' complex threads from Shakespeare's *As You Like It*, and these include the gender turbulence of its cross-dressing and the same-sex desires thereby cloaked.[58] As in Shakespeare, same-sex desire is to be sublimated in a marriage predicated on gender confusion.

Bight's initial proposal to Maud, which is suspended over the entire story, takes place in Richmond Park, London's 'Forest of Arden', and it is there that James explicitly resorts to the intricate codes of *As You Like It*:

> He turned a little, to rest on his elbow, and, cycling suburban young man as he was, he might have been, outstretched under his tree, melancholy Jacques looking off into a forest glade, even as sailor-hatted Maud, in—for elegance—a new cotton blouse and a long-limbed angular attitude, might have prosefully suggested the mannish Rosalind. (572)

Maud's female garb is queried by 'prosefully' and 'mannish' that cast it more as a disguise than a guise as Bight is softened by 'young' and 'melancholy'. Accentuated in the description of Maud, with her 'long-limbed angular attitude', are her phallic contours. The central intertextual question, however, is surely that of why James, in re-writing the plot, substitutes Jacques, the only principal character to avoid one of the four marriages with which *As You Like It* ends, for Orlando.

This substitution is far from capricious; it is reinforced by other adoptions, gratuitous if not pursued, of his character traits:

> with the life we lead and the age we live in, there's *always* something the matter with me—there can't help being: some rage, some disgust, some fresh amazement against which one hasn't, for all one's experience, been proof. (597)

That 'age we live in' reaches back to Jacques' soliloquy on the 'seven ages of man':

> All the world's a stage,
> And all the men and women merely players;
> They have their exits and their entrances,
> And one man in his time plays many parts.

(II vii 140–3)

If 'exits and entrances' is given its bawdy extensions, these lines not only relate to the malleability of self-produced personalities and celebrities in an age of publicity, but to the vagaries of selfhood in a world of unstable sexual boundaries and desires.

Also aggregated are fiction, journalism, the production of personal identity, acting, and all forms of sexual activity as areas of performance. Jacques escapes from the productions of heterosexual marriage in the forest to the 'religious life' recently adopted by the Duke in place of his 'pompous court' (V iv 180–1); and contrary to the conventional associations of marriage, this suggests retreat and celibacy for a Bight-as-Jacques who withdraws from his pursuit of Beadel-Muffet. 'Melancholia' can be interpreted as Shakespeare's code for unrequited, unrealizable, homoerotic desire, as with Antonio and his 'In sooth, I know not why I am so sad' (*The Merchant of Venice* I i 1). The overlaying of Jacques' identity on Bight heightens his predicament in a heterosexual society and appears to challenge the logic of the prospective marriage with which the story ends; unless, that is, James is attempting a union between what Haralson calls, in relation to Willa Cather's novels, 'successful (counter) masculinity and *or* successful (counter) femininity' (*Henry James and Queer Modernity* 137–8).

Homoerotic codes and the coding of the homoerotic hover closely in James when his work, as it frequently does, tests the limits of utterance and representation predicated on secrecy and obscurity. 'The Papers' is no more about the need for James to encrypt his sexuality than any of his other texts; it focuses on homoerotic desire and activity, scandal, and the press, and the interdependence of the three, but at the same time, it excavates homologies between this cluster and the origins and deep structures of fiction. Undoubtedly, James does have concerns about biography that relate to his profound misgivings about the uses other than his own of a potentially besieging past; but these concerns are always bound up with his sense of the requirements of, and for, art. These requirements, together with whether a writer has any 'private parts', and the degree to which they can, or should be, accessible, and how they might relate to his public self, or texts, is very much the territory of 'The Private Life'.

Doubleness, as Maurice Gedge discovers, is not a sufficient condition of art; also necessary is what the narrator of 'The Private Life' calls 'unabashed duplicity' (78). Privacy is essential to the existence of a text as a public entity, and to the process of which it is the result. But presence and the public, as distinct from absence and the private, are normative and passive states; privacy is an active affair of the imagination and has to be contrived; it requires duplicity.[59] 'Private' and 'privation' derive from the Latin *privatus*, which denotes a withdrawal, or being withdrawn, from public life.[60] In its earliest senses, it had aberrational and perverse connotations never quite lost (hence the ease with which it acquires an erotic edge, as in 'private parts'): to be in private was either to be secluded, like friars, or not to hold, or be deprived from holding, public office. 'Privacy' shapes St. Augustine's account of evil in a universe commensurate with the plenitude of God's goodness: 'evil is the privation of good' (Bk. 3, Ch. 7); it is a lack, or absence, not an entity that is positive, or created.[61] If privacy is vital to art, then it is a privacy whose close relatives are in the family of the 'obscure hurt': duplicity, secrecy, absence and lack, and the complications (of sin and evil perhaps) on which fiction is dependent. For James, and his sense of the art of fiction, nothing is more destructive than plenitude, or more profitable than absence. We are back with Maud and the treasures of a present soon to become the 'privations of the future' (593).

'The Private Life' is a story whose poles are privation and the private on the one hand, and a Lord Mellifont entirely defined by the public on the other.[62] The narrator, 'a searcher of hearts—that frivolous thing an observer' (69), had long 'secretly pitied' Mellifont 'for the perfection of his performance' and speculates about the impossible margin of compensating privacy it would require:

> He represented to his wife and he was a hero to his servants, and what one wanted to arrive at was what really became of him when no eye could see. He rested, presumably; but what form of rest could repair such a plenitude of presence? (79)

Art, as for Maud's tenuous experience of it in 'The Papers', is an affair of not seeing, and in the context of James's aesthetics 'presence', let alone 'a plenitude of presence', is a pathological state. Mellifont is a character who appears to have so little privacy, to exist so entirely in a public domain of representation and performance, that he disappears, in effect, when alone. Clare Vawdrey, a writer, has barely any public presence; in particular, his appearance, his conversation and general bearing, is utterly at odds with his writing.

This produces an inversion of a kind whereby Mellifont and Vawdrey double each other. Mellifont is 'all public and had no corresponding private life, just as Clare Vawdrey was all private and had no corresponding public one' (78). Mellifont the vacuous public figure plays the part of a Shakespeare Gedge's visitors queue to see, whereas Vawdrey seems in public to be a clumsy mediocrity whose writing cannot be accounted for: 'Clare Vawdrey's talk suggested the reporter contrasted with the bard' (65). If Vawdrey has become Bight, or Maud, rather, here, then Mellifont is only half-way towards Beadel-Muffet or Shakespeare. Lacking complication, he is too ponderable for the purposes of art. For Gedge, Shakespeare is beyond the reach of his talk; Mellifont, though, has no beyond. Like James in his essay on *The Tempest*, ultimately, Lady Mellifont is a preserver of mysteries; she prefers the 'relative grandeur of uncertainty (79) to what a look through the keyhole would reveal.

Writing in this story, as distinct from Mellifont's 'loud and cheerful and copious' performances (60), takes place in private in the sexually charged zone of Vawdrey's bedroom. The playwright, by contrast with Vawdrey's innocuous impersonation of him, is as invisible as the Shakespeare of his plays; he is available for speculation entirely because he is non-spectacular. In this respect, he represents the doubleness of Shakespeare, with that perceived disparity between man and plays that bedevilled both Delia Bacon and James in his introduction to *The Tempest*. So disembodied is Vaudrey-as-writer, that he can initially be mistaken for 'a travelling-rug thrown over a chair': 'his back was half turned to me, and he bent over the table in the attitude of writing'. The narrator rather understates his 'sense of mystification' given that 'to the best' of his 'belief', he had left Vawdrey 'below in conversation with Mrs. Adney' (72). He concludes that Vawdrey is two people so to speak, and that 'they're members of a firm'; 'one of them couldn't carry on the business without the other' (81). Beadel-Muffet and the journalists of 'The Papers' have an inter-dependency mapped in 'The Private Life' onto the one character of Vawdrey. In neither tale is there a sustained opposition between the public and the private, the latter being the necessarily obscure realm of generation. But by the time of 'The Papers', and after his forays into the tawdry realities of the market in 'The Birthplace', James can construct a public figure, Beadel-Muffet, who has some of the alchemy of art.

The narrator of 'The Private Life' resembles to an extent Mark Ambient of 'The Author of Beltraffio' in that his attraction to the author has strong homoerotic inflections. Blanche Adney and he seem to rival each other for Vawdrey's attentions, and the latter welcomes the storm which leaves him alone in a shelter with the object of his curiosity and desire, possibly. He cannot, however, satisfactorily express his adoration (90), for the playwright protects his private parts, and preserves his impenetrability, with endless prattle about 'Lady Ringrose', 'Mr. Chafer', and sundry other 'reviewers' (89). In a far from subtle code, the narrator expects Vawdrey, 'exposed to the fury of the elements', to 'assume' a 'Manfred attitude' (89).

Byron had long been a by-word for sexual incontinence, and his *Manfred* (1817), autobiographical in some of its resonances, dramatizes a hero whose love for his sister has doomed him to wander and suffer destruction in a world of darkness. Doubled, in a way that casts an interesting shadow on Vawdrey, is the playwright's doubleness in that Manfred, with his fantastic powers, lives half in the human world and half in the world of spirits. The narrator concludes, as the storm abates, that as he has experienced only 'responsive flashes', the real Vawdrey must be with Mrs. Adney. As an artist, Vawdrey can exercise an 'economy', rather than vaunt a 'plenitude of presence' like Mellifont, painful to a narrator relegated to the public sphere:

> The world was vulgar and stupid, and the real man would have been a fool to come out[63] for it when he could gossip and dine by deputy. None the less my heart sank as I felt my companion practice this economy. I don't know exactly what I wanted; I suppose I wanted him to make an exception for *me*. (89)

'The Birthplace', 'The Papers', and 'The Private Life' dramatize in disparate ways the extent to which obscurity and evacuation increase, rather than diminish, a critical curiosity on which, in any event, the literary text thrives. James's ambivalence about Shakespeare in his introduction to *The Tempest* arises in part because, like the narrator of 'The Private Life', he wants to reconcile the artist implied by the texts with the man. But Shakespeare-the-man, as constituted by the 'facts', is a fractured mediocrity, and any attempt to retrieve him as a supplement to his plays is fraught with contradictions.

(iv) 'The more extended lunge'

In his introduction to *The Tempest*, James has become a Howard Bight figure perpetuating the very mystery under investigation; and in the allusion to Macbeth—that 'sound and fury'[64]—a collaboration with the press in all its rapaciousness is implied:

> There are moments, I admit, in this age of sound and fury, of connections, in every sense, too maddeningly multiplied, when we are willing to let it pass as a mystery. (*IT* 1215)

Instructively, it is because 'the man everywhere, in Shakespeare's work' is 'so effectually locked up and imprisoned in the artist' that James finds himself hovering 'at the base of thick walls for a sense of him' (*IT* 1209), exercising his 'morbid and monstrous curiosity' (*IT* 1216).[65] This curiosity results in part from James's failure to find Shakespeare in the plays and not, as Vivian Jones has argued, because he detects there 'the complete formal transformation of private experience in the work of art' (199).[66]

The 'antique documents' left behind (or not) by Shakespeare, 'extricated, analysed, and compared', bore little resemblance for Emerson to the 'skyey sentences—aërolites' in the plays 'which seemed to have fallen out of heaven' ('Shakespeare; or, The Poet' 120), and this is one of the incongruities explored in 'The Private Life' and the introduction to *The Tempest*: in both, man, author, and texts seem greatly at odds with each other. James's 'imagination' and sharply honed reading skills reject the 'primitive simplicity' (*IT* 1215) of Halliwell-Phillips's facts.[67] 'The number of the mustered facts' is, in any case, irrelevant: what matters is 'the kind of fact that each may strike us as being' (*IT* 1208). Such relics of the past, as in 'The Birthplace', are incommensurable with Shakespeare the alluring and yet bedevelling 'monster and magician of a thousand masks' (IT 1209) who is both a Caliban suspicious of the curse of language and the imperatives of representation, exposure, and publicity, and a Prospero who concocts the empowering dissimulations of art.[68] In a formula familiar from Emerson and beyond, and tirelessly applied in 'The Birthplace':

> None ever appealed so sharply to some light of knowledge, and nothing could render our actual knowledge more contemptible. (*IT* 1215)

The Tempest shows 'us the artist consciously tasting of the first and rarest of his gifts, that of imaged creative Expression' (*IT* 1207), and this leaves James suspended between 'human curiosity' and 'aesthetic passion' (*IT* 1209); for where there are signs of expression, curiosity about the author's life is aroused; and if a text can no longer be detached from an expressive voice, or personality, the act of writing becomes more an affair of exposure, or possible discovery, than one of self-erasing and fiction-generating obscurity. James adhered, unsystematically, to an organicist aesthetic whose line stretches from Coleridge and the German idealists, and beyond, and through to Flaubert and his theories of impersonality.[69]

The central incoherence of organicism arises from its emphasis both on objective representation and writing as expression; the vital autonomy of a text depends on its detachment from an author whose impressions of experience it nevertheless expresses. But the artful means by which such impressions are objectified requires some knowledge of what, in the writer's experience, generated the material now transformed into art. If literature is a matter of style, and style is the man, then the more a reader knows about the man, the greater his knowledge of the technique and texts to which it might give rise, and the more significant, in turn again, the texts. But if the autonomy of texts depends on an author's severance from them, that 'stillness' of 'style' (*IT* 1209) James identifies in *The Tempest* calls the possibility of such an autonomy into question. 'It is one of my principles', wrote Flaubert, 'that one must not write oneself into one's work':

> The artist must be in his work as God is in creation, invisible yet all-powerful; we must sense him everywhere but never see him....Art should rise above personal feeling and emotional susceptibilities! (Letter to Mademoiselle Leroyer de Chantepie: 18 March 1857: 271)

'Doctor Hugh', in James's 'The Middle Years', a story much concerned with some of the paradoxes of this objectivist aesthetic, is an avid reader and admirer of Dencombe's work. The author deliberates, for 'a person was always a fool for calling attention to his work' (341), over whether to acquaint his reader with what is unavailable directly in the texts, his 'knowledge' and 'craft'. If 'he couldn't, the alternative was hard: Dencombe would have to surrender to silence, unvindicated and undivined' (348). Dencombe thinks, then, about the extent to which he could, or should, communicate to his reader what James calls the 'delicate debates and intimate understandings of an artist with himself' (*IT* 1210) to which he would like access in Shakespeare, or whether the 'concert' can only ever be for 'one, both performer and auditor' (*IT* 1211).[70] In the end, the processes whereby the writer 'renders the poverties and obscurities of our world....in the dazzling terms of a richer and better' appear to involve an incommunicable 'miracle' and obfuscations (*IT* 1211). On the one side, there is 'penetration, exploration, interpretation' and 'appreciation' (*IT* 1216), but on the other, somewhere in the vicinity of James's own self-fashioning manoeuvres at Newport—'the rhythmic play of my arms' (*HJA* 415) has its counterpart here in the 'waving arms'—there is 'an obscurity' which if 'endured, in fine, one inch further, or one hour longer'

> than our necessity truly holds us to, strikes us but as an artificial spectre, a muffled object with waving arms, set up to keep appreciation down. (*IT* 1217)

In reading over his own work, Dencombe reflects on the consequences for himself of an art that conceals art,[71] suggesting the costs to the writer of an obscurity, an anonymity and impersonality that prevents texts, nevertheless, from being mere biographical conduits:

> He recognised his motive and surrendered to his talent. Never, probably, had that talent, such as it was, been so fine. His difficulties were still there, but what was also there, to his perception, though probably, alas! to nobody's else, was the art that in most cases had surmounted them. (338)

If James attacked 'the mere muffled majesty of irresponsible "authorship"' (*PGB* 1323), he also recognized the importance of the 'author's voice' he now urgently seeks in *The Tempest*:

> There is always at best the author's voice to be kept out. It can be kept out for occasions, it can not be kept out always. The solution therefore is to leave it its function, for it has the supreme one. ('London Notes': 31 July 1897: 1404)

The 'unguessed riddle' of Shakespeare's life ('In Warwickshire' 175) and the ambivalence it generated about what can, cannot, and should not be known about a writer surfaces from the outset in the geometry and spatialization of James's hermeneutics. When recollecting in *A Small Boy and Others* an early experience of seeing *The Comedy of Errors*, which he enjoyed with almost 'unbearable intensity' (*HJA* 60), a dilemma is identified the usual terms of which are reversed. Consonant with his treatment of wars and soldiers, James configures the urge to see and know directly as passive, whereas a productive, imaginative, 'defiance'— in which 'presence is better than absence' only 'if you love excess' (Frank O'Hara 190)—is active. As he waited with his brother William for the play to begin, he remembers feeling (or needs, in 1914, to believe so) that 'the torment of the curtain was mixed, half so dark a defiance and half so rich a promise' (*HJA* 61). For James, as for Gaston Bachelard:

> there will always be more things in a closed, than in an open, box. To verify images kills them, and it is always more enriching to *imagine* than to *experience*. (88)

In a review of Henry Irving's *Richard III*, James associates Shakespeare and his plays with what is out of reach, intangible, and therefore intact. Play and playwright are imaginable only because they are remote and beyond representation. Whether

> such a Richard as this is or isn't...a 'comic character', leaves me cold compared with the opportunity of testifying afresh to an impression now quite wearily mature—an acute sense that, after all that has come and gone, the represented Shakespeare is simply no longer to be borne. The reason of this impatience is of the clearest—there is absolutely no representing him....The more it is painted and dressed, the more it is lighted and furnished and solidified, the less it corresponds or coincides, the less it squares with our imaginative habits. ('London', 23 January 1897: 490–1)[72]

James took the opportunity to involve Shakespeare in a modification of Violet Hunt's definition of 'genius' in a curious letter which reveals inconsistencies in his position on the enigma of Shakespeare similar to those visible in his introduction to *The Tempest*:

> Your comparison of genius to the passenger on the 'liner' with his cabin and his 'hold' luggage is very brilliant and I should quite agree

with you—and *do*. Only I make this difference. Genius gets at its *own* luggage, in the hold, perfectly (while common mortality is reduced to a box under the berth); but it doesn't get at the Captain's and the First Mate's, in *their* mysterious retreats. Now William of Stratford (it seems to me) *had* no luggage, could have had none, in any part of the ship, corresponding to much of the wardrobe sported in the plays. (11 August 1903: 4: 281)[73]

Some of the New York Edition prefaces uncertainly expose the 'private history' of the 'work' and partially reveal the '*accessory* facts in a given artistic case', although in an 'ambiguous aesthetic air' (*PRH* 1039). But the prefaces also declare other fiction to be 'fatherless and motherless' (*PTM* 1103), James choosing to deal coyly at times with the 'story of one's story itself' (*PA* 1309). There was always a fear of the 'terrible fluidity of self-revelation' (*PA* 1316), and 'the writer alone has the *secret* of the particular case', this renewing 'in the modern alchemist something like the old dream of the secret of life' (*PSP* 1141). James has a 'mysterious retreat' in which he fabricates his 'genius'; but in his letter to Violet Hunt, he regrets the inaccessibility of what others have stowed away, and speculates about the content of Shakespeare's wardrobe.

James's conclusion is not that an inspection of Shakespeare's 'luggage' would find him bereft of clothes, but that their discovery, or recovery—as with relics, documents, the germs of stories and novels, and the facts of life in general—would reveal items far from incidental yet inscrutable. Their relation to Shakespeare's work, like James's obscure hurt to his writing, would (of necessity) be skewed and oblique beyond measure at best. Tantalized by Shakespeare, James is anxious about the danger he represents, however, to the security of his own mysterious retreats. There are grounds for supposing that Delia Bacon was the kind of indomitable exhumer he feared when he wrote in one of his last letters, in answer to his nephew Harry's enquiry about his 'literary remains', that his 'sole wish' was 'to frustrate as utterly as possible the post-mortem exploiter', the 'invading chronicler'

which, I know, is but so imperfectly possible. Still, one can do something, and I have long thought of launching, by a provision in my will, a curse not less explicit than Shakespeare's own on any such as try to move my bones. Your question determines me definitely to advert to the matter in my will—that is to declare my utter and absolute abhorrence of any attempted biography or the giving to the world by 'the family', or by any person for whom my disapproval has any sanctity, of any part or parts of my private correspondence. One can discredit and dishonour such enterprises even if one can't prevent them.

Happy to contemplate the possible production of more 'passages of retrospect and reminiscence' of his own, James would not tolerate the prospect of rival fictions (Letter to Henry James III, 7 April 1914, *HJR* 4: 806), for 'a man has certainly a right to determine, in so far as he can, what the world shall know of him and what it shall not; the world's natural curiosity to the contrary notwithstanding' (Rev. of *Correspondence of William Ellery Channing* 212). James remained insatiably curious, however, about the lives of others, especially Shakespeare's, inferring thereby the threat to himself of posthumous enquirers.

Throughout his criticism, aware that 'to read between the lines of the best literature' is 'one of the most interesting pursuits in the world' (Rev. of *Mon Frère et Moi* 215), James vacillates over his revulsion and desire for 'searching, staring daylight' and the 'bereavement of privacy' (Rev. of *Ezra Stiles Gannett* 279). 'We always desire more information about the writers who greatly interest us than we find in their works' (Rev. of *Frülingsfluthen* 992), yet 'to be admitted behind the scenes of a man's personality', he wrote in 1875, is a 'privilege' that should be 'reserved for the few' ('Livingstone's Last Journals' 1142); and a year after the Civil War ended he reflected on 'how small is the proportion either of men or of women who could afford to have the last veil of privacy removed from their daily lives' (Rev. of *Lettres d'Eugénie de Guérin* 433). The 'eternal dispute' is 'between the public and the private, between curiosity and delicacy' (740) as the writer,

> the pale forewarned victim, with every track covered, every paper burnt and every letter unanswered, will, in the tower of art, the invulnerable granite, stand, without a sally, the siege of all the years. ('She and He: Recent Documents' 743)

James frets over the possibility of future biographies, however, not simply because he has things to hide, but because without the illusion of crypts more or less inaccessible, the mysteries on which fiction depends collapse.[74] If Gedge's 'excellent dumb discourse' (*The Tempest* III iii 39) in 'The Birthplace', under the influence of Irving's similarly artful ramblings, is one (counter-intuitive) form of preserving the nebulousness of entities in any case not susceptible to discursive access, then silence, a refusal to utter, or to represent, may be a superior one.[75] For James, and to a lesser degree Gedge, art is bound by Prospero's injunction:

> There's something else to do. Hush, and be mute,
> Or else our spell is marr'd.
>
> (*The Tempest* IV i 126–7)

The life-giving source of a work, especially in the form of the writer himself, its essence, perhaps its potential for autonomy, is buried: 'literature lives', wrote James in 'The Science of Criticism', 'in the sacred depths of its being'; but it is apparent from what immediately follows that he also believed that a text could resist the destructive invasions of criticism by remaining mute: 'nothing is better calculated than irresponsible pedagogy to make it close its ears and lips' (97). Both strategies, as in 'The Birthplace', work in a similar way: the idea of inaccessible depths that can never be plumbed both allures and holds off the critic; silence, on the other hand, amounts to much the same thing as emptiness but implies, by contrast, ineffable profundities.

When James reflected at Concord in *The American Scene* on the 'exquisite melancholy of everything unuttered' (569), making those connections explored in Chapter 1 between Shylock and an interest in history, he included the Birthplace at Stratford-upon-Avon as one of the 'rude relics...of greatness' (570) that 'resist their pressure of reference'. Recollecting 'the small hard facts of the Shakespeare house at Stratford', he sees them 'intrinsically...as naught—deeply depressing...to any impulse to reconstitute' (571). For Delia Bacon, Shakespeare, like his house, was a similar 'historic void' ('The Birthplace' 472); but from the perspective of Emerson and Very he was a definitive 'genius' unavailable to fact-mongering and its mundane discourses.[76] Either way, both Gedge's flamboyant inventions, his 'copious elements' in the presence of 'persistent ignorance' (*IT* 1205), and James's wavering commitments to silence trade heavily on an enigma they also construct.

Delia Bacon saw her task as one of dispelling through empirical investigation 'this great myth of the modern ages' ('William Shakespeare and His Plays' 169); but James in his introduction to *The Tempest* is much more perplexed about the issue in an essay that demonstrates by its own, sometimes incoherent, critical practice both the frustration and intensified curiosity that result from the resistance of art to artful penetration. That James could subject to ironic attack the very processes of interpretation and criticism which also supply the dynamics for much of his work is clear from 'The Figure in the Carpet'. The integrity of

Vereker's texts is a function of their impenetrability: endlessly available for interpretation, they must nevertheless remain uninterpreted. Significantly, Corvick's search for meaning is aligned with the futile pursuit of Shakespeare by legions of cryptographers at the end of the nineteenth century: 'He was like nothing, I told him, but the maniacs who embrace some bedlamitical theory of the cryptic character of Shakespeare' (588).[77]

James understands the mechanism whereby Shakespeare's 'career' has been taken as a 'transcendent "adventure"...of the mind of man' (*IT* 1219), and he nervously welcomes the power of the enigma thereby produced. But his hopes for the 'Criticism of the future', with his own forms of obscurity in play, are fearfully expressed:

> The figured tapestry, the long arras that hides him, is always there, with its immensity of surface and its proportionate underside. May it not then be but a question, for the fulness of time, of the finer weapon, the sharper point, the stronger arm, the more extended lunge? (*IT* 1220)

'One of the interesting things in big persons is that they leave us big questions' observed James ('London Notes', 21 August 1897: 1412), and his appetite for information about the bard was insatiable; he found the lure of the 'eternal mystery' (*IT* 1215), the 'strained and aching wonder' (*IT* 1205) of it all, however, an even more irresistible feast.

4
Grammars of Time, Senses of the Past

> That which hath been is now; and that which is to be hath
> already been; and God requireth that which is past.
>
> (Ecclesiastes 3: 15)

(i) 'A certain sense of proportion'

In *The Philosophy of History*, Hegel consigned America to the future and
thereby rendered it intensely susceptible in speculative and aesthetic
realms to present vicissitudes and the contingencies of an ever intangible beyond.[1] Hegel could argue, at least in the early eighteenth century, that 'the general object of the existence of this State is not yet
fixed and determined', for 'a real State and a real Government arise only
after a distinction of classes has arisen' (85). 'America is therefore the
land of the future', a 'land of desire for all those who are weary of the
historical lumber-room of old Europe':

> It is for America to abandon the ground on which hitherto the
> History of the World has developed itself. What *has* taken place in
> the New World up to the present time is only an echo of the Old
> World—the expression of a foreign life; and as a Land of the Future,
> it has no interest for us here, for, as regards *History*, our concern must
> be with that which has been and that which is. (87)

Emerson's reaction to the 'historical lumber-room' of the Old World,
which included Shakespeare and that pressure to cower imitatively in
his wake surveyed at the outset of the last chapter, was to seize with
great alacrity on the apparent detachment of America from history.
For Emerson and his Transcendentalist fellow-travellers, the local and

particular were valuable only as the means to, or types of, the universal; and temporal sequence, let alone the specific narratives of history, was a distraction from the progression, however inchoately expressible, to things spiritual and divine. America, and its cognates of poetry and 'wonder', like the Shakespeare Emerson had envisaged, could 'spring', 'from the invisible, to abolish the past' ('Shakespeare; or, The Poet' 119).

But for Henry James as an aspiring novelist, a vacuous beyond was as inconvenient as the insubstantial American past and present given the complexities and obscurities on which he saw fiction as depending. James specified Hawthorne's problems as a writer as arising in no small measure from the 'so thin and impalpable a deposit' left by 'history' in the 'United States' (*Hawthorne* 327). After making his observations that 'it takes a great deal of history to produce a little literature', and 'that it needs a complex social machinery to set a writer in motion' (*Hawthorne* 320), James offered his notorious inventory of what he called the 'negative side of the spectacle on which Hawthorne looked out':

> No State, in the European sense of the word, and indeed barely a specific national name. No sovereign, no court, no personal loyalty, no aristocracy, no church, no clergy, no army, no diplomatic service, no country gentlemen, no palaces, no castles, nor manors, nor old country-houses, nor parsonages, nor thatched cottages nor ivied ruins; no cathedrals, nor abbeys, nor little Norman churches; no great Universities nor public schools—no Oxford, nor Eton, nor Harrow; no literature, no novels, no museums, no pictures, no political society, no sporting class—no Epsom nor Ascot! (*Hawthorne* 351–2)

In his *Parables of Possibility*, Martin locates James's rhetorical strategies in a long tradition of the *via negativa*, of defining America not in terms of what it is and has but in those of what it is not and does not have, a discourse that stretches back at least as far as Montaigne, and the effect of which is the 'negative invention' of a country 'endowed with simplicity and a fundamental purity' (48). As Mr. Evelyn tells Sylvester Judd's eponymous Margaret in an account of a shipwrecked (*Tempest*-like) America on which James appears to have drawn: 'We have no traditions, legends, fables, and scarcely a history', for 'a good part of the Old World on its passage to the New was lost overboard':

> We have no monarchical supremacy, no hereditary prerogatives, no patent nobility, no Kings, and but few Bishops....we have no

Haddon Hall or Raby Castle Kitchen; no chapels or abbeys, no broken arches or wasted crags....Our atmosphere is transparent, unoccupied, empty from the bottom of our wells to the zenith, and throughout the entire horizontal plane. (246–8)

The accumulation of anaphoric negatives in James's identification of what America lacks, together with his imitation of a form, the list, that avows the paratactical assembly of data at the expense of the hypotaxis of densely connected prose with its syntax of intricate subordination, is the idiom, in part of Emerson, Thoreau, Whitman, and others, and can be seen as characterizing, for example, approaches to American literary history before the Civil War.[2] By 1883, when James Herbert Morse's two major essays on the history of American literature were published in the *Century Magazine* ('The Native American Element in American Fiction: Before the War', and 'The Native American Element in American Fiction: Since the War'), retrospective inventories of its fiction in particular had become commonplace. Naming, listing, and the production of catalogues constitute modes of orientation and acts of possession and self-fashioning; and as such, these formations are the indispensable morphemes of narrative and history. Morse can predicate his history on what Brodhead calls the 'past-establishing' systems (5) of abundant lists already in circulation. The question of why his essays are able to adopt narrative principles apparently unavailable, or uncongenial, to many of his predecessors can be construed as being closely related to James's appropriation of, and involvement in, post-bellum initiations of proportion, obscurity, and senses of the past.

Among literary critics and historians, there was a growing sense of a distinctively American literature, with its antecedents stretching beyond the War of Independence, well before the Civil War.[3] Typical of an approach in which the complications of narrative are rejected or unavailable is George Tucker's 'A Discourse on American Literature' (1838). Rather than ranking and estimating quality, Tucker catalogues and measures abundance:[4]

The names of Halleck, Percival, Bryant, Sigourney, Willis, Allston, and Mellen, have ably vindicated the claim of their country to poetical talent....In essay writing and miscellaneous literature....we may mention Irving, Paulding, Cooper, Wirt, Walsh, Everett, Ingersoll, Jefferson, John Quincy Adams, Cass, Flint, Dwight. (213)

Two years later, an anonymous writer of 'The Inferiority of American Literature' identifies what he calls the 'constellation' of 'Bryant, Brainard, Dana, Halleck and Percival, Sigourney, Gould, Embury and Davidson' (256), and such evaluations as he offers borrow their vocabulary and syntax, given the plethora of em dashes, isocolons, and formulaic premodifications, from trade catalogues and newspapers. There are

> the strong and nervous writing of Jefferson and our lamented Hamilton—the deep, logical reasonings of Edwards—the wild force and energy of Dana—the pensiveness and natural imagery of Bryant—the bold originality of Halleck—the versatile and beautiful productions of Irving—the inimitably striking descriptions of Cooper. (257)

And so it goes on.

With Morse's 1883 essays, it is immediately apparent that we are in the presence of narrative. Significantly, Morse allocates only writers he deems as minor to the indignity of the list. Major writers are given miniature biographies, becoming narrative agents in effect, and their works are treated thematically and ranked, rather than merely enumerated and classified. In Hayden White's terms, there is 'emplotment' here (*Metahistory* 7): the movement tracked, or constructed, is from the novels of Charles Brockden Brown, James Fenimore Cooper, and William Gilmore Simms, towards the summit of Hawthorne and, more dubiously, to William Dean Howells, James, and the realist school, where French-inflected theories and technical sophistications cast their shadow. Morse early signals the genre to which he aspires, the post-Darwinian context on which he draws, and his dense plot: 'Let us trace, as well as we can, the history of these changes in our fiction, and note the growth in it of a native as well as an artistic element' (106). The essays as a whole, then, have an evident teleology and sense of closure. Annals and chronicles are subjected to a narrative momentum involving intricate hierarchies and evaluations. Anachronies replace chronologies as Morse establishes relations between writers and texts by orchestrating analepses and prolepses.[5] He foreshortens to sharpen the focus on the worthy; and the overlay is of a densely cohesive syntax, the hypotaxis of cause-and-effect sequences displacing the parataxis characteristic of many earlier essays in the genre.

In a Hegelian vein, Hayden White has emphasized narrative as the distinguishing feature of 'history' rather than 'chronicle'. White's line in *The Content of the Form* is that annals and chronicles, like historical grand narratives, are 'particular products of possible conceptions of historical reality' (5), and that it is the

> need or impulse to rank events with respect to their significance for the culture or group that is writing its own history that makes a narrative representation of real events possible. (10)

It is only in sufficiently elaborate societies that the 'diacritical markers' (10) of the hierarchies necessary to narrative history are available. The demand for narrative closure—as annals evolve into chronicles and not history, merely, but a narrative history commensurable with fiction—is a function of an imperative of 'moral meaning' (21) and the values attached not to the real, but to its representation. Rather than the past, whatever that might be, the focus is on its uses. The pressure is on the real to 'display the coherence, integrity, fullness, and closure of an image of life that is and can only be imaginary'. 'Does the world', asks White, 'really present itself to perception in the form of well-made stories?' (24).

The continuity of what could have been one long essay, for Morse, is ruptured by the Civil War; and towards the end of his first piece, singled out for consideration is what White calls a 'principle', a complication in the form of a 'social center...for assigning importance or significance to events' (11) which makes possible narrative history:

> The war had disturbed the old monotony of healthy and regular growth in the nation, forcing old blood into new channels; and out of the change and ferment was to come a more vigorous and much more original novelistic growth....The wheels of time had got a fresh jog, and were rolling on a little faster than usual. (121)

Disturbance and the end of monotony, change, and ferment were among the advantages of the Civil War identified by Henry James when he observed that it 'introduced into the national consciousness a certain sense of proportion and relation', the world now 'being a more complicated place than it had hitherto seemed, the future more treacherous, success more difficult' (*Hawthorne* 427–8). For James, what mattered about the complications he saw as arriving with the advent of the Civil War was the more convoluted experience of the present it enabled together with a keener, yet also troublesome, sense of the exigencies of space and time. The 'obscure hurt' is both an objective correlative[6] for these seismic shifts and a displacement of them for a writer formed in part by the opening up of an individual, social, and national past whose spectres of lost innocence and guilt in hypotactical relation would be the compelling factors of his narrative fiction. Nietzsche is apposite here: 'in order that there might be some degree of conscious-ness in the world, an unreal world of error had to arise' (Vaihinger 346), and 'consciousness is something essentially falsifying' (Vaihinger 358n). Henceforth, punctuating past, present, and future, in an age of dawning relativities at all levels of thought and experience, would be a much more perilous activity: a ramifying and increasingly bewildering American present could increasingly be regarded as an unfathomable function of a future-limiting past.

What began in America as a celebration of its freedom from history was to develop into forebodings, as the past opened up behind a nation no longer youthful, about the power of a burgeoning anteriority. In this respect, not least in the productive inconsistencies of his position, James is thoroughly American: he seeks security in the 'nearer distances and clearer mysteries' (*PAP* 1177), and Gabriele D'Annunzio is acclaimed for his 'imaginative development of observable things, things present, significant, related to us, and not in a weak false fumble for the remote and the disconnected' (932). James's approaches to the challenges posed by the past for the present and the future were to become ever more radical as he surveyed the unstable intersections between the 'superfluous, abundance of the eventual' (Letter to the Hon. Robert S. Rantoul, 10 June 1904: 470), 'far recessional perspec-tives' (Preface, *Letters from America* 751), and the 'retrospective present' (Rev. of *The Schönberg-Cotta Family* 828). Paradoxically, an intensifying awareness of a future restricted by the past resulted for many writers, and especially for Henry James, in a relocating of potential from the future to the past, and in a greater investment in disruptions of anisotropic time.[7] Purdy has argued that 'linear time', 'time with a dependable "arrow"', has always been treated as 'counterintuitive' in 'the history of literature' (71); and for James, 'man is a retrogressive as well as a progressive being' ('Thomson's Indo-China and China' 1309).

When a mere twenty-seven years of age, James felt able to write of 'the enormous bulk of the still lingering ineradicable past' (Letter to Charles Eliot Norton, 25 March 1870: 33). This precocious nostalgia was in some measure provoked by the death of his cousin Minny Temple; but James also saw her relegation to what he was later to call the 'early dead' as a good speculation ('The Author of Beltraffio' 907). 'Twenty years hence what a pure eloquent vision she will be', James confided to his mother, 'it will count in old age, when we live, more than now, in reflection, to have had such a figure in our youth' (Letter to Mary Walsh, 26 March 1879: 37–8); and forty-five years later (in 1914), looking over a photograph of Minny he had long 'secreted and brooded over', he considered the return on his investment: 'I prize the ghostly image all the more for the lapse of time'.[8] Apparent in these incoherent rhetorical manoeuvres is an ambivalence about the 'eternal time-question' (*PRH* 1048) and the past, with its 'pleasant promiscuous patina of time' (*The American Scene* 436), with which James was to struggle throughout his career. If the Civil War had made the 'future more treacherous' (*Hawthorne* 428) there was also the problem of 'treacherous History' (*IT* 1207); and if James delighted 'in a palpable imaginable *visitable* past' (*PAP* 1177), there was always that 'abundance of the eventual' (Letter to the Hon. Robert S. Rantoul: 10 June 1904, 470).

In 1904, after an absence of nearly twenty years, James returned to America to gather impressions for *The American Scene*. The 'post-major' or 'fourth' phase of writing the visit initiated involves a good deal more than the 'racism and xenophobia' McWhirter establishes a range of critics as seeing ('"A Provision Full of Responsibilities": Senses of the Past in Henry James's Fourth Phase' 162n, 152), and much less than a discovery for James of 'who he is' (162). What James determines is more the futility of searching for a stable sense of self amidst models of time and history under siege from turn-of-the-nineteenth century shifts in scientific and philosophical thinking.[9] The fulcrum of this final phase, which Gard simply dismisses as containing 'the side productions ... of an extremely fevered later life' (1), is James's volatile apprehension of both 'the lost and regretted period and chance, always, to fond fancy, supremely charming and queer and exquisite' ('The Story-Teller at Large' 286) and of what Georges Poulet identified as the 'charm of the bygone future' (353).

In itself, James's interest in time, the problems of negotiating it in narrative—he wrote of it as 'the stiffest problem that the artist in fiction has to tackle' ('London Notes', 31 July 1897, 1404)—and the mapping of such concerns onto the cycle of his own life, was far from new. In many of the short stories in particular, imperatively—but often impossibly, and usually transgressively—the past is resurrected, investigated, and embraced, or (re)presented as synthetic, a variably delightful fiction vulnerable to multiple interpretations, and better excoriated and expunged. There are characters trapped in the present struggling for the 'long backward reach into time' ('Frances Anne Kemble' 1073) and others, haunted and transfixed, who seek to expiate or redeem the past.

More rarely, there are viciously satirized Americans 'who quietly' feel that they 'have the Future' in their 'vitals' ('The Point of View' 561). By going back in time in *The Sense of the Past*, Ralph Pendrel makes a pre-emptive strike against T. S. Eliot's 'If all time is eternally present/ All time is unredeemable (*Four Quartets* 171). James left the novel unfinished, however, and like counterparts seemingly less fortunate, who resemble Prufrock 'etherised upon a table' ('The Love Song of J. Alfred Prufrock' 13), he remains suspended in an arena of querulous enquiry. There is also the familiar James strategy of declaring the past to be inaccessible, unspeakable, or unutterable. Beyond the pale of discourse, past experience is often projected as unrepresentable and unamenable, in particular, to historical methods anchored in a reverence for facts. More and more, and in ways relevant to both 'The Jolly Corner' and *The Sense of the Past*, James came to see the past in a mixed idiom of the natural and the super-natural, and as embodied only in people such as Frances Anne Kemble who are 'historic' because of the 'curious contacts' with it that they are 'able, as it were, to transmit' ('Frances Anne Kemble' 1074–5).

But what characterizes James's interest in time in 'The Jolly Corner' and beyond is the extent to which it seemed increasingly available in the early twentieth century, along with the past, as a synthetic category, a discursive formation, for use and abuse. For William James, for example, the 'soul is only a succession of fields of consciousness', and 'perspective' is entirely a matter of the words—'"here", "this", "now"', and so on—we 'apply' (*The Varieties of Religious Experience* 182). 'We assume for certain purposes', he argues in *Pragmatism*, 'one "objective" Time', but 'we don't livingly believe in or realize any such equally-flowing time' (566). William James's affinities are with Henri Bergson, of course, and nowhere is this more the case than in *A Pluralistic Universe*, published in the same year as 'The Jolly Corner'.[10] 'The essence of life is its continuously changing character; but our concepts are all discontinuous and fixed':

> Past and future, for example, conceptually separated by the cut to which we give the name of present, and defined as being the opposite sides of that cut, are to some extent, however brief, co-present with each other throughout experience. The literally present moment is a purely verbal supposition.[11]

For William James, 'the only present ever realized concretely' is the '"passing moment" in which the dying rearward of time and its dawning future forever mix their lights' (746). 'In the pulse of inner life immediately present now in each of us is a little past, a little future, a little awareness of our own body' and of the 'direction of history' (760); 'all real units of experience *overlap*' (761). William James even does a little dabbling, trading in the medium of the subjunctive and the hypo-thetical in the process, in a little time-travelling of his own: 'our judge-ments at any rate change the character of *future* reality by the acts to which they lead' (876):

> Future and present really mix in such emergencies, and one can always escape lies in them by using hypothetic forms. (877)

In ways that Spencer Brydon is to discover, as William James draws on Kierkegaard, 'we live forwards', but 'we understand backwards' (*Pragmatism* 584).

Of great significance in all this is the distinction William James makes between 'percepts and concepts', between what the individual experi-ences and what he treats merely in abstraction as an intellectual object: 'percepts are continuous and concepts are discrete' (*Some Problems of Philosophy* 1007). The contention in *The Will to Believe* is that

> the world's contents are *given* to each of us in an order so foreign to our subjective interests that we can hardly by an effort of the imag-ination picture to ourselves what it is like. We have to break that order altogether—and by picking out from it the items which con-cern us, and connecting them with others far away, which we say 'belong' with them, we are able to make out definite threads of sequence and tendency...and to enjoy simplicity and harmony in place of what was chaos. (545)

If a 'collateral contemporaneity, and nothing else, is the real order of the world' (546), then the scope for each individual, for Spencer Brydon, Ralph Pendrel, and Henry James, for arranging suitable sequences, and for fabricating useful junctions and disjunctions, might be immense. In any event, that sense of 'proportion' introduced for some by the Civil War looms larger than ever as Spencer Brydon in par-ticular attempts to 'feel at home'. For William James, 'we break' the chaotic sequence in which we are inserted

> into histories, and we break it into arts, and we break it into sciences; and then we begin to feel at home. We make ten thousand separate

serial orders of it, and on any one of these we react as though the others did not exist....Essential these relations are, but only *for our purpose*, the other relations being just as real and present as they. (546)

(ii) 'Tense situations'

'Sailing into New York Harbor on August 30, 1904', Kaplan speculates, James 'saw for the first time technology triumphant': 'the Republic' he had left 'twenty-one years before had been transformed into a great modern state' (478). There is no doubt that this trip to America, which ended in July, 1905, sharpened James's apprehension of the perplexing inseparability of time and space: to move from the Old World to the New was, in effect, to journey into the future and to a zone with a quite different basis for calculating time. When writing on Nathaniel Hawthorne in 1879, James remarked that he had used the 'epithets "ancient" and "near"...according to the American measurement of time and distance' (*Hawthorne* 389). Spencer Brydon, a character who exemplifies the collision between the 'backward view' (358) and the 'tangled actual' (368) of *The American Scene*, and a man, like James, engaged in a 'strangely belated return to America', similarly observes that

> He had been twenty-three on leaving New York—he was fifty-six today: unless indeed he were to reckon as he had sometimes, since his repatriation, found himself feeling; in which case he would have lived longer than is often allotted to man. (697)

'The biographical elements in the story are clear enough', suggests Buitenhuis, and very few approaches to 'The Jolly Corner' reach beyond those elements (211). This critical emphasis has left comparatively unexplored the situation of James's story within the contemporary discourse of time and space, especially as inflected by post-Kantian notions of time as a subjective category, synthetic and regulatory (as for William James) rather than absolute and essential.[12] Above all, 'The Jolly Corner' and *The Sense of the Past* are James's 'liberties taken with time and space' (James, 'The Third Person' 271) at the syntactical level.[13] James exploits the arbitrary relation between tense and time, and the temporal indeterminacies of the modal auxiliary, to indulge in some rather arcane time travel.[14] What make this possible, in part, are debates then current among scientists, philosophers of time, and grammarians.

J. Ellis McTaggart's 'The Unreality of Time', an essay that was to shape philosophical approaches to the issue for the rest of the century, appeared in the same year as 'The Jolly Corner'. Momentarily at least, but less certainly in *The Sense of the Past*, the temporal terrain charted by McTaggart seems both congenial and usable to James.[15] The residual relevance of the essay to much of the fourth-phase writing is in the contingent sense of time it releases for the active, and imaginative, appropriation of the experiencing and perceiving subject. 'In all ages', asserts McTaggart, a 'belief in the unreality of time has proved singularly attractive' (457); and his project is to prove that very 'unreality'. The essay differentiates between 'A series' events, in which the distinction between the past, present, and future obtains, and 'B series', where events are classified as 'earlier' or 'later'. But 'it is clear', McTaggart continues, 'that we never *observe* time except as forming both these series'. Rather than being an objective entity, time ('as observed by us') is constituted by individual perception and perspective. So it may be that the distinctions of the 'A series' between 'past, present and future' are 'merely subjective' and 'simply a constant illusion of our minds', and that 'the real nature of time only contains the distinction of the B series' between what is earlier and later in a sequence (458). If this were the case, 'we could not *perceive* time as it really is, but we might be able to *think* of it as it really is' (459).

But McTaggart insists that

> the A series is essential to the nature of time, and that any difficulty in the way of regarding the A series as real is equally a difficulty in the way of regarding time as real.

'If, then, a B series without an A series can constitute time, change must be possible without an A series' (459); but only in the A series does an event change its characteristics and yet remain the same event. The death of Queen Anne, for example, will always be that, but 'it began by being a future event' and 'became every moment an event in the nearer future' until 'at last it was present'; then 'it became past, and will always remain so, though every moment it becomes further and further past'. (460)

> Without the A series then, there would be no change, and consequently the B series by itself is not sufficient for time, since time involves change.

As the 'B series' is ineluctably temporal, 'it follows that there can be no B series where there is no A series, since where there is no A series there is no time' (461).

But there is also a 'C series' (like the alphabet, or a sequence of numbers): here the elements do not change and they may have no specific direction. Once 'change and time come in', a C series develops 'relations of earlier and later, and so it becomes a B series' (462).

> Besides the C series and the fact of change there must be given—in order to get time—the fact that the change is in one direction and not in the other.

It follows, then, 'that the A series, together with the C series, is sufficient to give us time'. There 'can be no time unless the A series is true of reality', and 'no other elements are required to constitute a time-series except an A series and a C series' (463). Crucially, the distinction between earlier and later of the B series is unnecessary to the concept of time: 'it is only when the A series, which gives change and direction, is combined with the C series, which gives permanence, that the B series can arise' (464).[16] The A series is as indispensable to time, however, as it is inexplicable: 'We cannot explain what is meant by past, present and future. We can, to some extent, describe them, but they cannot be defined' (463):

> I am endeavouring to base the unreality of time, not on the fact that the A series is more fundamental than the B series, but on the fact that it is as essential as the B series—that the distinctions of past, present and future are essential to time, and that, if the distinctions are never true of reality, then no reality is in time. (464)

McTaggart has 'succeeded in proving', he believes, 'that there can be no time without an A series', and that as 'an A series cannot exist...time is not real at all', 'since it is admitted that, the only way in which time can be real is by existing' (467). 'Past, present, and future are incompatible determinations', yet 'every event has them all':

> If M is past, it has been present and future. If it is future, it will be present and past. If it is present, it has been future and will be past. Thus all the three incompatible terms are predictable of each event, which is obviously inconsistent with their being incompatible, and inconsistent with their producing change. (468)

He reaches the conclusion that 'the application of the A series to reality involves a contradiction, and that consequently the A series cannot be true of reality' (470). We experience senses of past, present, and future, but they have no objective reality; they arise from 'certain perceptions', 'the memory of certain other perceptions, and the anticipation of others again' (471).

Drawing, as we shall see, on William James's formulation of the 'specious present' in *The Principles of Psychology* (573), McTaggart holds that 'a direct perception is present when I have it, and so is what is simultaneous with it' (471). But

> the direct perceptions which I now have are those which now fall within my 'specious present'. Of those which are beyond it, I can only have memory or anticipation. Now the 'specious present' varies in length according to circumstances, and may be different for two people at the same period. (471–2)

But this means that the A series must be 'purely subjective', for

> the event M may be simultaneous both with X's perception Q and Y's perception R. At a certain moment Q may have ceased to be part of X's specious present. M, therefore, will at that moment be past. But at the same moment R may still be part of Y's specious present. And, therefore, M will be present, at the same moment at which it is past.

The 'present through which events really pass, therefore, cannot be determined as simultaneous with the specious present' (472), and 'neither time as a whole, nor the A series and B series, really exist' (473).[17]

The only reality is in William James's 'collateral contemporaneity' (*The Will to Believe* 546), or in what McTaggart specifies as the 'C series' of order; and the task is that of making ourselves at home there by forging grammars of time and senses of the past. For a Henry James disdainful of history's way with the past, propelled, in any event, by a present and continuing obscuring of an 'obscure hurt' as a defining element of his fiction, and increasingly absorbed by his need for a flexible past, there are welcome coincidences between the temporal liberties and challenges to logic in 'The Jolly Corner' and *The Sense of the Past* and Mc Taggart's declaring that

> it is, therefore, possible that the realities which we perceive as events in a time-series do really form a non-temporal series. It is also possible, so far as we have yet gone, that they do *not* form such a series, and that they are in reality no more a series than they are temporal. (473)

If 'time' is 'a loose image confusedly thrown together, and that, as we gaze, falls asunder' (Bradley, *Appearance and Reality* 85–6), it becomes available, perhaps, for those with a more pragmatic gaze. Four years before Bradley's *Appearance and Reality* (1897), James looked forward with considerable avidity to that 'some day or other' when

> surely we shall all agree that everything is relative, that facts themselves are often falsifying, and that we pay more for some kinds of knowledge than those particular kinds are worth. ('Gustave Flaubert' 297)

For Spencer Brydon, with his Old and New World perceptions, time— as for Einstein, McTaggart, and William James—'is something that is tied to the position of an observer' (Purdy 76). Three years before McTaggart's essay, Einstein published his *Special Theory of Relativity*, developing and extending its ideas at the height of the First World War in his *Relativity: The Special and the General Theory* (1916).[18] Time and space, he argued, 'are free creations of the human intelligence, tools of thought, which are to serve the purpose of bringing experiences into relation with each other' (*Relativity* 99). When Spencer Brydon left New York for Europe, the Old World, as it had been for much of James's life, was for many the point of absolute reference in the domains of history, time, and culture. On their return, both James and Brydon had to confront the turbulence of a world in which America, too, could be a 'reference-body', and where at best, 'absolute time...is an idle metaphysical conception' (Mach 127):

> the fictitious rigid body of reference is of no avail in the general theory of relativity....The general principle of relativity requires that all these mollusks can be used as reference-bodies with equal right and equal success. (Einstein, *Relativity* 98–9)

In Newtonian mechanics, there had only been one clock, but after Einstein, there were 'as many clocks as we like' (Albert Einstein and Leopold Infeld, *The Evolution of Physics* 181):[19]

> Now before the advent of the theory of relativity it had always tacitly been assumed in physics that the statement of time had an absolute significance. (Einstein, *Relativity* 27)

James was certainly in the vanguard of such reasoning, reflecting as he did on the particularities of American and European society and culture. There is a 'sense of...relativity, in a word', he wrote in *Hawthorne*, which 'replaces that quiet and comfortable sense of the absolute' that has reigned 'supreme in the British and in the Gallic genius' (435).

Such senses of relativity were eventually to shape the casuistical acrobatics of a range of logicians, philosophers, and grammarians, and artists and writers everywhere, who seized on the creative possibilities offered by the unmooring of time. For Peirce, the present could be dispersed as the 'Nascent State between the Determinate and the Indeterminate'; and 'future facts are the only facts that we can, in a measure, control' ('Issues of Pragmaticism' 312). 'As for that part of the past that lies beyond memory', the 'Pragmaticist doctrine'

> is that the meaning of its being believed to be in connection with the Past consists in the acceptance as truth of the conception that we ought to conduct ourselves according to it (like the meaning of any other belief).[20]

Thus 'a belief that Christopher Columbus discovered America really refers to the future'. The 'consciousness of the present is then that of a struggle over what shall be'; and we emerge from studying it with 'a confirmed belief that it is the Nascent State of the Actual' (313). In 'Humanism and Truth Once More', which appeared in the same year as Peirce's 'Issues of Pragmaticism' (1905), William James, as he inadvertently outlines a dimension of 'The Jolly Corner', concludes that there is

> no absurdity whatever in the notion of a retrospective hypothesis having for its object the very train of experiences by which its own being, along with that of other things, has been brought about. (1197)

Whereas absolute time, within Newton's framework, postulated stable and essential senses of the past, present, and future, turn-of-the nineteenth century thinking focused not just on the radical indeterminacy of these concepts, but also on complex durations of the present. Henry James's distinction between 'a palpable imaginable *visitable* past' and the shrinking, more remote 'element of the appreciable', stems from these developments in the philosophy of time. The present is a zone with its own past, present, and future, and it may recruit for use and abuse the obscurities of a more distant past otherwise irrelevant to it. What is beyond the 'nearer distances and clearer mysteries' is less 'appreciable'; on offer, perhaps, 'is mainly a view of barriers' (*PAP* 1177). This form of punctuation can serve, self-protectively, to seal off segments of the past; but periods can give way to semicolons or commas, for example, depending on the needs of particular acts of memorialization, reconstruction, and representation. For Henry James, as for Henri Bergson,

> we trail behind us...the whole of our past; but our memory pours into the present only the odd recollection or two that in some way complete our present situation. (*Creative Evolution* 167)

In *Matter and Memory*, the concept of 'duration' (*durée*) sets Bergson's entire agenda; but it is a 'duration...lived by our consciousness', and 'very different', therefore, 'from the time of the physicist' (205).[21] Its present 'has one foot' in the 'past' and 'another in the future' (138). At the centre of Bergson's (and William James's) sense of the past are perception and experience; for both thinkers, as for Henry James, there is no past as such, only a usable past amidst 'our helpless promiscuity in the crucible of time' (Henry James, 'The After-Season in Rome' 468):

> The essence of time is that it goes by; time already gone by is the past, and we call the present the instant in which it goes by. But there can be no question here of a mathematical instant. No doubt there is an ideal present—a pure conception, the indivisible limit which separates past from future. But the real, concrete, live present—that of which I speak when I speak of my present perception—that present necessarily occupies a duration. (*Matter and Memory* 137)

Similarly, William James believed that the 'specious present'[22]

> is no knife-edge, but a saddle-back, with a certain breadth of its own on which we sit perched, and from which we look in two directions into time. The unit of composition of our perception of time is a *duration*, with a bow and a stern, as it were—a rearward- and a forward-looking end. (*The Principles of Psychology* 574)

The concept of the 'saddle-back', and the extensive but fugitive present it implies, can be construed as a specifically American response to anxieties about senses of a thin past and fears about an uncertain future; and it operated as a seminal element in the dislocation, everywhere evident in the James of the fourth phase, of linear, unidirectional notions of time.[23] The fixed metrics of anisotropic time with its arbitrary divisions between past, present, and future, as distinct from the subjective schema of individual experience and perception, are exactly what the notion of a 'stream' of time discourages:

> The knowledge of some other part of the stream, past or future, near or remote, is always mixed in with our knowledge of the present thing. (*The Principles of Psychology* 571)[24]

With the house on the jolly corner in prospect, it is significant that William James also held that 'Space...is quite analogous to time in this regard' and that 'date in time corresponds to position in space' (575).[25] Stalking round the house, as the intensity of his perceptions begins to increase, Spencer Brydon testifies to the validity of Vaihinger's contention that 'the fictive activity of the mind is an expression of the fundamental psychical forces' (12); he is like a participant in one of William James's 'action–time experiments' where so 'many impressions follow in excessively rapid succession in time' that 'we may be quite at a loss to tell which comes first and which last; or we may even invert their real order' (575).

For Henry James, objects, and especially houses, are often attractive because they spatialize and inscribe time in ways that disrupt linear, chronological, models. If this is Spencer Brydon's experience in New York, it is certainly Ralph Pendrel's anticipation for the house he inherits in England. He had earlier written, in a book that explores an expression, 'the sense of the past', that has much 'worked' (32) on Aurora Coyne, that

> there are particular places where things have happened, places enclosed and ordered and subject to the continuity of life mostly, that seem to put us into communication, and the spell is sometimes made to work by the imposition of hands, if it be patient enough, on an old object or an old surface. (*The Sense of the Past* 34)

The 'lingerings of old objects' and the 'incomings of the new' are 'the germs of memory and expectation, the retrospective and prospective sense of time' (*The Principles of Psychology* 571); and more than whole archives of documents and fragmentary relics, such vitalized spaces and 'sentient' ruins ('Roman Rides' 441) offer fractious, tenuous, and appropriative possibilities for Henry James of a creative communion with the past. 'Call it much or call it little', James writes in 'Florentine Notes', 'the ineffaceability of this deep stain of experience', yet it is the interest of old places and the bribe to the brooding analyst. Time has devoured the doers and their doings, but there still hangs about some effect of their passage. (567)

That his family have lived and died in the house on the jolly corner 'represented, within the walls', for Brydon, 'ineffaceable life' (705).

When Spencer Brydon returns to New York after a life of unspecified dissipation in Europe, he is not—unlike James, periodically at least— propelled into the past as a consequence of recoiling against the present.[26] On the contrary, he revels in his newly discovered business acumen as he deals in property and supervises the erection of a lucrative skyscraper on the site of one of his two houses.[27] His plan is to preserve the house of his birth, where he finds the 'impalpable ashes of his long-extinct youth, afloat in the very air like microscopic motes' (704), and develop the site of what was his second, now demolished, house. Wandering in the old house, as he speculates on how an alternative past might have shaped the present, Brydon begins to resemble Roderick Chisholm's logical neophyte on the brink of a 'crucial experiment' (483) whose object is to test the validity of those 'deliberative' conditionals which, according to Peirce, express the 'real generals' of the universe ('Issues of Pragmaticism' 453):[28]

He found all things come back to the question of what he personally might have been, how he might have led his life and 'turned out', if he had not so, at the outset, given it up. (706)

There are distinct parallels between Robert Frost's 'The Road Not Taken', which appeared in 1916, and 'The Jolly Corner'. Frost's poem depicts two diverging roads—temporal or spatial, imaginary or real; both, in any event, intensely and poignantly symbolic—as 'one traveler' wistfully contemplates future recollections of an absent alternative which would then be forsworn in favour of 'the one less traveled by'. Frost's traveller is left not only with an oppressive sense of the road taken, but the paralyzing fact that it 'has made all the difference' (105). The classically American predicament is that of pondering (prospectively and retrospectively) the foreclosure of choice, the ultimate unavailability of ubiquity, even for citizens of the New World, and the evanescent fantasy of sustaining endless possibility, and the impossibility of doing so.[29]

Henry James's late fiction specializes in constructing, within the volatile framework of philosophies of time then current, decadent mutations of Amerca's vanishing dreamers, characters arrested, like Kate Croy at the close of *The Wings of the Dove*, by the forlorn realization that 'we shall never be again as we were!' (457). But in Brydon, James constructs a surrogate who can put what is 'forsworn' (711) to use as he seeks to escape the limitations of being merely 'one traveler' by traversing, however enigmatically, the 'wanton line between the past and the present' (*HJA* 598). Brydon is suspended throughout in phrases like 'were it possible', 'since he *had* supposed himself' (697), the 'wonderment' of considering the consequences 'if he had but stayed at home' (701), and 'I *might* have lived here...then everything would have been different enough' (704); and, finally, there are Alice Staverton's thoughts, so 'worked' over, about 'what you might, what you mighn't have been' (730). If the future and the present mix in hypothetical and subjunctive forms for William James (*A Pluralistic Universe* 876–7), such forms abound in 'The Jolly Corner' as the means by which the story negotiates the past to exploit the unreality of time, constituted in part by confused and confusing temporal significations of tense, to dislocate chronological sequence (McTaggart's A and B series) into 'collateral contemporaneity' (William James, *The Will to Believe* 546).

The generic strategy of 'The Jolly Corner'—with its recuperation of Hawthorne's spectral world of the gothic, as James reaches back to antebellum spaces and forward to modish theories of the *alter ego*— dramatizes William James's 'saddle-back' conception of the 'specious present' (*The Principles of Psychology* 573–4).[30] Brydon's belief that he has a 'strange *alter ego* deep down somewhere within', and somehow 'blighted' by his migration to Europe (707), develops into the conviction that the house contains that other self, that self that would have been had he remained in America. If 'time' is 'nothing but the ghost of space haunting the reflective consciousness' (Bergson, *Time and Free Will* 99), Brydon engages in a form of exorcism which allows, transiently, an experience of 'both the past and the present states' as an 'organic whole', together with a 'reversibility' of 'order' (*Time and Free Will* 100–1). Momentarily, and even horrifically, the 'self...broken to pieces' by the 'social life' of Europe merges with a 'fundamental self' recovered by 'the unsophisticated consciousness' (*Time and Free Will* 128–9). 'We do not *think* real time', argues Bergson in *Creative Evolution*, 'but we *live* it, because life transcends intellect' (46), and the 'intellect', by contrast with the intuition, can only form a 'clear idea' of the 'discontinuous' (154).

What James creates for Brydon in 'The Jolly Corner' is an experience whereby 'the state of consciousness overflows the intellect' (*Creative Evolution* 200), as he represents (however bizarrely) 'the contrast of what is, not only with what has been, but also with all that might have been' (*Creative Evolution* 295). But whereas Bergson sees language as stifling the 'processes' of the soul by isolating and naming, the 'word' covering over 'the delicate and fugitive impressions of our individual consciousness' (*Time and the Free Will* 131–2), James experiments in 'The Jolly Corner' at least, with its potential fluidities in relation to tense and time.

'What he personally might have been' (706) can be read as the consequent of a counter-factual conditional with a suppressed antecedent ('if he had stayed in America, then he wondered what he personally might have been'). In this context, however, 'what might have been' could also be construed as both a question and a statement. But questions cannot be true or false; and whatever the underlying logical form of Brydon's predicament, or James's formulation of his sense of it, no modal logic, however sophisticated, is available for it.[31] This counter-factual conditional with its interrogative consequent occupies as a 'disorderly element' that realm of apparently 'unactualized possibilities' identified by Quine as 'incorrigible', and to which James was addicted (4). What Spencer Brydon experiences in part, however, is the release into a realm of perceivable simultaneities by a heightening apperception, or self-consciousness; in such situations, as Vaihinger concludes, deductions about self and the world can be made from the unreal:

> In the conditional clause something unreal or impossible is stated, and yet from this *unreality* or *impossibility* inferences are drawn. In spite of its unreality or impossibility the assumption is still formally maintained. It is regarded as an apperceptive construct under which something can be subsumed and from which deductions can be made. (92–3)

The formula of the 'as if' manoeuvre that structures appearances operates in exactly the same way as the phrase 'what might have been' in that 'the particular, is *compared* with something whose impossibility and unreality is at the same time admitted' (Vaihinger 93).

'What might have been' is further complicated by a two-dimensional, or 'saddle-back', dynamic in that although nominally the preterite of 'may', it functions as an unreal past expression of the conditional and leaves indeterminate what would otherwise clearly be its present-perfect tense ('have been'). By analogy, 'might' seems to operate as the past tense of 'may', even though the 'past-tense uses' of the modal, according to Warner, have 'steadily' diminished (25). Preserved in its form, 'might' being more uncertain than 'may', is the adoption of an '"unreal", "tentative", or past tense' (Warner 9) for hypothetical situations past, present, or future:

> *Might*, the remote tense of MAY, never has a real-past meaning in modern English; its remoteness is that of *unreality*. (Joos 187)

The use of the past for the hypothetical present or future ('would you read this', rather than 'will you', for example), together with the temporal obscurities of the present-perfect itself, makes isotropic time much less counter-intuitive at the grammatical level than elsewhere as James is able to exploit 'the growing opacity of the semantic relationship between the present and the preterite' (Warner 150). Warner goes on to suggest that 'it is far from clear that *might* contains the same morpheme "past" as verbs' (59), and that

> the typical subjectivity of modals also clearly accounts...for their predisposition to interpretations in present time, and for their disregard of the opposition of tense. (60)[32]

Otto Jespersen was one of the first philologists systematically to insist on the importance of keeping the 'two concepts time and tense strictly apart' (*A Modern English Grammar on Historical Principles* 4: 1), and this bifurcation, along with the unrealities of time posited by William James, Bergson, Einstein, McTaggart, and others, enabled Henry James to register not only the extent to which senses of time are synthesized in language, but to explore the liberation of such senses in linguistic domains, together with the usable forms, or transformations, of the past that may result. A saddle-back geometry is visible throughout Jespersen's innovative taxonomy of time-tense correspondences. He sees the 'perfect', 'composed by means of the present of an auxiliary', as having the principal function of making that connection between 'the present time' and 'the past' (4: 47) which is at the core of Bergson's model of duration. In terms increasingly familiar by the time of 'The Jolly Corner', Jespersen holds that 'the present moment...has no dimensions, but is continually fleeting' (4: 1), and that '"now" means a time with appreciable duration' (4: 16–17). English had only two tenses: 'the Present and the Preterit' (4: 3); but its creative adaptation of what James called its 'precious auxiliaries' (Introduction, *Madame Bovary* 345), allowed Jespersen to construct a thirteen-part model of time references which included extravagant isotropous categories such as the 'restrospective past', 'retrospective present', and 'retrospective future', the 'prospective present', 'prospective past', and 'prospective future', and the 'imaginative past', 'imaginative present time', and 'imaginative future time' (4: 361–2).

The observations on tense and speech in Jespersen's *A Modern English Grammar on Historical Principles* are of considerable relevance to an analysis of the form and function of 'might' within its 'might have been' structure in 'The Jolly Corner'.[33] He identifies 'back-shifting', where the 'tenses are often very different from what they would have been in direct speech', as the 'most important case of tense-shifting in indirect speech': 'I am glad to see you', for example, becomes 'he was glad to see me' (4: 151). But modal structures are like the pluperfect in that they cannot be 'further shifted' (4: 152). In indirect speech, 'I wonder what might have been' is simply 'he wondered what might have been', and 'it is impossible to see whether the shifted tense is in the indicative or subjunctive' (4: 157). This narrative obfuscation of Brydon's speculations about 'what...might have been' (706) has among its consequences a prodigious complicating of the relation between time, tense, mood, and the moment of utterance. 'What might have been' falls into the category of what Reichenbach terms the 'token-reflexive' because it refers to its own utterance (*Elements of Symbolic Logic* sec. 50–1).[34] It is the precise location of Brydon's utterance in the past–present continuum, however, that is indeterminable; and it is often extremely difficult to ascertain whether the speculating voice, with its miscegenation of the hypothetical and the subjunctive, is the narrator's rather than Brydon's.

It is hardly surprising, then, that Brydon on the brink of stalking a ghost putatively haunting him, in yet another rupture of the linear, should look 'again at his watch' to see 'what had become of his time values' and observe that 'he had taken hours for minutes—not, as in other tense situations, minutes for hours' (721).[35] Tense and intensity conspire to bring about the conditions for Brydon's retrospections: the 'positive mystification he felt himself create' (704) arises during frequent vigils that begin at the 'crepuscular' hour in the 'autumn twilight' (709)—in that liminal, threshold space to which Gedge is devoted in 'The Birthplace'—as James exploits the resources of a grammar under pressure from contemporary conceptions of time to develop in language the kind of access to fluidity that Bergson reserved for intuition. H. G. Wells's time machine may have been a cumbersome contraption initiating a perilous journey, but at the grammatical level James has been able to exploit the problematic boundary between past and present to construct a much more subtle and effectual form of transport. In 'The Jolly Corner', the past, or a sense of it, is recuperated and inserted into a present from whose vantage-point it can be revisited. If time is unreal other than from an individual perspective, and if it exists only as a purposive intuition of the experiencing subject, the imaginative writer whose business with the past is always unfinished has a licence, and even a responsibility, to maintain vigilant negotiations with it.

James, like Jespersen, then, was attracted by the temporal instability of the present-perfect tense ('have been') and the degree to which boundaries between the past and the present, under siege from post-absolute models of time and space, had become usefully insecure. The intriguing conspiracy in 'The Jolly Corner' between narrative discourse and the modal auxiliary 'might' is heightened by the nebulous character, in terms of temporal reference, of the present perfect 'have been'. If the 'current relevance' (Palmer, *The English Verb* 50) of an indeterminate past for an unspecified moment in the present is one way of defining the present-perfect, then James's ghost can be construed as an agentive manifestation of that temporally sprawling tense. In what could serve as a summary of the projects of 'The Jolly Corner' and *The Sense of the Past*, Jespersen observes in *The Philosophy of Grammar* that the 'perfect cannot be fitted into the simple' tense 'series', for 'besides the purely temporal element it contains the element of result' (269); and the 'double-sided character of the perfect' (272) makes it 'difficult to keep up the sharp distinction between the idea of the present result of past events and that of these past events themselves' (270).

Amidst these temporal vagaries, what Brydon finally encounters is not the *alter ego* he had envisaged but an 'evil, odious, blatant, vulgar' (725) monstrosity with a' hand mutilated by the loss of two fingers. Such a face, as he returns to consciousness, he rejects as 'unknown, inconceivable, awful, disconnected from any possibility' (725). One of the principles of all this, as the Civil War beckons once more, is announced by Ralph Pendrel in *The Sense of the Past*: 'There might always be something to be gained so long as anything to be renounced was left' (*The Sense of the Past* 7). If the reader focuses on Brydon's overwrought state and his obsession not only with what survives of the past in the present, but what it could tell him about what might have been, the events of the story can be interpreted in terms of his imaginatively contrived double consciousness. But available in ways far from incompatible with that consciousness is a sense of his having returned to a futuristic New York from the Old World to encounter a man from the past he had abandoned once he had set sail for Europe: the character he would have been had he remained in America. Again, this is less a travelling back, or the simple reversal of a sequence, and more the giddying experience of simultaneity as the unreality of time, and its insecure arrangements in the compartments of the past, present, and future, is discovered. To return to his old home has not been enough for Brydon; he has had to make himself at home by arranging a journey, more discursive than real or spectral, to reach an accommodation with a past the negation of which, unknown to himself so far, has constituted what he has been and is.

(iii) The 'gaping abyss'

Saul Rosenzweig sees the death of John Ford in 'The Story of a Year' as releasing the ghost that is to haunt many of James's subsequent tales, and he argues that in leaving America James materialized Ford's death (89). The return to America in 1904–5 is part of the process, for Rosenzweig, whereby James finally confronts, compensates for, and exorcises a failure to fight in the Civil War, a treachery compounded by his flight to Europe:

> Henry James's visit to America…was largely actuated by an impulse to repair, if possible, the injury and to complete the unfinished experience of his youth. He was, as it were, haunted by the ghost of his own past and of this he wished to disabuse his mind before actual death overtook him. (92)

In 'The Jolly Corner', 'the ghost of Spencer Brydon' is obviously his rejected self'; and the 'injury', the 'two lost fingers', 'stands in some relation to the fact that the life was not lived or that, in other words, a kind of psychological death had occurred'. This contortion of the significance of Ford's death in 'The Story of a Year'[36] allows Rosenzweig to suggest that 'The Jolly Corner' complements, or therapeutically completes the earlier story, and that the 'identity of the characters is established by the injuries each suffered—James's "obscure hurt", Ford's wounds, and Brydon's missing fingers'. Alice Staverton, as a complement to Elizabeth Crowe, redeems the faithless Alice (93).

> In 'The Jolly Corner' one finds a coalescence of revisit and revision which satisfactorily explains the complementary relationship of this story to the first ever written.[37] (94)

James's American visit also precipitated his autobiographical writings, however, and the careful strategies there for elevating art to that position of heroic mastery over the Civil War discussed in Chapter 3. In *The American Scene*, James again subjects the heroic to the aesthetic, observing on his visit to the 'great hall of the Union' at Harvard (405) that the

> recording tablets of the members of the University sacrificed, on the Northern side, in the Civil War, are too impressive not to retain here always their collective beauty; but the monumental office and character suffer throughout from the too scant presence of the massive and the mature. (406)

Similarly, the position James occupies in Richmond, as he reflects on the Civil War, is that of a sage Northern interpreter rather than that of an abject non-combatant. Consonant with his emphasis on the need for a 'prepared sensibility' (566) at Concord, he argues that in the South 'if one doesn't know *how* to look and to see, one should keep out of it altogether' (656), for Richmond, as he evacuates the 'blood-drenched', 'tragic ghost-haunted city' of history and the popular imagination, 'in a word, looked to me simply blank and void' (657–8).

After the failure of Reconstruction, the poetry of the Civil War moved South;[38] and it is there that James vanquishes it, calling into question the entire rationale of the War and what it had come to represent: 'There were no *references*—that had been the trouble; but the reaction came with the sense that the large, sad poorness was in itself a reference'.

> I was tasting, mystically, of the very essence of the old Southern idea—the hugest fallacy, as it hovered there to one's backward, one's ranging vision, for which hundreds of thousands of men had ever laid down their lives. (659)

Sitting in the very pew of the Richmond Church where Jefferson Davis first heard of Lee's surrender in 1865, James rises above and masters, as a *faux*-Union soldier, remains that result only in the 'trivialization of history': 'the news had been big, but the place of worship was small' (668).

At the Richmond Museum, James sees only objects that bring 'home' the 'humiliation of defeat'. He carefully includes military uniforms, along with the detritus of country fairs in general, and aligns himself with victory, literacy, and culture:

> The sorry objects...brought it home—so low the aesthetic level: it was impossible, from room to room, to imagine a community, of

equal size, more disinherited of art and letters. These about one were the only echoes—daubs of portraiture, scrawls of memoranda, old vulgar newspapers, old rude uniforms, old unutterable 'mid-Victorian' odds and ends of furniture, all ghosts as of things noted at a country fair. (671)

There is a Southerner in the museum, a 'young man of stalwart and ingenuous aspect' (672), who relates to James 'felicitously, some paternal adventure'

Of which I have forgotten the particulars, but which comprised a desperate evasion of capture, or worse, by the lucky smashing of the skull of a Union soldier.

The young man declares the he would 'be ready to do...all over again' what James calls 'these old, unhappy, far-off things'. From a vantage-point, however, not just of military supremacy, but of a superiority to that supremacy in terms of aesthetic mastery and appropriation, James feels able to indulge in post-bellum moralizing at the expense of the South. 'He was a fine contemporary young American, incapable, so to speak, of hurting a Northern fly':

So I wondered till it came to me that, though he wouldn't have hurt a Northern fly, there were things (ah, we had touched on some of these!) that, all fair, engaging, smiling, as he stood there, he would have done to a Southern Negro. (673)

James's visit to America, like Brydon's encounter in 'The Jolly Corner', is not an act of contrition but an exercise in what Theweleit has called 'self-maintenance'(*Male Fantasies*, Vol. 2: 319–20) as he recuperates a sense of the sense of a past ever more, if tenuously, useful to him. James saw the Civil War, especially in the proxy of that 'obscure hurt', as the advent of a specious present whose complications arose from its endless entanglements with the past and an uncertain reach into the future. Spencer Brydon is not simply what he is, for he is also not the man he encounters; his life in Europe, correspondingly, has been a function of the life he did not lead in America. To have a 'social reality' which 'is uniquely that of the Not', and 'a personality' which is 'a perpetual negation' (Sartre 47), is normative for James and some of the 'poor sensitive gentlemen' he constructs (*PAD* 1250). This is what Brydon has lacked, or a consciousness of it at least, hitherto. His return to New York allows a discovery of the imperatives not just of denial and renunciation for the purposes of self-production, but the necessity of defining the self in terms of obscure renunciations of the complicated, enigmatic, and even heroic, in order to achieve superior forms of mastery. It is important not to overlook the irony by which Brydon detaches himself from his final destination in a sentimental romance he nevertheless finds useful: 'Ah I've come to myself now—thanks to you, dearest' (730). His is the willing retention of a 'charming mono-cle', of a vision deliberately narrowed to screen out what makes him perpetually interesting, rather than the adoption of his *alter ego*'s indis-criminate 'great convex pince-nez' (731) which, whatever his 'ruined sight', gives him a broader horizon than Brydon's.[39]

Without a sense of the past that the present is not, and the endless pursuit of obscure relations between the present and the obscurities of the past, the dynamics of James's kind of fiction and self-fashioning are lost. For Brydon and James, 'the nature of consciousness simultaneous-ly is to be what it is not and not to be what it is' (Sartre 70). What we are and do is trivial by comparison with what we are not and do not do, as long as what we are is dependent on forms of obscurity screened out in the main, and our present is a function of a past foreshortened and mutilated, among other reasons, for the sake of interest. The past is there to temper a present which, in turn, it temporizes. In 'The Jolly Corner', James renovates and regenerates an isometry of the past and present on which his fictions of the self have thrived. If the Civil War had resulted for James and others in more complex senses of the pres-ent, the 'specious present' involves recruiting the past, and keeping it in play, for the purposes of that present, which is also the scene of any writing. The present is 'specious' for William James and McTaggart because it also includes elements of the past and the future, but what is specious is also an affair of appearances, falsifications, and pretexts in a world where there is only ever less matter and more art.[40]

Both Rosenzweig and Edel extend their schemes to the First World War and beyond, Rosenzweig seeking a corroboration of his theories in what Edmund Gosse regarded as James's premature death.[41] Rosenzweig won-ders whether it is 'too much to suggest that the unparalleled fervor' of James's First World War activity 'is to some extent explained by a belated compensation for his failure at the time of the Civil War' (95), and he treats an analogy James made between the American Civil War and the war of 1914 as the clinching 'testimony' in his case, although there is plenty of prevarication, fanciful speculation, and confused interpretation:

> The analogy of the wars in his own consciousness thus attested, it is
> not difficult to believe that a common motivational tie was at least

implicitly at work. He might have been found wanting in 1861, but he would not be found so on this second and doubtless final occasion....Instead of hanging his head as a war disability, he would stand forth as a war hero.

It is within this context, Rosenzweig believes, that the 'mooted question of James's assumption of British citizenship a few months before his death' becomes 'intelligible' (96). 'So at last', Rosenzweig concludes, 'the pattern of the genius which was Henry James emerges':

Suffering from childhood with a keen sense of inadequacy, he experienced in his eighteenth year an injury that sharply crystallized this attitude into a passional death. The ghost which as an apotheosis of his unlived life appears repeatedly in his later tales was liberated from this 'death'. (97)

This is the Henry James of Edmund Wilson's *The Wound and the Bow*, a book Rosenzweig acknowledges (97), with its 'myth of the sick artist' (Trilling, *The Liberal Imagination* 162). Philoctetes is Wilson's representative artist, 'forced', as Trilling puts it, 'to live in isolation because of the disgusting odor of a suppurating wound', yet 'sought out by his countrymen because they had need of the magically unerring bow he possessed' (*The Liberal Imagination* 162). Rosenzweig's 'crystallized' leaves everything unexplained, and James's 'passional' state, as a corporeal or psychological matter, is inaccessible and unfathomable. As for lives unlived, or journeys not taken, or for what is not, rather than what is, these are structures of absence, denial, and renunciation fundamental to the individual subject whatever the contingencies in play. Inadequacy and injury are universally available; it is the uses James made of them, and the imaginative alliances he sought in the realms of epistemology, philosophy, linguistics, and science that result in his distinctive art of fiction. 'The Jolly Corner' is an affirmation of the denials on which the use and abuse of the past depend and without which fiction would be impossible. This is an affair of aesthetics and lives constructed, however, rather than a case for the marauding hands of the psychoanalyst. 'We cannot...make the writer's inner life exactly equivalent to his power of expressing it', Trilling contends, and 'anyone might be injured as Henry James was' and 'yet not have his literary power' (*The Liberal Imagination* 171).

In his eagerness to press James's analogy into service, Rosenzweig misses the fact that it collapses utterly after only one paragraph. There is no doubt that at the outbreak of the First World War, James was struck, or wanted to be struck, by what he has Spencer Brydon call 'the tremendous force of analogy' (712):

> The first sense of it all to me after the first shock and horror was that of a sudden leap back into life of the violence with which the American Civil War broke upon us, at the North, fifty-four years ago, when I had a consciousness of youth which perhaps equalled in vivacity my present consciousness of age.

'The illusion was complete, in its immediate rush; everything quite exactly matched in the two cases', and the 'analogy quickened and deepened with every elapsing hour'. But in the extremity of the circumstances, this is a resort to fiction—it 'added' an 'inexpressible romantic thrill' to 'the harsh taste of the crisis'—which is tested to destruction ('Within the Rim' 177). Tellingly, it is the 'support obscurely derived' from the Civil War analogy, and hence the whole discursive strategy of obscurity and the 'obscure hurt', that comes under re-vision:

> My point is, however, that upon this luxury I was allowed after all but ever so scantly to feed. I am unable to say when exactly it was that the rich analogy, the fine and sharp identity between the faded and the vivid case broke down, with the support obscurely derived from them; the moment anyhow came soon enough at which experience felt the ground give way and that one swung off into space, into history, into darkness, with every lamp extinguished and every abyss gaping. (178)

In 1879, when James was 36, he wrote 'The Diary of a Man of Fifty', a story which playfully establishes the follies and limits of making analogies. The narrator returns to Italy, in search of the past, and experiences there, in ways similar to Brydon's, 'a certain sense of loss lurking in the sense of gain; a tendency to wonder, rather wishfully, what *might* have been' (454). He meets a young man who has fallen in love with the daughter of the seemingly heartless woman he, long ago, had given up, as ever in James, for flinching, self-protective reasons. 'To me', he reflects, 'everything is so perfectly the same that I seem to be living my youth over again' (453). As an enthusiast for recycling, he is reminded of 'something else, and yet of itself at the same time; my imagination makes a great circuit and comes back to the starting-point' (454). On encountering Stanmer and learning of his relationship, the narrator hastily declares that 'the analogy is complete' (460). It may be the 'same story' (476) but Stanmer, the narrator's *protégé*, ends it differently by marrying the daughter of the Countess he had rejected. Challenged in the process is the narrator's imaginative, artistic proclivity for analogy, for imposing patterns on the chaos of experience: 'Don't you think you rather overdo the analogy?' asks poor Stanmer (469) in the presence of the narrator's 'dangerous comparisons' (464), eventually writing to him: 'A fig for analogies unless you can find an analogy for my happiness!' (483).

At this point in James's literary trajectory, and in keeping with views expressed in the preface to *The Spoils of Poynton* that 'life' is 'all inclusion and confusion', and 'art...all discrimination and selection' (1138), the reader is left to assume that life, rather than art, is the worse for its failure to respond to the analogies of fiction. In ways unknown to 'The Diary of a Man of Fifty', however, there are auguries there of upheavals in these wilful designs in which art appears to shape life into significance. Analogies, as fictions, establish relations that are 'in the last analysis unfitting' (Vaihinger 173); and if Brydon's is a purposive rejection of the analogy with which he is confronted, it is the very structure of analogy-making processes that disintegrates for James in 1914.

As 'space' and 'history' disappear into gaping abysses in 'Within the Rim', a schematization of James's evolving sense of time can be advanced. The American Civil War, marking as it did for James the boundary between a vaguely timeless past, the ramifying present, and what was to come, precipitated a post-lapsarian consciousness of a conventional logic of time with which, however, he was already disaffected. His fiction, not least because of the fluid negotiations with the past thereby enabled, became increasingly more hospitable towards counter-essentialist appropriations of neo-Kantian conjectures and the veritable carnival of relativity of turn-of-the-nineteenth century culture. Ever frustrated by disparities between the potential of art for 'a projected result' and life as 'the unconscious, the agitated, the struggling, floundering cause' ('The Lesson of Balzac' 119), and wary of the pressures of the real (merely an artless fiction after all) on the forms of obscurity that compel artful fiction, James was able to take advantage at the levels of aesthetic theory and practice of the correspondences between art and life offered by subjective, isotropic, accounts of time and space; for 'life' is 'at best good prose—when' it isn't 'bad' (*The Sense of the Past* 44), and

> we may polish our periods till they shine again, but over the style of life our control is necessarily more limited. ('Gustave Flaubert' 301)

Approaches to time which emphasized analogy, symmetry, and an infinite but bounded universe, were intensely congenial to a writer for whom illimitable relations, imaginatively circumscribed by artists, had always been the deep structure of his art. There are affinities, for instance, between James's encapsulation of these views in his preface to *Roderick Hudson* and theories being formulated by Einstein at the very time the New York revisions were underway:

> Really, universally, relations stop nowhere, and the exquisite problem of the artist is eternally but to draw, by a geometry of his own, the circle within which they shall happily *appear* to do so. (*PRH* 1041)

> Space is primarily a bounded space. This limitation does not appear to be essential, however, for apparently a larger box can always be introduced to enclose the smaller one. In this way space appears as something unbounded. (Einstein, *Relativity* 138)

This aesthetic, and its contemporary philosophical and scientific framework, is one constituent of the fantastic journeys of Spencer Brydon and Ralph Pendrel, but it supplied James with only the most fleeting of paradigms within which to process the horror of the First World War. In a poignant move with its own backward reach, James wrote on the very day war broke out to Edward Emerson, Ralph Waldo Emerson's son, that:

> It fills me with anguish & dismay & makes me ask myself if *this* then is what I have grown old for, if this is what all the ostensibly or comparatively serene, all the supposedly *bettering* past, of our century, has meant & led up to. It gives away everything one has believed in & lived for—& I envy those of our generation who haven't lived on for it. (4 August 1914: *LL* 542)

Percy Lubbock, who oversaw the posthumous publication of the unfinished *The Sense of the Past* in 1917, believed that James

> Went back to it again during the first winter of the war, having found that in the conditions he could not then go on with *The Ivory Tower* and hoping that he might be able to work upon a story of remote and phantasmal life. (Preface, *The Sense of the Past* v)[42]

From its inception, James was bedevilled by the 'damnable *difficulty*' of the story: 'I have rarely been beaten by a subject', he wrote to Howells, 'but I felt myself, after upwards of a month's work, destined to be beaten by that one' (29 June 1900: *HJL* 4: 151). In the novel, Ralph Pendrel, as a historian 'oddly indifferent to the actual and the possible' as distinct from 'the spent and the displaced' (48), attempts to substitute the real—or the 'ineffable genius itself of the place' (55), 'a museum of held reverberations' (67–8)—for its discourse by journeying back into a past that he can reconfigure for the purposes of the present and beyond.[43] If the 'bettering past' James bewails in his letter to Edward Emerson could be bettered, then a control over the future might be possible, perhaps; and initially at least, the novel is far from being 'remote and phantasmal' from James's searing anxieties about the bellicose present. 'I've been ridden all my life', Ralph tells the American ambassador he visits in London,

> by the desire to cultivate some better sense of the past than has mostly seemed sufficient even for those people who have gone in most for cultivating it. (103)

Aurora Coyne has rejected his offer of marriage because she wants an American uncontaminated by the Old World, and Ralph embarks on an adventure that would dwarf the cowboys (28) and soldiers (11) he sees as his only rivals for the category of the pure 'American' (27). When Ralph is on the brink of his campaign, with Aurora's words lingering— 'I like men of action...Men who've been through something' (11)— James finds a military metaphor irresistible as he trumpets the superiority of a historian-containing fiction and the battles it involves over conventional combat:

> Recovering the lost was at all events on this scale much like entering the enemy's lines to get back one's dead for burial; and to that extent was he not, by his deepening penetration, contemporaneous and present? 'Present' was a word used by him in a sense of his own and meaning as regards most things about him markedly absent. It was for the old ghosts to take him for one of themselves. (49–50)

In part, *The Sense of the Past* is 'A Passionate Pilgrim' refracted through 'The Jolly Corner' as James persists in applying the discourse of time's unreality which proved serviceable for the latter tale. 'Nights spent in peculiar houses', as Ralph muses, perhaps, on 'The Jolly Corner', 'were a favourite theme of the magazines, and he remembered tales about them that had been thought clever' (82).[44]

The property Ralph inherits in England has been bequeathed to him by his 'late kinsman', a 'Mr. Philip Augustus Pendrel' (40) on the strength of his having read his 'young relative's remarkable volume, "An Essay in Aid of the Reading of History"',

> and, wishing somehow to testify to the admiration he felt for it, had come to consider that no symbol would be so solid as the old English house forming the sole item, in a long list of heavily hampered possessions, that he was free thus to dispose of. (42)

'Mansfield Square' appears to be, in so far as chapters of 'history' go, the real thing; but embedded in Ralph's assessment of his enthusiasm for it, there is a hierarchy reminiscent of James's 'The Art of Fiction': 'it was for the historic, the aesthetic, fairly in fact for the cryptic, that he cared' (43). Ralph's encounter with a portrait of this forebear, and the endless scrutiny to which he subjects it, results, as the portrait comes to life and the two exchange places in some wondrous and inexplicable way, in that reciprocation of the past and present for which James had long uncertainly sought.[45] Ralph's ancestor married the elder daughter of the Midmore family, and was on the point of doing so before he hurtles forward to exchange places with Ralph in the future. Ralph, however, falls in love with Nan, the younger daughter, and threatens a rupturing of the past from the illicit vantage-point of the present, or future. In the meantime, what James calls a 'malaise' emerges as the family perceives, uneasily, Ralph's 'strange cleverness' (298), the preternatural wit and apparent clairvoyance of what is, as yet unbeknown to them, a ghost from the future haunting the past. This, at the end of an incomplete fourth chapter, is where James came to a halt.[46]

Increasingly restive in the past, and eager to escape, Ralph's obsessive desire for it has turned into a nightmare in which the future, his present, seems forever lost.[47] Like Wells's protagonist, the Time Traveller, Pendrel realizes that in 'losing' his 'own age', he is now 'helpless in this strange new world' (*The Time Machine* 34).[48] In Pendrel, James has taken the historian at his word partly to demonstrate how unreal and intangible such researches have to be; and if the 'future' is substituted for the past, he is as much a victim of a curiosity comfortable only in the abstract as Wells's Time Traveller left contemplating

> the thought of the years I had spent in study and toil to get into the future age, and now my passion of anxiety to get out of it. I had

made myself the most complicated and the most hopeless trap that ever a man devised. (*The Time Machine* 38)

In his scenario, James rehearses the complications of Nan's renouncing her love for Ralph so that he can be returned to the London of 1910. There, Aurora (who, anxious about him and despite her earlier resolve against it, has came back to the Old World) awaits him; and they are to marry. For Beverly Haviland, James's uniting of the two in London, where they are to remain, can be 'seen' as a 'love-gift' to 'the Europe that had sustained him and his art for so long' (30).[49] But this is to disregard the fact that James's notes for a continuation were never transposed into the novel itself. Whereas Spencer Brydon, having retrieved from his experience a usable sense of the past, emerges into the welcome arms of Alice Staverton and enters, ironically, the genre of a romance, Ralph Pendrel is left suspended in the past contemplating a future once present and now forever inaccessible. Stillborn in the paratext of the novel is a plot resolution in which Alice Staverton's counterpart (putatively), Nan, renounces her relationship with the time-trespassing Ralph so that he is somehow free to return to the present (future). If Brydon, Pendrel, and the James of the autobiographical writings are caught in fugal states, only Brydon manages to achieve an escape of a kind.

In *The Great Gatsby*, Nick Carraway beats on against the current of time only to 'be borne back ceaselessly into the past' (188), whereas the easy continuities presupposed by images of the stream of time are, ultimately, inconceivable for James. To the 'treatment of time', George Stransom woefully observes in 'The Altar of the Dead', 'the malady of life begins at a given moment to succumb' (459), but even this limited comfort is disavowed by James as he contemplates the loss of a 'still-felt past and a complacently personal future' (HJA 199). The difficulty of clinging to an 'indestructible presence' stretching 'away into the past' ('Owen Wingrave' (275)), of hovering 'between prospect and retrospect' (Rev. of *Middlemarch* 958), has given way to sheer impossibility. The outbreak of the Great War of 1914 and the disabling incongruities that arose almost immediately between it and the Civil War, had a shattering effect on James's way with the past, both at the personal and aesthetic levels: henceforth, ludic, abstract, engagements with grammars of time and senses of the past, however radical, experimental, and interesting, were simply irrelevant.

Lured by what he laments as the 'massacre and ravage and anguish' ('Within the Rim' 180) of the war into giving a rare press interview,

James found himself reverting to the arcana of syntax, tense, and perspective, elements of a time-consuming grammar he immediately consigns to other worlds, like the plots of 'The Jolly Corner' and *The Sense of the Past*, as futile anachronisms:

> a fine sense for the semicolon, like any sort of sense at all for the pluperfect tense and the subjunctive mood, on which the whole perspective in a sentence may depend, seems anything but common....But what on earth are we talking about? And the Chairman of the Corps Committee pulled himself up in deprecation of our frivolity. ('Henry James's First Interview' 142)[50]

In 'The Long Wards', James returns to instincts voiced in *William Wetmore Story and His Friends*, where 'speculations as to what might have been are ever' the 'prey of mere beguilement', and are 'almost as futile as they are fascinating' (2: 223). Abandoned to languish, in the presence of 'unutterable things' and 'something unspeakably different' ('Within the Rim' 180), is the besetting, yet now overwhelmingly meaningless question posed by 'The Jolly Corner':

> We have left immeasurably behind us here the question of what might or what should have been. That belonged, with whatever beguiled or amused ways of looking at it, to the abyss of our past delusion. ('The Long Wards' 171)

Obliterated for a moment that James was not to outlive, by a war that had 'used up words', were some of the very terms on which the past had been available for use and abuse ('James's First Interview' 144).

Afterword

'Untruth is a condition of life'
(Nietzsche)

To see fully is to locate chaos, such a vision being more perilous than the liberating errors or fictions available to imaginative individuals who have discerned that 'Chaos' is the 'law of nature' whereas 'Order' is the 'dream of man' (*The Education of Henry Adams* 1132). By the time Maisie reaches Boulogne at the end of *What Maisie Knew*, she understands that 'appearance' and 'illusion' are the 'necessary' presuppositions of 'art as well as of life' (Vaihinger 343)[1] and that 'it isn't knowledge', but a vigilant 'ignorance that—as we've been beautifully told—is bliss' (James, 'The Tree of Knowledge' 224). But at Folkestone in the meantime, as the novel takes on apocalyptic dimensions, she begins to grasp the extent of her egregious misunderstanding of the relationship between her mother and a Captain now 'the biggest cad in all London'. Imposed upon Maisie by a narrator who also silences her is a grammar of the sublime which collapses into incoherence:

> There rose in her a fear, a pain, a vision ominous, precocious, of what it might mean for her mother's fate to have forfeited such a loyalty as that. There was literally an instant in which Maisie fully saw—saw madness and desolation, saw ruin and darkness and death. 'I've thought of him often since, and I hoped it was with him—with him—' Here, in her emotion, it failed her, the breath of her filial hope. (*What Maisie Knew* 187)

Maisie first encounters the Captain in a Kensington Gardens likened to the 'Forest of Arden'; and there, as part of a romance in which

Sir Claude has adopted for Maisie and himself the roles of 'banished duke' and the 'artless country wench' (115), she struggles to extract the Captain's protestations of 'loyalty' towards her mother: 'Of *course* I love her, damn it, you know!' (128). What Maisie experiences at Folkestone is the foundering of a construction about the past. Hers is the momentary confrontation of a failure to make valid connections in Kensington Gardens: a failure which, in a quixotic way, exposes the fictive and uncovers the literal and threatens her with the atomization of that fiction of which she is a product. But there is enough of the literary about that 'literally' ('there was literally an instant') to suggest that making fictions has as much to do with what is conventionally taken as being reality as it has with the unreal. If Maisie is an artist-manquée exploring the artifices by which a coherent appearance of an essentially chaotic and meaningless reality is synthesized, she is also as a character in fiction, and is herself constructed. The fiction of this novel is more than an analogue of the principles on which the world of appearances is ordered, for

> it must be remembered that the object of the world of ideas as a whole is not the portrayal of reality...but rather to provide us with an *instrument for finding our way more easily in this world.* (Vaihinger 15)

'Philosophy', wrote Adam Smith, 'is the science of the connecting principles of nature'. 'Wonder', he continues, is a condition brought about by an 'unusual succession of things' which results in 'disjointed' objects with a 'gap or interval betwixt them'. When there is a 'clear discovery of a connecting chain', the difficulties 'vanish', along with that sensation of having 'been admitted behind the scenes' (16). Discursive formations such as James's 'obscure hurt', rather than the incoherent event in itself, and fictions in general can be prophylactics against chaos:

> Nature, after the largest experience that common observation can acquire, seems to abound with events which appear solitary and incoherent with all that go before them, which therefore disturb the easy movement of the imagination....Philosophy, by representing the invisible chains which bind together all these disjointed objects, endeavours to introduce order into this chaos of jarring and discordant appearances. (20)

William James posits in *The Principles of Psychology* that alternative which, for 'literally an instant', Maisie 'fully' sees but counters it by emphasizing the extent to which 'the consciously-false, plays an enormous part in science, in world-philosophies and in life' (Vaihinger xli):

> We may, if we like, by our reasonings unwind things back to that black and jointless continuity of space and moving clouds of swarming atoms which science calls the only real world. But all the while the world *we* feel and live in will be that which our ancestors and we, by slowly cumulative strokes of choice, have extricated out of this, like sculptors, by simply rejecting certain portions of the given stuff. Other sculptors, other statues from the same stone! (277)

'No possible number of entities', William James asserted, 'can sum *themselves* together'.

> Each remains, in the sum, what it always was; and the sum itself exists only *for a bystander* who happens to overlook the units and to apprehend the sum as such. (161)

Two years later, Karl Pearson argued in a similar vein that

> The universe is a variable quantity, which depends upon the keenness and structure of our organs of sense, and upon the fineness of our powers and instruments of observation....the universe is largely the construction of each individual mind. (18)

Pearson sees 'science' as 'more artistic than modern art' (20). 'The real world lies for us', with an ambiguous 'lie' in play, 'in constructs and not in shadowy things-in-themselves' (68); 'it is meaningless', and 'exists only when formulated by man' (73). The transcendent realms posited by Kant (as he acknowledged),[2] perhaps even the Shakespeare of our imagination, the real of history, or James's actual experiences at Newport, like the Aspern of the papers, are all 'relative to the human mind' (88) for Pearson:

> What we have no right to infer is that order, mind, or reason—all human characters or human conceptions falling on this side of sense-impressions—exist on the other side of sense-impressions.... Briefly chaos is all that science can logically assert of the supersensuous. (94–5)

'What we generally call truth', suggests Vaihinger, 'namely a conceptual world coinciding with the external world, *is merely the most expedient error'*. The 'conceptual world' is 'subjective in its forms', '*subjective is fictional; fictional is false; falsehood is error*' (108). It is 'as if', given that all discourse is necessarily a 'deviation' from the chaos of 'reality' (Vaihinger 97), James experienced not just a 'hurt' but an 'obscure hurt', and that his reconstructions and interpretations of it in the auto-biographical writings are for real, for 'there is *only* a perspective seeing, *only* a perspective "knowing"' (Nietzsche, 'On the Genealogy of Morals' 555). Or as William James expresses it, in an essay whose title, 'On a Certain Blindness', implies a necessary conspiracy between partial, rather than full, seeing and fiction:

> neither the whole of truth, nor the whole good, is revealed to any one single observer, although each observer gains a partial superiority of insight from the peculiar position in which he stands. (860)

For 'experience is what I agree to attend to':

> Only those items which I notice shape my mind—without selective interest, experience is an utter chaos. Interest alone gives accent and emphasis, light and shade, background and foreground—intelligible perspective, in a word. ('Brute and Human Intellect' 929–30).

If 'so-called agreement with reality must finally be abandoned as a criterion' for truth (Vaihinger 108) then, as Maurice Gedge discovered in a limited way, the imaginative resort must be to fictions that are superior in form to what are, in any event, only fictions. As the French physiologist and medic Claude Bernard wrote in the year the American Civil War ended and as James was beginning his career in fiction (1865):

> The words life, death, health, disease, have no objective reality. When a physiologist calls in vital force, or life, he does not see it; he merely pronounces a word. (Bernard 71)

'Life', George Henry Lewes contended, 'is a fiction; but we do not on that account reject it. Fictions are potent' (1: 46).

When Mrs. Wix first mentions her idea of a curious *ménage à trois* comprising Sir Claude, Maisie, and herself, 'it hung before Maisie...like a glittering picture and she clasped her hands in ecstasy' (85). This arrangement excludes Mrs. Beale; and Maisie's insistence on that exclusion at the end of the novel suggests that she has figured out how to avoid disabling disconnection and incoherence by averting the collapse of enabling fictions in a world of the 'as if'. No longer available to her is a passive 'overlooking' of the surface as a 'bystander' (William James, *The Principles of Psychology* 161), for she has become aware of the necessary mendacities of fiction after being 'admitted behind the scenes' (Adam Smith 16) at Folkestone. As James's surrogate, Maisie now possesses the capacity to construct life-saving appearances contingent on absence, deferral, and potential in a world where what appears is not an appearance of the real, but a not-chaos formation of the individual mind, and where 'language' is perpetually in 'flight', 'running after a reality which it can only define negatively' (Macherey 63).

Appearances, or realms of the 'as if', are constituted by an absence of the real, and the more enigmatic and unrepresentable it seems to be, the greater the power of the fiction thereby engendered. As Macherey holds:

> The speech of the book comes from a certain silence, a matter which it endows with form, a ground on which it traces a figure. Thus, the book is not self-sufficient; it is necessarily accompanied by a *certain absence*, without which it would not exist. (85)

The 'discourse of a work' is 'sealed and interminable, completed or endlessly beginning again, diffuse and dense, coiled about an absent centre which it can neither conceal or reveal' (27). Infinite, however, are the ways of being silent or absent, and some are much more interesting and productive than others. 'There is no binary division to be made between what one says and what one does not say', Foucault suggests, and

> we must try to determine the different ways of not saying... things....There is not one but many silences, and they are an integral part of the strategies that underlie and permeate discourses. (*History of Sexuality* 1: 27)

If our beginning is in the yarns we spin, we also tell tales, like Scheherazade, to postpone the end; and forced upon us in the process is Nietzsche's contention that 'untruth' is a 'condition of life' (*Beyond Good and Evil* 202). But with the boundless reverberations of Lear's 'nothing will come of nothing' in play,[3] and with the realization that 'chaos', the 'real', and 'obscurity' are no more than 'summational fictions' at best (Vaihinger 211), there may always be another turn of the screw, penultimately.

List of Abbreviations

Henry James

CS—*Complete Stories*. 5 vols. Library of America. New York, N. Y.: Literary Classics of the United States, Inc., 1996–99.

CTWGB—*Collected Travel Writings: Great Britain and America: English Hours, The American Scene, Other Travels*. Library of America. New York, N. Y.: Literary Classics of the United States, Inc., 1993.

CTWTC—*Collected Travel Writings: The Continent: A Little Tour in France, Italian Hours, Other Travels*. Library of America. New York, N. Y.: Literary Classics of the United States, Inc., 1993.

HJA—*Henry James: Autobiography*. Ed. Frederick W. Dupee. London: W. H. Allen, 1956.

HJL—*Henry James: Letters*. Ed. Leon Edel. 4 vols. Cambridge, Massachusetts and London, England: Belknap Press, Harvard University Press, 1974–84.

IT—Introduction. *The Tempest. The Complete Works of William Shakespeare*. Ed. Sidney Lee. 1907. *LCEL* 1205–20.

LCEL—*Essays on Literature, American Writers, English Writers. Literary Criticism*. Vol. 1. Library of America. New York, N. Y.: Literary Classics of the United States, Inc., 1984.

LCFW—*French Writers, Other European Writers, The Prefaces to the New York Edition. Literary Criticism*. Vol. 2. Library of America. New York, N. Y.: Literary Classics of the United States, Inc., 1984.

LL—*Henry James: A Life in Letters*. Ed. Philip Horne. London: Allen Lane, 1999.

N—*The Complete Notebooks of Henry James*. Ed. Leon Edel and Lyall H. Powers. New York and Oxford: Oxford University Press, 1987.

NY—*The Novels and Tales of Henry James*. New York Edition. 24 vols. New York: Charles Scribner's Sons, 1907–9.

PA—Preface. *The Ambassadors*. 1907–9. *LCFW* 1304–21.

PAD—Preface. 'The Altar of the Dead'. 1907–9. *LCFW* 1246–68.

PAP—Preface. 'The Aspern Papers', 'The Turn of the Screw', 'The Liar', 'The Two Faces'. 1907–9. *LCFW* 1173–91.

PDM—Preface. 'Daisy Miller', 'Pandora', 'The Patagonia', 'The Marriages', 'The Real Thing', 'Brooksmith', 'The Beldonald Holbein', 'The Story In It', 'Flickerbridge', 'Mrs. Medwin'. 1907–9. *LCFW* 1269–86.

PGB—Preface. *The Golden Bowl*. 1907–9. *LCFW* 1322–41.

PLM—Preface. 'The Lesson of the Master', 'The Death of the Lion', 'The Next Time', 'The Figure in the Carpet', 'The Coxon Fund'. 1907–9. *LCFW* 1225–37.

PPC—Preface. *The Princess Casamassima*. 1907–9. *LCFW* 1086–1102.

PR—Preface. *The Reverberator*, 'Madame de Mauves', 'A Passionate Pilgrim', 'The Madonna of the Future', 'Louisa Pallant'. 1907–9. *LCFW* 1192–1207.

PRH—Preface. *Roderick Hudson*. 1907–9. *LCFW* 1039–52.

PSP—Preface. *The Spoils of Poynton*. 1907–9. *LCFW* 1138–55.

PTM—Preface. *The Tragic Muse*. 1907–9. *LCFW* 1103–19.

PWM—Preface. *What Maisie Knew,* 'The Pupil', 'In the Cage'. 1907–9. *LCFW*
1156–72.

Other

AS—*Americans on Shakespeare,* 1776–1914. Ed. Peter Rawlings. Aldershot:
Ashgate, 1999.
AF—*Americans on Fiction, 1776–1900.* 3 vols. Ed. Peter Rawlings. London and
Vermont: Pickering and Chatto, 2002.
WJ1—William James. *Writings, 1878–1899.* Library of America. New York, N. Y.:
Literary Classics of the United States, Inc., 1992.
WJ2—William James. *Writings, 1902–1910.* Library of America. New York, N. Y.:
Literary Classics of the United States, Inc., 1987.
OED—*Oxford English Dictionary.* 2nd edn. 1992.

Note
All references to Shakespeare are to: *The Riverside Shakespeare.* 2nd edn. Ed.
G. Blakemore Evans. Boston and New York: Houghton Mifflin Company, 1997.

Notes

Introduction: 'We Want None of Our Problems Poor'

1 See Silverman for a discussion of James and more conventional (Freudian) senses of the primal scene.

2 Roosevelt regarded the Civil War as the principal agent of a national unity predicated on the memories, and on the history, fabricated in its name: 'The captains and the armies who, after long years of dreary campaigning and bloody, stubborn fighting, brought to a close the Civil War have likewise left us even more than a reunited realm. The material effect of what they did is shown in the fact that the same flag flies from the Great Lakes to the Rio Grande, and all the people of the United States are richer because they are one people and not many, because they belong to one great nation, and not to a contemptible knot of struggling nationalities. But besides this, besides the material results of the Civil War, we are all, North and South, incalculably richer for its memories' ('True American Ideals' 744). See Robert Penn Warren's observation (as evidence for the prevalence of the myth, rather than of the fact): 'The Civil War is, for the American imagination, the great single event of our history. Without too much wrenching, it may, in fact, be said to *be* American history. Before the Civil War we had no history in the deepest and most inward sense' (3). The drift of Mark Twain and Charles Dudley Warner's comments on the Civil War in *The Gilded Age* is broadly comparable in substance to James's, but they are entirely negative in cast, projecting the war in destructive rather than constructive terms: 'The eight years in America from 1860 to 1868 uprooted institutions that were centuries old, changed the politics of a people, transformed the social life of half the country, and wrought so profoundly on the entire national character that the influence cannot be measured short of two or three generations' (228–9). It is interesting to note that in Louis Menand's *The Metaphysical Club*, the Civil War continues to be regarded as a paradigm shift for America: 'The war was fought to preserve the system of government that had been established at the nation's founding....And the system was preserved; the union did survive. But in almost every other respect, the United States became a different country. The war alone did not make America modern, but the war marks the birth of modern America' (ix). For the purposes of my argument, it is less that this was, or could have been the case, more that it is a common, and usable, perception.

3 James had distinguished non-combatant company, of course: 'Henry Adams anxiously watched the grand spectacle from London....William Dean Howells, his literary plans momentarily "deranged" by Fort Sumter, sailed for Venice in November 1861 and served there as United States consul general until his return in 1865. And Mark Twain, after a brief and not entirely creditable or credible few weeks as a lieutenant in a Rebel company of Home Guards, defected and accompanied his abolitionist brother to Nevada' (Aaron 91–2).

4   Leon Edel gives a detailed account of the incident, correcting in the process James's skewed sense of the dates in his *Notes of a Son and Brother*; see *Henry James: The Untried Years* (167–88). But this date has been disputed by Hoffman (530).

5   Aaron also writes of James 'trying to screen the story of his nonparticipation behind a fog of words' (107–8).

6   I agree with much of Savoy's discussion of the 'the hermeneutic desire awakened by queer figuration' in James, although I see the queerness as a means of staging fundamental issues of epistemology, language, and representation to which gender and sex are subordinate.

7   For Rebecca West, in the first book-length study of Henry James, the 'obscure hurt' was literally an accident that simply prevented James from fighting: 'he sustained an injury so serious that he could never hope to share the Northern glory' (20); Edmund Gosse agreed: 'Henry James's health forced him to be a spectator of the war' (21). But a view developed in the 1920s and 1930s that James had been castrated in 1861. Edel challenges this, concluding that it was nothing more than a back injury which became chronic. James elucidated the 'hurt', Edel believes, as an 'unconscious identification' with a father whose leg was amputated as a result of a fire-fighting accident (*Henry James: The Untried Years*: 180). Similarly, R. W. B. Lewis has observed that 'the painful incident had an almost uncanny family aspect to it. Young Henry James may or may not have known about the nocturnal occasion when his grandfather feverishly worked the pumps on the Albany wharf in a dangerous and unsuccessful effort to save his shops from being gutted by fire. But his father's cork leg was a daily reminder of the catastrophe that befell Henry Senior when *he* attempted to put out a stable fire' (117). Eakin is right to describe Edel's 'well-intentioned attempt to demystify the hurt' as 'wrong-headed', but not because the obscurity of the hurt is constituted merely by the raft of psychoanalytical complexities for which he pitches ('Henry James's "Obscure Hurt": Can Autobiography Serve Biography?' 689). The possible psychological dimensions of the accident are difficult to deny, but that is not the same as categorizing it as a 'psychological event' (108), or an 'inward psychological reality' that exceeded 'the capacity of autobiographical discourse to express it' (Eakin, *Fictions in Autobiography: Studies in the Art of Self-Invention* 113). On the origins of the castration theory in the 1920s and 1930s, see Haralson, *Henry James and Queer Modernity* (194–200). Stephen Spender suggested that the rumour of 'castration seems exaggerated and improbable' (37n), but Glenway Wescott was more confident in his belief that James's 'pre-Civil-War accident' had resulted in castration or some form of impotence (523). The rumour was prevalent enough in the 1920s, as Haralson observes, for Ernest Hemingway's manuscript to link the mutilated Jake of *The Sun Also Rises* with Henry James (*Henry James and Queer Modernity* 194). Halperin sees the 'hurt' as more psychic' than 'physical,' and his emphasis on James's passiveness is exactly what I want to oppose ('Henry James's Civil War' 25). The most schematic, psychoanalytical, interpretation of the 'obscure hurt', and one which Edel clearly draws on, is Saul Rosenzweig's essay 'The Ghost of Henry James: A Study in Thematic Apperception'. Rosenzweig argues that James's 'Oedipus situation...included a highly individualistic father— a cripple—and a gifted sibling rival (William)', both of whom 'dwarfed'

Henry. 'The problematic relationship to father and brother was solved submissively by a profound repression of aggressiveness'. The 'obscure hurt', Rosenzweig contends, combined a 'keen sense of created impotence' with 'a possible suspicion of unconscious malingering' and 'crystallized his early sense of inferiority into "castration anxiety"'. It was 'at any rate after his injury that James turned to the art of fiction. His writing served him both as an escape from frustration by way of fantasy and as a partial means of solving his problems through sublimation'. This escape proved insufficient, and James left an American scene no longer tolerable to him. In the final third of his life (this argument is considered in Chapter 4), 'a resurgence of his buried drives occurred' as the repressed returns in the guise of the ghosts that haunt stories such as 'The Jolly Corner'. World War I, and James's work on behalf of the American Volunteer Ambulance Corps for example, amounted to an 'over-compensation' for the cluster of problems organized around the 'obscure hurt' (98–9). On the issue of the 'masochistic aesthetic' and William James, see David McWhirter, 'Restaging the Hurt: Henry James and the Artist as Masochist'. Like Edel, Rosenzweig, Eakin, and McWhirter, Wendy Graham is locked into a psychological, or psychoanalytical, paradigm whose explanatory reach, and all-embracing extent, is taken too much for granted: rather fancifully, if creatively, she reads the 'obscure hurt' as signifying 'an unconscious attempt to bring gender identity, sexual preference, and anatomy into pseudocoherence by effecting an imaginary sex change' (71–2). Graham acknowledges that the 'obscure hurt' could be regarded as James 'unconsciously' choosing (a problematic formulation) 'disability as a way out of the trials of masculinity that surrounded him in 1861' (12), but her principal emphasis is on James's 'effemination' as (again) 'an unconscious response to his incestuous longings for his father and brother' (13). The homosexualization of the relationship between William and Henry James, and the proposal that the 'obscure hurt' was William's marriage, is a line pursued in a number of articles by Hall; and this is also Feinstein's trajectory, along with that of the intense bond of sickness between the two. Similarly, Sarotte makes much of Henry's being 'rejected' by William, but his reading of the 'obscure hurt' is severely afflicted by the dubious benefits of hindsight: 'Cannot this *obvious desire to pass for a eunuch* be read as an attempt to make excuses for James's attitude toward women and his lifelong bachelorhood by a completely involuntary physical accident....Is this not a means of forestalling an accusation of homosexuality?' (199). Jacob Jacobson speculates that James experienced a 'surprise seminal discharge' (208) at Newport and that his subsequent traumatization fits 'historical accounts of...masturbation phobia and the threat of spermatorrhea assaulting America' (209). Kaplan is sceptical about the extent to which Henry James Senior's injunction against William and Henry's going to war was resisted by the non-combatants: 'According to Henry senior, his two elder sons strongly fought against his prohibition. The record is minimal, motivations and struggles unclear' (54). Menand comments, in relation to William James, that 'no doubt the father preferred to keep his older son out of danger. Still, William does not seem to have pulled very hard at the leash' (74). Surprisingly, there is no mention of the 'obscure hurt' or the Civil War in John R. Bradley's *Henry James's Permanent Adolescence*.

8 For anti-positivism and its context, see Hughes. Two books which by title seem directly relevant to this chapter are, however interesting in other respects, at a considerable distance from its concern with James's senses of the past and his theory and practice of history: Ian F. A. Bell, *Henry James and the Past: Readings into Time* and Roslyn Jolly, *Henry James: History, Narrative, Fiction.* Bell's successful and stimulating project is to locate James's fiction in the context of America's developing market economy in the nineteenth century. His argument examines James's awareness of the extent to which the market, with its emphasis on the 'performative', reconstructs the 'person' as a 'personality' (12). The 'Romance form' (ix), he argues, is reworked by James in the interests of going 'beyond the confinements of the rhetoric of realism' to the essential 'exercises of power in history' (x). I like Bell's emphasis on the 'air' in the 'air of reality' in 'The Art of Fiction' (*Washington Square: Styles of Money* 25) and the need, therefore, in James to be 'alert to the indirection of testimony, to omissions and suppressions, completing suggestions' (26); although I am far from convinced that there is a balance, even in the James of the 1880s, between a '"latitude" advocated by Hawthorne' and an 'admiration for the Balzacian fact' (39). The early James, Jolly believes, authorized his fiction in terms of history as part of a broader 'anti-romance' campaign (vi). Alfred Habegger, in *Gender, Fantasy, and Realism in American Literature*, is much more convincing on James's tactical, and temporary, deployment of the genre of 'realism' in the early phases of his writing. Increasingly, Jolly suggests, James came under siege from characters who imply that 'fiction is most valuable not as a record of experience, but as mode of encountering and shaping it' (vii–viii). I shall argue, however (especially in Chapter 1), that James never subscribed to the view that fiction could simply be a 'record of experience'.

9 Three critics, in particular, emphasize the importance of the Cleveland Street scandal and the Wilde trials for James's writing, but with very different agendas from this one. See Stevens; Graham; Haralson (*Henry James and Queer Modernity*).

10 On the origins of this 'fourth-phase' category, see McWhirter, '"A Provision Full of Responsibilities"' 149.

11 Poverty is not something from which Rowe's *Henry Adams and Henry James* suffers. But its sense of James's sense of the past is, in my view, unduly present-oriented; and it concedes too much power to the aesthetic, and the impressionistic, and not enough to James's tactical acumen.

12 Dr. Henry J. Bigelow (1818–90), professor of surgery at the Harvard Medical School (Feinstein 198).

1 'The Exquisite Melancholy of Everything Unuttered': History and the Abuse of the Past

1 Rowe is relevant here: 'The kind of history with which' James 'is concerned is intimately related to his sense of the aesthetic process' (*Henry Adams and Henry James* 133).

2 Whilst Donoghue is certainly right to say that 'James's sense of the past...is opportunistic rather than devout', I cannot agree that James, of all writers,

is 'metaphysically incurious', 'the past' being 'just another subject to him' (123).

3   Fritz Stern's account of the development of historiography emphasizes objectivity, or what he calls the extinguishing of the self (15), as the principal feature of the movement from the 'century of ideas to the century of facts' (17) in the period from 'Niebuhr's work in 1811' to the early twentieth century (16). By the end of the nineteenth century, there was a strengthening opposition to the aridities of scientific history, Nietzsche's 'The Use and Abuse of History' (1874) being one of the first salvoes in this direction. For Nietzsche, in a position far from unattractive to James, the task of history is not to venerate the past but to vitalize the present. 'To value' the study of history 'beyond a certain point mutilates and degrades life' (3), and 'if the historical sense no longer preserves life, but mummifies it: then the tree dies, unnaturally, from the top downwards, and at last the roots themselves wither. Antiquarian history degenerates from the moment that it no longer gives a soul and inspiration to the fresh life of the present' (27).

4   The novels were *The Household of Sir Thomas More* and *Jacques Bonneval; or, The Days of the Dragonnades*.

5   For one map of these developments, see Marwick 34–55. Collingwood, however, gives a much more coruscatingly philosophical account of the naïve commitment to scientific procedures and principles by historians later in the nineteenth century.

6   In 1875, James even suggested that Mrs. Annie Edwards' *Leah: A Woman of Fashion*, in a genre he despised, was 'so much more exciting' than 'Motley or Buckle' ('Recent Novels' 40). Conversely, Francis Parkman's *The Old Régime in Canada* is praised for its novelistic qualities: it is a 'thrilling volume' (577) with 'abundantly dramatic' episodes (579).

7   See Stern 17.

8   'Three generations of German, British, and even French historians marched into battle intoning the magic words "*Wie es eigentlich gewesen*" like an incantation....The Positivists, anxious to stake out their claim for history as a science, contributed the weight of their influence to this cult of facts. First ascertain the facts, said the Positivists, then draw your conclusions from them. In Great Britain, this view of history fitted in perfectly with the empiricist tradition....The empirical theory of knowledge presupposes a complete separation between subject and object' (Carr 9); see Carr generally on facts and history (7–30).

9   James is in line with Collingwood here: a 'fact,' for the positivistic historian, 'is something immediately given in perception' (132); but 'no historical testimony can establish the reality of facts that have no analogy in our present experience' (138). Compare Oakeshott: 'there is no fact in history which is not a judgement, no event which is not an inference' (100); or Bradley (in 1874): 'our facts are inferential, and their actuality depends on the correctness [or not] of the reasoning which makes them what they are [or are not]' (*The Presuppositions of Critical History* 90).

10 James overlooks in *Middlemarch* the concentration on the sterilities of Casaubon's researches. The contrast between Will Ladislaw and Casaubon is central to this project. For the former, 'the very miscellaneousness of Rome...made the mind flexible...and saved you from seeing the world's ages

as a set of box-like partitions without vital connection'. Ladislaw is in the James mould, for 'the fragments stimulated his imagination and made him constructive' (244). Both 'The Art of Fiction' and *Middlemarch*, though James was unwilling to acknowledge the affinities, are conceived in the paradigm of organicism. The artist 'on whom nothing is lost' in 'The Art of Fiction' (53) has a forebear in Ladislaw's poet, whom he defines as having 'a soul so quick to discern, that no shade of quality escapes it' (256). Whereas Casaubon's is the futile attempt, in the spirit of Buckle, 'to reconstruct a past world' (40) and to find the 'key to all mythologies' (412), Ladislaw shares James's suspicion of facts: 'he said he should prefer not to know the sources of the Nile, and that there should be some unknown regions preserved as hunting-grounds for the poetic imagination' (106–7).

11 Macaulay's approach (and hence a partial resemblance between 'History' and some features of 'The Art of Fiction') is an indication of the extent to which 'in Britain the main thrust of Ranke's immediate contemporaries was to re-emphasize history as a literary art rather than as a science' (Marwick 43).

12 In a similar vein, James regrets Victor Hugo's 'useless enumerations' (Rev. of *Quatrevingt-treize* 457) and 'researches' that are 'pedantically exhibited' (Rev. of *Légende des Siècles* 461). Paul de Musset is castigated for producing a book that 'is decidedly poor as fiction, but tolerably good, probably, as history' ('Alfred de Musset' 605). By contrast, Guy de Maupassant has a 'visual sense' that is 'never prolonged nor analytic'; it has 'nothing of enumeration, of the quality of the observer, who counts the items to be sure he has made up the sum' ('Guy de Maupassant' 526).

13 Relevant here are Millicent Bell's remarks on 'James's fear of an excess of real record' and its inhibiting effect on the 'free imagination of the artist' (122).

14 Aristotle distinguished between four causes: material (what something is made of), formal (what it is in essence), efficient (what brought it into being), and final, or teleological (what its function or purpose is) (*Physics* 98–100).

15 The three volumes of autobiographical writings comprise: *A Small Boy and Others* (1913); *Notes of a Son and Brother* (1914); *The Middle Years* (1917). These volumes are collected in *Henry James: Autobiography*, ed. Frederick W. Dupee.

16 'The ordinary novel would trace the history of the diamond—but I say, "Diamond, what! This is carbon". And my diamond might be coal or soot, and my theme is carbon' (D. H. Lawrence 290).

17 John Keats, 'Ode on a Grecian Urn' (209).

18 See Matthew 25.

19 The narrator is also imbued with many of the characteristics of Delia Bacon, the American historian who sought to prove that Shakespeare was not the author of his plays. This element of the tale, and its uses of and allusions to Shakespeare, will be considered in Chapter 3.

20 Rivkin sees the tale as revolving around 'gain and loss' rather than presence and absence, observing that 'lest we be tempted to deem the narrator's fail-ure to represent Aspern adequately his greatest moral shortcoming, we must consider the similar moral failure that would await his success' ('Speaking with the Dead: Ethics and Representation in "The Aspern Papers"' 141).

21 See Carton (118) on the commodification of the women in 'The Aspern Papers'.

22 I am drawing on Jacques Lacan's concept of the 'réel', as adopted and adapted by de Certeau. The 'real', for de Certeau, as for Lacan, is 'a world of unmarked space and time that cannot be mediated by language or signs' (Conley xvi). My interest is not in a systematic application of Lacan's 'real', 'imaginary', and 'symbolic' orders, but with connections between this general scheme and James's preoccupation with a world beyond appearances—the social world of linguistic communication, intersubjective relations, and ideology of Lacan's 'symbolic order'—fabricated by discourse. See Lacan 279–80.

23 See the discussion of these texts in Chapter 4.

24 For an application of this aspect of de Certeau's thinking, see Fradenburg.

25 The only book-length study of James and science is Purdy's *The Hole in the Fabric: Science, Contemporary Literature, and Henry James*. It has nothing to say about the impact of scientific thinking on James's unease with language.

26 Ernst Mach's *The Science of Mechanics: A Critical and Historical Account of Its Development* appeared in 1883 and was translated into English in 1893, a year after the publication of Pearson's *The Grammar of Science*.

27 'Yes! in the sea of life enisled,/ With echoing straits between us thrown,/ Dotting the shoreless watery wild,/ We mortal millions live *alone*' (Matthew Arnold, 'To Marguerite—Continued' 197).

28 The failure of this retreat is considered in Chapter 4.

29 2 Corinthians 3: 6.

30 The 'minute-men' (local militia) fired on British forces advancing on Concord (20 April 1775); this 'shot heard around the world' is traditionally taken as the starting-point for the War of Independence (1775–83).

31 Compare Collingwood: 'What the historian is doing, when he fancies he is merely cognizing past events as they actually happened, is in reality organizing his present consciousness' (153).

32 Compare Charles Bellingham in Howells' *The Rise of Silas Lapham*: 'The past of one's experience doesn't differ a great deal from the past of one's knowledge. It isn't much more probable; it's really a great deal less vivid than some scenes in a novel that one read when a boy' (186).

33 'Major phase' is from F. O. Matthiessen, *Henry James: The Major Phase*. James first used the phrase 'remount the stream of time' in his short story 'Sir Dominick Ferrand' in 1892 (199), and it occurs frequently in the prefaces to the New York edition. The 'stream of time' was the common currency of William James and Henri Bergson. William James first wrote of streams of time and consciousness in 'On Some Omissions of Introspective Psychology' in 1883 (987).

34 Meissner suggests that 'the thing itself, James demonstrates, can never be known since reality is always larger than any attempt to capture it'; perhaps, but I find this argument, in its unwillingness to take on the Kantian dimensions of that 'thing itself', a little impressionistic and under-theorized (190).

35 Certainly by the end of his career, aspects of James's work, not least in his suspension of *The Sense of the Past*, have all the signs of what Trilling terms in *Sincerity and Authenticity* the 'drastic reduction in the status of narration, of telling stories' (134), and not simply the 'disfavour into which narrative history has fallen' (139).

2 'Wars and Rumours of Wars': Among the Soldiers

1 The 'compulsive chasing of working-class contacts', and especially of recruits, was 'undoubtedly a major component of the sub-culture of homosexuality in late-Victorian England. It was a world of promiscuity, particularly if you had the right contacts, and many sections of the working-class were drawn in, often very casually, as the Post Office messenger boys in the Cleveland Street scandal of 1889–90 and the stable-lads, newspaper sellers, bookmakers' clerks in the Wilde trial vividly illustrate' (Weeks, *Sex, Politics, and Society* 113).

2 'Gamin': 'a neglected boy, left to run about the streets; a street Arab'. (*OED*)

3 Mark André Raffalovich (1864–1934) was a Russian Jew reared in France. In his *Uranisme et unisexualité*, published in 1896, he attacked the theory that homosexuality was either a psychiatric disorder that could be treated or that such characteristics were the product of a degenerate heredity. He became a Dominican, calling himself 'Brother Sebastian', and moved with the poet John Gray (1866–1934) to Edinburgh where Raffalovich built St Peter's Church for Gray. Henry James took a keen interest in the relationship between the two, writing to Hugh Walpole: 'When you refer to their "immorality on stone floors", and with prayerbooks in their hands so long as the exigencies of the situation permit of the manual retention of the sacred volumes, I do so want the picture developed and the proceedings authenticated' (*LL* 531). In his pocket diary for 10 February 1914, James records 'Raffalovich and friend lunch 1.45' (*N* 391).

4 *Studies in the Psychology of Sex* was published in 1897; Symonds died in 1893. In its second edition, 'Appendix A: A Problem in Greek Ethics. By J. A. Symonds' was omitted.

5 Stories about James's liaisons with soldiers were peddled, apparently, by Hugh Walpole. Leeming recounts that Stephen Spender 'became a frequent guest at my house during his Storrs [University of Connecticut] visits. There he told spicy stories about the rich and the famous, always with a tone of naïveté, as if he did not quite understand the significance of the spice. The young Hugh Walpole had told him about Henry James's affairs with the royal horse guardsmen' (xii).

6 On *A Problem in Modern Ethics*, James observed (with an interesting deployment of 'exhibition' and 'queer') that 'J. A. S. is truly, I gather, a candid and consistent creature, and the exhibition is infinitely remarkable'; but 'it's on the whole, I think, a queer place to plant the standard of duty, but he does it with extraordinary gallantry. If he has, or gathers, a band of the emulous, we may look for some capital sport' (Hyde 50). See Hyde's discussion of James and the Wilde affair (47–54). Hyde concludes that 'on the subject of homosexual relationships Henry seems to have held an open mind' (47).

7 Xavier Mayne is the pseudonym of an expatriate American, Edward Irenaeus Prime-Stevenson (1868–1942); his *Imre: A Memorandum*, an overtly homosexual novel, appeared in 1906.

8 See my "Grotesque Encounters in the Travel Writing of Henry James."

9 This essay has the same title as the book, *A Little Tour in France*, but it is distinct from it.

10   See Haralson (*Henry James and Queer Modernity*) on strategies of 'illegibility'
      for eluding the new 'sexological order' (*Henry James and Queer Modernity* 57).

11   See *Beloved Boy: Letters to Hendrik C. Andersen, 1899–1915*. Jobe (292–3) spec-
      ulates about Edel's late work on an edition of these letters and Henry James
      III's earlier blocking of their publication.

12   Both Kaplan and Cannon seem to take their cue from Edel. Kaplan consid-
      ers the homoerotic pull of a number of James's texts, especially 'The Author
      of Beltraffio' and 'The Pupil', within the context of the Cleveland Street
      scandal and the Wilde trials, and in the light of James's knowledge of and
      acquaintance with the life and work of John Addington Symonds, the clos-
      eted Edmund Gosse, and others, and reaches the conclusion that James
      'allowed himself the feelings and the language of transgression' in his 'rela-
      tionships, but not more' (454). Similarly, Cannon (like Kirby) argues that
      'James confined his homosexuality', a misnomer for 'homoeroticism' given
      the tenor of his book, 'to thoughts and mild acts of affection such as hugs
      and kisses' (71). There is a spirited rebuttal of all this in Zwinger. In ascrib-
      ing the desire, yet proscribing its satisfaction, neither writer seems aware of
      how incredible it is to be so categorical about genital activity. To look for evi-
      dence of what was is one thing; to offer unsupported statements about what
      was not is quite another. As ever, writing of both James M. Barrie and Henry
      James, Sedgwick assumes a much more intelligent poise: 'each author seems
      to have made erotic choices that were complicated enough, shifting enough
      in the gender of their objects, and, at least for long periods, kept distant
      enough from *éclaircissement* or physical expression, to make each an
      emboldening figure for a literary discussion of male homosexual panic'
      (*Epistemology of the Closet* 195).

13   Sheldon M. Novick's *Henry James: The Young Master*, irrespective of the huge
      disparity between the claims it makes and the evidence on offer, has an
      oddly regressive biographical enthusiasm. Novick also exudes an innocent
      confidence in the stability of phrases such as 'sexual orientation', which she
      construes as somehow timeless (xiii). Philip Horne's question, that of 'what
      we do, as literary critics, with biographical homosexuality in an author even
      when established', remains a pertinent one in this context ('The Master and
      the 'Queer Affair' of 'The Pupil'' 116).

14   'Homosexuality' emerged as sex became the subject of diagnostic, criminal,
      and pathologizing discourses in the later nineteenth century. See Foucault,
      History of Sexuality (Volume 1): *An Introduction*. The reach and context of
      turn-of-the-nineteenth-century 'homosexuality', Sedgwick speculates, are
      very different from that of 'gay' in its 1980s environment: 'Thus 'homosex-
      ual' and 'gay' seem more and more to be terms applicable to distinct,
      nonoverlapping periods in the history of a phenomenon for which there
      then remains no overarching label' (*Epistemology of the Closet* 17). The first
      use of 'homosexual' cited in the *OED* is from Krafft-Ebing's *Psychopathia
      Sexualis*, translated by Charles Gilbert Chaddock in 1892 (the German orig-
      inal is 1886). This is even later than the 'last third of the nineteenth centu-
      ry' specified by Sedgwick in *Epistemology of the Closet* (2). Also, the OED
      traces the use of 'gay' for 'homosexual' to underworld and prison slang in
      the 1930s. It certainly had this sense long before the 1980s.

15 Haralson's *Henry James and Queer Modernity* everywhere attests to the validity of complex senses of the 'queer' in James.

16 I find it hard to accept Person's view that 'recent scholars...have brought James and James studies out of the closet to the point where we can almost take James's homosexuality for granted', largely because I cannot see what evidence would allow such critics to establish so categorically what is not a transhistorical identity, but a shifting pattern of behaviour constituted by specific and unstable discursive formations. Person also makes the dubious assumption that 'homosexuality' and 'male desire', and its 'poetics', are necessarily linked ('James's Homo-Aesthetics: Deploying Desire in the Tales of Writers and Artists' 188–9). He seems unwilling to push beyond these limited concerns to the wider questions of epistemology and representation involved.

17 'Many other unnamable things', Horne continues, 'creep in under the same umbrella' ('The Master and the "Queer Affair" of "The Pupil"' 120). But Horne underplays the highly public association between what could not be named, the reporting of the Wilde trials, and the role of the press and salacious silence in the popular construction of 'homosexuality' at the time. For a writer preoccupied with language and silence, sex was much more of an imperative resort than ever at the end of the nineteenth century; see Cohen 142–72.

18 James is consigned to a life of guilt and compensation by a large number of critics. See, for example, Dupee, *Henry James* 50.

19 Haralson conducts a useful survey of James's fiction in relation to what he describes as 'not just the depth but the *durability* of James's interest in things military' ('Iron Henry, or James Goes to War' 39) emphasizing his 'commitment to an *alternative* heroism in art' (41). I entirely agree that 'masculinity' is the issue, but not at all with the idea that James feels 'anxious to verify his [fictional] men's masculinity by equipping them with the standard military instinct' (43)—and Rowland Mallet will be my case in point in section iii of this chapter—nor with the notion that James has any sense whatever, on the contrary, that his was a 'failure of masculinity during the Civil War' (44). For reasons that will become evident as I discuss the three Civil War tales later in this chapter, 'failed masculinity' is a pleonasm in James.

20 Beebe's rebuttal of Rosenzweig squares with mine, although he disregards the seminal and interrogative power of the 'obscure hurt' for James: 'the injury was not...the cause either of James's detachment or of his decision to become a writer....the injury was followed not so much by regret as by relief, not so much by a sense of guilt as by a conviction of strength....James never repudiated the attitude of detachment' (529–30). Henry James Senior and his wife moved from Newport to Boston in 1864 and Henry and William James, both at Harvard at the time, joined them there (Edel, *Henry James: The Untried Years*: 202–3).

21 There is much more at stake here than a 'conjunction of the historical and biographical' that enabled James 'to view the war in aesthetic terms' (Charles and Tess Hoffman 552).

22 Linderman also discusses the war as a 'test of male maturity' and of the extent to which men could cast off 'womanly influences' (27).

23   Relevant here is Gilmore: 'manhood is the social barrier that societies must erect against entropy...and all the human weaknesses that endanger group life' (226). Theodore Roosevelt delivered his address, 'The Strenuous Life', in 1899. Earlier, in 'What "Americanism" Means', he has a writer like Henry James firmly in his sights: 'The man who becomes Europeanized, who loses his power of doing good work on this side of the water, and who loses his love for his native land, is not a traitor; but he is a silly and undesirable citizen' (199). More tellingly, as a 'second-rate European', 'over-civilized, over-sensitive, over-refined', such a man 'has lost the hardihood and manly courage by which alone he can conquer in the keen struggle of our national life. Be it remembered, too, that this same being does not really become a European; he only ceases being an American, and becomes nothing.... Thus it is with the undersized man of letters, who flees his country because he, with his delicate, effeminate sensitiveness, finds the conditions of life on this side of the water crude and raw; in other words, because he finds that he cannot play a man's part among men....This *émigré* may write graceful and pretty verses, essays, novels; but he will never do work to compare with that of his brother, who is strong enough to stand on his own feet, and do his work as an American' (201). James commented on Roosevelt's 'violent' patriotism in 'American Letters', 23 April 1898: 664. 'Mr. Roosevelt', retaliates James, 'makes very free with the "American" name, but it is after all not a symbol revealed once for all in some book of Mormon dug up under a tree....the national type is the result, not of what we take from it, but of what we give to it' (665). In 1901, James wrote to Jessie Allen: 'I don't either like or trust the new President, a dangerous and ominous Jingo' (19 September 1901, *HJL* 4: 202). For a discussion of James and Roosevelt, see Banta, 'Men, Women, and the American Way' 21–39.

24   'In Charleston Bay, Wilky was interviewed by the *Tribune* for an article syndicated in the Boston *Journal*. It pictured Wilky sitting against the flagstaff at Fort Sumter, gazing in a melancholy way at Fort Wagner' (Gordon 58). William wrote to Alice James that he 'must have been behaving in a very theatrical way. I made a caricature of him brandishing his foot [which Wilky had previously injured] at Fort Wagner, which I sent him' (quoted in Maher 53). 'From his foot drip three drops of blood, his measly badge of courage' (Gordon 58).

25   *Ore rotundo*: with a loud, resounding voice.

26   Kaplan also sees 'The Story of a Year' as a 'sharply ironic story that uses the Civil War for its situational background' (69).

27   The main line on these tales is often crudely bio-critical. Buitenhuis's views are characteristic: 'James's protagonists seem to be invested with their creator's sense of his own inadequacy', and the stories are a 'representation of pain, guilt, and frustration' (36–7). For Wilson, 'the idea of incapacitation for military service was to become involved in James's mind with sexual incapacity', and 'this is borne out by the three early stories of James that are concerned with the Civil War' (*Patriotic Gore* 659). In Kaplan, there is a simple association between James and the 'frustrated, self-tormented young men' he represents (70). The starkest, and most simplifying, application of the 'obscure hurt' comes in Halperin's interpretation of 'A Most Extraordinary Case': it is 'about a veteran of the Civil War who, though apparently healthy, loses the will to live, and dies of some unnamed and

unnameable disease, obviously psychosomatic. Wounded by the war in invisible ways, he dies, in fact, of an obscure hurt' (*Novelists in their Youth* 34).

28 James is often ignored, or marginalized, in historical surveys of Civil War fiction. See, for example, Thompson; Lively. For the continuing impact of the Civil War on the fiction of the 1880s, and especially on James's *The Bostonians*, see Limon; Silber.

29 See Dawson: 'the idea of the martial woman is deeply transgressive' (13). Wheelwright is also relevant here.

30 James writes close to Pope's 'The Rape of the Lock' here. There is the witty, yoking of uneven things together, along with a characterization of Lizzie resembling the battle-ready Belinda, especially in the closing cadence of the 'smile' in the description of the party preparations:

> First, rob'd in White, the Nymph intent adores
> With Head uncover'd, the *Cosmetic* Pow'rs.
> A heav'nly Image in the Glass appears,
> To that she bends, to that her Eyes she rears;
> Th'inferior Priestess, at her Altar's side,
> Trembling, begins the sacred Rites of Pride.
> [....]
> Smooth flow the Waves, the Zephyrs gently play,
> *Belinda* smil'd, and all the World was gay.
>
> (222, 224)

Belinda's defences against rape are presented throughout in war-like terms: 'And swell her Breast with Conquests yet to come./ Strait the three Bands prepare in Arms to join' (227); and 'Now move to War her Sable *Matadores*'; and she is depicted, in gender inversions exploited by James, as a 'warlike *Amazon*' (228).

31 Civil War narratives continued to populate magazines on a large scale at least until 1876. For an excellent categorization of these tales, and a shrewd analysis of their impact not only during the war period itself, but also on continuing debates over emancipation, reconstruction, and re-union, see Diffley, *Where My Heart is Turning Ever: Civil War Stories and Constitutional Reform, 1861–1876*. The stories themselves can be sampled in *To Live and Die: Collected Stories of the Civil War, 1861–1876*, ed. Diffley. A broader selection of Civil War prose is in Masur.

32 Buitenhuis takes a rather severe view of Lizzie: 'selfish and impulsive', she is the 'first of' James's 'long line of American women whose behaviour makes them at least as potentially destructive as the Vénus d'Ille' (18). In Prosper Mérimée's story, 'La Vénus d'Ille' (1837)—'The Venus of Ille'—Alphonse, has a fatal engagement with a Greco-Roman statue discovered by his father, and with whose 'affections' he has toyed. It seems to me that neither Ford nor the story as a whole resemble Mérimée's tale. James was reading and translating 'La Vénus d'Ille' in Newport, however, just before the Civil War began (*HJA* 292).

33 To 'bob-tail' is to cut short a tail (*OED*); it also means 'shorter or briefer than usual'. For horses, bob-tails are formed by 'cutting a muscle' in the tail.

See *Random House Webster's Unabridged Dictionary*, revised and updated (New York: Random House, 1998), 232.

34   Similarly, as Rotundo reminds us, 'if a man was without "business", he was less than a man' (168).

35   The phrase 'feminine fifties' derives in part from Pattee's *The Feminine Fifties*. Pattee sees Susan B. Warner's *The Wide, Wide World* (1850) as the beginning of a 'flood of novels' (66)—'there are 245 tear-flows in the 574 pages of the novel' (57)— in which Dickens, and the widespread adoption of his 'sentimentalism', was to blame for adding 'emotion' to 'an over-emotional age' (72). Pattee was unable, and Habegger seemingly unwilling, to incorporate the sophisticated and complex work of Tompkins in this area: 'the *popularity* of novels by women has been held against them' (xiv), yet the 'popular domestic novel of the nineteenth century represents a monumental effort to reorganize culture from the woman's point view' (124). The notion that women dominated American fiction in the 1850s is highly contentious for Romero: 'assertions that women dominated literary production appear as dubious as the claims made about their role in cultural consumption'; but 'even if (as it indeed appears) the best-selling novels of the period written by women outsold the best-sellers written by men, the book-publishing industry was almost entirely in the hands of men'; irrespective of sales, 'at mid-century men authored more than twice as much fiction as women' (13).

36   For subtle alternatives to Habegger's approach to homosexuality in *Roderick Hudson*, see Haralson, *Henry James and Queer Modernity*; Walton.

37   I think that Born fails to make out a convincing case for William James's being the model for Roderick Hudson; and in the process, he misses the correspondences between Wilky and Hudson.

38   I believe that Rebecca West's emphasis on passivity is entirely wrong: 'And so he worked out a scheme of existence...in which the one who stood aside and felt rather than acted acquired thereby a mystic value, a spiritual supremacy, which...would be rubbed off by participation in action' (21).

39   These views are tackled directly by Roosevelt in 1894: 'There are philosophers who assure us that, in the future, patriotism will be regarded not as a virtue at all, but merely as a mental stage in the journey toward a state of feeling when our patriotism will include the whole human race and all the world....philosophers of this type are so very advanced that they are of no practical service to the present generation.' It is in this article that Roosevelt goes on to attack the 'Europeanized' man as a 'silly and undesirable citizen' ('What "Americanism" Means' 199).

40   'We work in the dark—we do what we can—we give what we have. Our doubt is our passion and our passion is our task. The rest is the madness of art' (Henry James, 'The Middle Years' 354).

41   On the myth of the lost cause and the construction of a romance of the Old South, see Simpson; Osterweis; Cash; Taylor.

42   In a novel where all the relationships are acutely predatory, and especially that between Rowland Mallet and Roderick, there is never a question of a 'well-developed relationship between Rowland and Roderick' (Sofer 187).

43   Jeffords uses a concept of 'remasculinization' when exploring representation and the Vietnam War (xi). The trope of war was a frequent critical resort for James. So it is that James Russell Lowell, 'in poetry, in satire, in prose...was

essentially a fighter; he could always begin the attack; he could always in criticism as in talk, sound the charge and open the fire' ('James Russell Lowell' 550); and Daudet 'is a novelist to his finger-tips—a soldier in the great army of constant producers' ('Alphonse Daudet' 223).

44 I take the phrase 'biographical act' from Caramello.

45 Oakeshott comes to James's rescue here: 'The fact is, then, that the past in history varies with the present, rests upon the present, is the present (107); 'for no fact, truth or reality is, or can be, past' (146).

46 'Prosthetic memory' is from Landsberg.

47 Cf. Bataille: 'Primitive war is rather like a holiday, a feast day, and even modern war almost always has some of this paradoxical similarity. The taste for showy and magnificent war dress goes very far back, for originally war seemed a luxury. It was no attempt to increase the peoples' or rulers' riches by conquest: it was an aggressive and extravagant exuberance. Military uniforms have carried on this tradition right up to modern times; the preponderant consideration now, however, is to avoid attracting the enemy's fire' (76).

48 The relegation of the British army to passivity and the ornamental has a specific historical edge, as James bays for blood, regretting that 'England and Russia have stood glaring at each other across the prostrate body of the expiring yet reviving Turk' (3), and musing over 'this heavy-burdened slow-moving Old England making up her mind' (7).

49 According to the *OED*, 'flasher' was in common use in the late nineteenth century as a term for a person indecently exposing himself.

50 'Within nationalist discourse, narratives about soldier heroes' may well be 'underpinned by, and powerfully reproduce, conceptions of gender and nation as unchanging essences' (Dawson 11), but this is not a uniform feature of all such (or other) discourses.

51 Theweleit has argued that a 'homosexual act' in a military context can be understood 'as a *maintenance process*' in which soldiers 'use the degradation of others as a means of maintaining their own services' in the presence of 'threats of devouring dissolution; but they may not be "homosexual"' (318). The anus, or anal sex, he sees as offering the 'opportunity...to circumvent devouring femininity...for men whose fear of re-engulfment by erotic femininity becomes so great that they can no longer countenance the slightest contact with the dangers represented by women' (*Male Fantasies*, Vol. 2: *Male Bodies: Psychoanalyzing the White Terror* 319–20). Elsewhere, Theweleit posits that 'in patriarchy where the work of domination has consisted in subjugating, damming in, and transforming the "natural energy" in society, that desiring-production of the unconscious has been encoded as the subjugated gender, or femaleness'; 'men themselves were now split into a (female) interior and a male' exterior as represented, in military contexts, by 'body armor'; the 'interior was allowed to flow only within the masculine boundaries of the mass formations' (*Male Fantasies*: Vol. 1: *Women, Floods, Bodies, Histories* 432, 434). Whatever the apparent rigidities of armor, the uniform is a much more fluid affair; and in this context, Theweleit fails to take into account the carnivalesque, performance, elements of military rituals and war and the gender turmoil they produce.

52 Ironic distance, rather than 'tragic fellowship' (Cox 248), is the note struck here.

3 Shakespeare and the 'Long Arras'

1 Rupert Brooke's was a 'pre-war' death (on Easter Sunday, 1915) in that he died of blood-poisoning on the way to Gallipoli.

2 See Fussell on the 'frantic popularity of Rupert Brooke' (272) and the 'wider homoerotic conception of soldiering' at the time of the First World War (284).

3 'We are such stuff/ As dreams are made on, and our little life/ Is rounded with a sleep.' *The Tempest* 4 i 156–7.

4 For an earlier treatment of some of these ideas, see my 'Henry James, Delia Bacon, and American Uses of Shakespeare', *Symbiosis* 5 (2001): 139–58.

5 Budd further suggests that 'although a corollary movement arose in Great Britain, wide agreement assigns to Americans the dubious honor of publicizing the belief that Francis Bacon really wrote the Shakespeare plays' in a fashion whose main impetus was 'from 1860 to 1900'. He believes that 'Delia Bacon was surprised in 1856 when an Englishman, William Henry Smith' simultaneously 'advanced the idea' that Francis Bacon had written the plays (359), and that neither Smith nor Bacon seem to have been aware of an earlier voyage into these waters in the American Joseph C. Hart's *The Romance of Yachting* (1848) (360). *The Romance of Yachting* is extracted in *Americans on Shakespeare, 1776–1914*, ed. Rawlings (140–50). William Henry Smith's *Was Lord Bacon the Author of Shakespeare's Plays? A Letter to Lord Ellesmere* appeared in 1856. Budd's is a simplified charting of the issues. Delia Bacon, a 'groupist' rather than preoccupied simply with Bacon, was concerned more with depriving Shakespeare of his authorship, than with the question of specific attribution. Questions about Shakespeare's authorship arose in the early eighteenth century in Captain Goulding's *Essay Against Too Much Reading* and surfaced again in Herbert Lawrence's *The Life and Adventures of Common Sense: An Historical Allegory* (1769). The next intervention seems to have been James Wilmot's in 1785: he could find no evidence attesting to Shakespeare's authorship and fearing the consequences of such a revelation, burned his notes; see Schoenbaum 397–99. James Wilmot first came to attention in an article by Allardyce Nicoll, 'The First Baconian' in 1932. Anti-Stratfordians proliferated as the nineteenth century wore on, as did the number of writers surveyed as alternatives to Shakespeare. James Greenstreet, in a series of articles in *The Genealogist*, nominated William Stanley, 6th Earl of Derby. Thomas William White, taking a 'groupist' approach, attempted to prove that the plays were written collectively by Christopher Marlowe, Robert Greene, George Peele, Thomas Nashe, Thomas Lodge, Francis Bacon, and others; *Our English Homer; or, Shakespeare Historically Considered* (1892). Wilbur Gleason Zeigler, by contrast, recruited Marlowe as the sole playwright in his rather sensationalized *It was Marlowe: A Story of the Secret of Three Centuries* (1895). The main rival to the Bacon Society (founded in 1886) is the Shakespeare Oxford Society. It was established in 1957 (stemming from the Shakespeare Fellowship of the 1930s) to propose Edward de Vere, 17th Earl of Oxford, as the real bard. This branch of the argument grew out of Thomas Looney's *'Shakespeare' Identified in Edward de Vere, the Seventeenth Earl of Oxford* (1920). I am grateful to David Chandler (Doshisha University, Japan) for information about James Wilmot, Allardyce Nicoll, and the origins of the Shakespeare Oxford Society.

6   Brooks coined the phrase a 'usable past' in *America's Coming of Age* (1915).

7   On Melville and Shakespeare, see Matthiessen, *American Renaissance. Art and Expression in the Age of Emerson and Whitman.*

8   This is, in part, a riposte to Sidney Smith's 'Who reads an American book?' (Rawlings, Introduction: 'Who Reads an American Book?' xiii).

9   For a discussion of American expropriations of Shakespeare, see my 'Shakespeare Migrates to America' where a version of some of these ideas first appeared. Jones Very (1813–80) was a Harvard graduate, Transcendentalist poet of a kind, and a friend of Emerson's. His essay on Shakespeare is a culmination of his life-long fanatical advocacy of the need to destroy all traces of the sensuous self.

10 The object of Emerson's attack here is John Payne Collier, an English Shakespeare critic, and his *New Facts Regarding the Life of Shakespeare. In a Letter to Thomas Amyot* (1835). Collier, along with a group of other Shakespeare scholars, established the Shakespeare Society in 1840. The society, eventually 'discredited and ingloriously dissolved', became renowned for invention and criminal forgery; see Schoenbaum 251–2.

11 William Wordsworth, 'Intimations of Immortality from Early Recollections of Childhood. Ode' (1807). The lines, from Wordsworth's 'My Heart Leaps Up' (1802), form part of the poem's epigraph.

12 'Delia espouses Bacon's claim to the plays but never names him, preferring to speak of "ONE"....But elsewhere the one becomes several, for Sidney is quoted and Raleigh is unmistakably hinted at' (Schoenbaum 389)

13 For information about Delia Bacon's life, and her unsuccessful occupation of the lecture platforms of Boston and Cambridge, Manhattan and Brooklyn, see Schoenbaum 385–94.

14 Carlyle wrote to his brother John on June 13, 1853: 'For the present we have (occasionally) a Yankee lady, sent by Emerson, who has discovered that the *"Man* Shakespeare" is a *Myth*, and did *not* write those Plays which bear his name....*Ach Gott!* (Schoenbaum 387).

15 On anti-Stratfordian thinking in America after Delia Bacon, see Falk 102–18.

16 See Budd 359–68.

17 See Falk; McManaway; Thorndike; Bristol; Levine.

18 'But one of the soldiers with a spear pierced his side, and forthwith came there out blood and water' (John 19: 34).

19 On James and 'a burgeoning mass culture' (6) in the later nineteenth century, see Strychacz.

20 James Halliwell (later Halliwell-Phillips), one of the most eminent and prolific nineteenth-century Shakespearean antiquarians and biographers, was a persistent advocate of the authenticity of Shakespeare's birthplace, although there were many sceptics. He believed that the tradition is 'as well authenticated as any of the kind, referring to so remote a period, can be expected to be,—there is certainly not the shadow of a known fact that is inconsistent with' its 'truth;—and it will be a pity if the pilgrim, without an adequate reason, is unable to direct his steps towards the venerated room in Henley Street without entertaining a suspicion that he may become the victim of an inglorious deception' (*New Evidences in Confirmation of the Traditional Recognition of Shakespeare's Birth-Room, A.D. 1769—A.D. 1777*: 5–6). Predictably, given their vigorously partisan perspective (The Bacon

Society), Habgood and Eagle insist that the birthplace 'has no claim whatever to this honour, except a very doubtful traditional one' (1), and that 'no part' of the house 'as occupied in 1575 survives' (7). The American Shakespeare scholar Richard Grant White was equally dubious: 'In 1847 the Shakespeare house passed into the hands of the association under whose care it has been renovated; but unfortunately, like some of the Shakespeare poetry, not restored to a close resemblance to its first condition; though that was perhaps impossible. Whether it was in this house that John Shakespeare and his wife, with their only previous child, staid out the plague, which visited Stratford in 1564, or whether they fled to some unfinished place, we do not know' ('Memoirs' I: xiii). According to Fox, 'there is documentary proof that John Shakespeare, William's father, was living in Henley Street as early as 1552, and records survive which prove that the premises were occupied and owned by him. Tradition assigns the western portion of the building as the poet's birthplace' (*Shakespeare's Birthplace* 2).

21   In 1866, the property was conveyed to the Corporation of Stratford-upon-Avon. The Shakespeare Birthplace Trust Act formally incorporated the Trustees and Guardian of the Henley Street house in 1891. See Brown and Fearon.

22   See Mark Twain's 'Is Shakespere Dead?'

23   Agnew endorses this point, noting that 'Barnum had built his success less upon the credulity of his public than upon its suspicion' (80).

24   See Hodgdon on the commodification of Shakespeare in Stratford-upon-Avon.

25   The major essays on 'The Birthplace', all of which ignore Marie Corelli and the Baconian dimension of the tale, are McMurray; McDonald; Tanner, 'The Birthplace'; Nakamura; Cowdery, *The Nouvelle of Henry James in Theory and Practice*; Holleran; Arms; Ross.

26   Marie Corelli, the best-selling author of romances such as *The Sorrows of Satan* (1895), is reputed to have been one of Queen Victoria's favourite novelists. Andrew Carnegie (1835–1919) was born in Scotland and emigrated to the United States at the age of twelve. By the time of his death, he had donated '$56,162,622 for the construction of 2509 library buildings throughout the English-speaking parts of the world' (Bobinski 3). Carnegie 'made an open offer to all English-speaking towns to contribute £10,000 towards the erection of a free library, provided that the local authorities' would 'spend not less than £800 a year on its maintenance' (Alderson 183–4).

27   See Halliwell-Phillips, *New Evidence in Confirmation of the Traditional Recognition of Shakespeare's Birth-Room*.

28   Tanner is especially acute on this aspect of the tale; see his 'The Birthplace'.

29   James does not withhold the name in the notebook entry, however: 'The other day at Welcombe...Lady T. spoke of the case of the couple who had formerly (before the present incumbents) been for a couple of years—or a few—the people in charge of the Shakespeare house—the Birthplace—which struck me as possibly a little *donnée* (N 195).

30   For a discussion of these issues, see my 'A Kodak Refraction of Henry James's "The Real Thing"'.

31   The narrator of 'The Figure in the Carpet' early announces of the ill-fated Corvick, and others, that 'for the few persons, at any rate, abnormal or not, with whom my anecdote is concerned, literature was a game of skill, and

skill meant courage, and courage meant honour, and honour meant passion, meant life' (591).

32 I think Tanner, in arguing that the allusions to Shakespeare should not be seen 'as doing heavy intertextual duty' ('The Birthplace' 81) misses the power and skill with which James deploys the plays in his tale, especially *The Merchant of Venice*.

33 Despite the apparent oddness, 'become' is what James wrote here and not 'becoming'.

34 Marcia Jacobson has explored James's complex relation to the 'mass market' (14). Margolis observes that James 'was an artist who repeatedly called for the overthrow of the most cherished conventions of Anglo-American fiction', yet, 'at the same time, he was a writer who evinced a chronic obsession with the idea of popular success on a grand scale' (xiii).

35 *Hamlet* V ii 358.

36 A number of critics have been curiously censorious about what they see as Gedge's 'lies'. One of the most simplistic approaches is Holleran's. See also Andreas: Gedge 'becomes completely fraudulent as a commentator and guide, only then does he please his masters' (137–8). A similar line is pursued in Ross. Other critics defend Gedge, allying him with James's belief in the 'futility of Fact'; see Nakamura; Hartstock.

37 *Macbeth* I vii 60.

38 *Macbeth* V v 17.

39 'Adieu, adieu, adieu! remember me; *Hamlet* I v 91.

40 Stafford is right, I think, when he says that 'the Hayeses somehow appear to be more interested in the increasingly tense relation of Gedge to Shakespeare than they are in Shakespeare himself'; 'James Examines Shakespeare: Notes on the Nature of Genius' (127).

41 *Hamlet* II ii 604–5: 'the play's the thing/ Wherein I'll catch the conscience of the King'.

42 *Hamlet* III i 55.

43 In arguing that Mrs. Gedge's 'position subsumes the whole question of poet and critic', affirming 'values more central to the human condition than those of aesthetic or literary history', I believe that Stafford radically misunderstands not only this story, but James as a whole: nothing was more 'central' to him than questions of art and the aesthetic (*Books Speaking to Books: A Contextual Approach to American Fiction* 117–18).

44 'O well-divided disposition....O heavenly mingle!' *Antony and Cleopatra* I v 53–9.

45 Nathaniel Hawthorne's account of his visit to Stratford-upon-Avon is in 'Recollections of a Gifted Woman': 'Thence I was ushered up stairs to the room in which Shakspere is supposed to have been born; though, if you peep too curiously into the matter, you may find the shadow of an ugly doubt about this, as well as most other points of his mysterious life' (220). Hawthorne purchased a 'good many' of the 'various prints, views of houses and scenes connected with Shakspere's memory' and concluded that 'this respectable lady perhaps realizes a handsome profit' from such articles (221).

46 'The tale can be taken as the depiction of the process by which Morris Gedge flowers into a superb ironic artist' (Vaid 170); but I want to emphasize the distance, ultimately, between James and his protagonist.

47 Relevant here is Mayne's observation that 'nowhere else does blackmail operate with such terrible alertness as in the uranian world' (455).

48 According to the *OED*, the first use of 'spunk' for seminal fluid is in Walter's *My Secret Life*, published in 1890–95, written in 1871.

49 Stevens works hard to prove that 'queer' had homosexual denotations long before the *OED*'s first ascertainment of this usage as being in 1922 (1–19). I believe he is probably right, although the life of my argument does not depend on the fact. A much subtler treatment of the question can be found in Haralson's *Henry James and Queer Modernity*.

50 'What, a play toward! I'll be an auditor,/ An actor too perhaps, if I see cause' (*A Midsummer Night's Dream* III i 79–80).

51 Mayne recounts an event whose features closely resemble aspects of James's 'The Papers', or the plot he eventually refuses, and which took place in the year of the story's publication (1903); Beadel-Muffet has plenty of actual progenitors, and their demise is often closely associated with newspaper reports and the threat of blackmail and discovery: 'Within a few weeks of the time when these pages were written, England and Continental Europe were shocked by a notable loss to the British army, and by a melancholy social tragedy—the death in Paris of Major-General Sir Hector Macdonald, who died a suicide, in consequence of uranistic intimacies....During the last days of March, 1903, incognito, he took up his quarters in a Paris hotel. One morning he was found dead in his room, having shot himself. The episode excited much grief in Great Britain. Indeed, British hypocrisy in speaking or writing of homosexualism, on this occasion was considerably laid aside' (194). 'Often', Mayne reports, 'one meets with a newspaper-reference similar to this one...."No further light can be thrown as yet on the suicide of Lieutenant R—B last Sunday. The personal and professional affairs of the deceased young man were in good order"' (197). 'British "high society"' figures frequently take up 'persistent residence abroad in countries where they can feel safer from suspicion and from blackmailing scandals' (237). The 'police-annals of all countries' seem to have informed James's story and Maud's vision, for they 'witness...melancholy episodes': 'broken careers, shipwrecked lives, disappearances, interrupted marriages, inexplicable money-embarrassments, murders, suicides by hundreds'; and the 'incessant examples of "unaccountable affairs" too often mean that some intersexual victim, persecuted by a grasping enemy, threatened with exposure as an uranian, can hold out no longer' (457).

52 Burns (although his focus is on American journalists) takes a similarly one-sided view; and in restricting James to protecting the 'private sphere' (1), he overlooks its radical dependence on the 'public' side of the binary. Much more usefully, Salmon suggests that the tale 'recognizes its own immanence in the object of its critique'; but he otherwise fails to see the erotic charge of 'The Papers' and its anchorage in James's pervasive aesthetics of obscurity (148).

53 For a discussion of possible correspondences between Shakespeare's retreat to Stratford-upon-Avon, *The Tempest*, and James's 'The Lesson of the Master', see Horne, *Henry James and Revision: The New York Edition* (312–14). Horne is good at spotting allusions in James to Shakespeare, although any interpretative yield is often ignored. His approach, on a much bigger scale, has the limited rewards of Melchiori's little piece 'Shakespeare and Henry James'.

54 Kramer, like many other critics, sees James as 'disparaging' (140) Ransom;
    but the relation between Ransom and author, as distinct from narrator, is
    more complex than this suggests. Trilling's reading of *The Bostonians* (*The
    Opposing Self*), in which he speculates about Ransom as a vague anticipator
    of the Southern Agrarian cultural rebellion against the North, is still one of
    the shrewdest; and his emphasis on the Civil War context of the novel, and
    the question of 'manhood' (114) is highly productive.

55 On the context of degeneration, see Greenslade.

56 For a consideration of salient aspects of the situation of the popular press at
    the time of 'The Papers', see my 'Mythologies of Cultural Decline and
    Aspects of the Newspaper Industry'.

57 McColley's emphasis on the brutality of the final scene of the novel, on
    Ransom's 'assertiveness and possession' (165), is especially telling.

58 Tintner has no interest in the erotic reaches of the tale's relation to *As You
    Like It*, confining herself to commenting on the 'challenge' of 'transposing'
    one of Shakespeare's 'most enchanting...fantasies' on to the 'world of
    London journalism' (34).

59 This aspect of the tale is overlooked in Kappeler's analysis of 'the writer's
    dilemma, his inner division in an artist and a social persona' (91). John H.
    Pearson has an interesting approach to the 'relation between reality and
    irreality' in the tale, but there are too many simplifications involved in see-
    ing the 'origins and signifieds' of 'texts' as 'embodiments of the author'
    (124). Rivkin offers a powerfully illuminating treatment of the 'dual econ-
    omy of the representational supplement' in 'The Private Life' (*False
    Positions: The Representational Logics of Henry James's Fiction* 26–39).

60 I am drawing here, and in the discussion that follows, on the *OED*. Duby has
    excavated the meaning of '*privatim*' in Cicero's vocabulary as: 'to act not as
    a *magistratus* invested with a power emanating from the people' (4); in the
    Middle Ages, he continues, 'the word *privatus* also came to mean "in
    retreat"' (5): this suggests connections, of course, between characters like
    Prospero, the Duke in *Measure for Measure*, and Hermione in *The Winter's
    Tale*, and Vawdrey, Beadel-Muffet, and James (in the sense of 'in retreat
    from') (3–32).

61 St. Augustine discusses 'plenitude' in Book XIII, Ch. 2 of *The Confessions*
    (AD 367).

62 See Bresnick for a more narrowly ethical approach to the tale, and Griffin for
    an interesting treatment of doubling and selfhood.

63 Although 'coming out' relates to public declarations of homosexuality only
    from the late 1960s, the phrase has denoted 'to show oneself publicly', or to
    'declare oneself in some way', since the early seventeenth century (*OED*).
    Perversely, or paradoxically at least, the narrator is looking for a 'public'
    revelation of Vawdrey's privates, or his private self, here.

64 'It is a tale/ Told by an idiot, full of sound and fury/ Signifying nothing'
    (*Macbeth* V v 26–8).

65 I am unconvinced by Schwartz's attempts to interpret the '"torture"
    Shakespeare's reader suffers at the writer's hands...as a manifestation of the
    Oedipal drama' (74). A little over-dramatically perhaps, Cowdery captures
    some of the feverish atmosphere of James's piece on *The Tempest*: 'But it
    is exactly as a hunt for big-game that this essay ranks with 'The Beast in
    the Jungle' and 'The Jolly Corner' for risk, excitement and the complexity

of the relation between the stalker and stalked' ('Henry James and the "Transcendent Adventure": The Search for the Self in the Introduction to *The Tempest*' 145).

66 I also think Holland mis-reads the introduction by suggesting that for James 'instead of being obliterated the dramatist is in effect enclosed and diffused, still present, in his art' (180).

67 James Orchard Halliwell's (later Halliwell-Phillips) biography of Shakespeare is *The Life of William Shakespeare. Including Many Particulars Respecting the Poet and his Family Never Before Published* (London: n.p. 1848); he also wrote, in addition to numerous books and pamphlets about the bard, *Outlines of the Life of Shakespeare* (Brighton: privately printed, 1881), which went into seven editions during his life-time (and which is probably the book James was reading at the time of his introduction to *The Tempest*). *Outlines* grew out of the earlier *Illustrations of the Life of Shakespeare in a Discursive Series of Essays* (London: n.p., 1874).

68 'Monstrosity' has its roots in display and immediacy, whereas 'art' has allies in concealment and deferral: 'Until the beginning of the nineteenth century…madmen remained monsters—that is etymologically, beings or things to be shown' (Foucault, *Madness and Civilization: A History of Insanity in the Age of Reason* 70). Cf. 'monstrant', meaning 'showing and declaring' (*OED*).

69 For a discussion of this context, see my: 'Henry James and "Brooksmith": Circumscribing the Task of Reading'; 'Pater, Wilde, and James: "The Reader's Share of the Task"'; 'Resisting Death: Henry James's "The Art of Fiction"'; 'Henry James and the Discourse of Organicism', PhD thesis, University of Cambridge (1991). The classic study of the aetiology of organicism is still Abrams.

70 The allusion is to Shakespeare's *A Midsummer Night's Dream* (see note 50); and James refers to the play on p. 1210.

71 The gnomic 'Ars est celare artem' ('it is art to conceal art') is often attributed to Ovid's *Ars Amatoria* (1 BC); but the nearest phrase to it there is 'si latet, ars prodest' in Book 2: 213 ('art works when it is hidden').

72 This is the conventional post-Romantic view of Shakespeare, of course: 'It may seem a paradox', wrote Charles Lamb, 'but I cannot help being of opinion that the plays of Shakspere are less calculated for performance on a stage than those of almost any other dramatist whatever' (223).

73 Tanner quotes this letter in his 'The Birthplace', but does not relate it to the strategies of the introduction to *The Tempest* (89).

74 Meissner is right to emphasize that James's autobiographical writing is the 'creation, not the accounting of, a life', but I dislike the ascent, and the terms in which he articulates it, to some transcendent position he outlines for James: 'autobiography could be nothing less than an exemplary mode of self-construction which fuses the human and the aesthetic so as to get behind and beyond both' (195).

75 James's Gedge is not dealing with the simple absence of facts John H. Pearson focuses on, but with their obscurity, and the disparity between the myth of Shakespeare and his plays: 'Gedge…can be a historian silenced by the absence of validating facts, or he can become an artist, and find glory in the absence' (119).

76 This is the tradition in which Thoreau writes: 'Shakespeare's house, how hollow it is! No man can conceive of Shakespeare in that house' (*Journal*, 27 October 1857: 97).

77 Cryptology, especially in the service of ousting Shakespeare from his perch as the author of his plays, was much in the air at the time of James's introduction to *The Tempest*; see Schoenbaum (415–24). One of the most extensive, and influential (American) books in the area (and possibly the target of James's satire in 'The Figure in the Carpet') was Ignatius Donnelly, *The Great Cryptogram: Francis Bacon's Cipher in the So-Called Shakespeare Plays* (1888).

4 Grammars of Time, Senses of the Past

1 For an earlier mutation of some aspects of this chapter's treatment of time, syntax, and 'The Jolly Corner', see my 'Grammars of Time in Late James'.

2 Parataxis is 'the placing of propositions or clauses one after another, without indicating by connecting words the relation (of co-ordination or subordination) between them'; 'hypotaxis' is 'subordination', or a 'subordinate construction' (*OED*).

3 Seminal essays would include: Edward Tyrell Channing, 'American Language and Literature' (1815) and 'Reflections on the Literary Delinquency of America' (1815); James Kirke Paulding, 'National Literature' (1820); 'American Literature' (1833); James Ewell Heath, 'Southern Literature' (1834); H. J. Groesbeck, 'American Literature: Its Impediments' (1835); B, 'Literature of Virginia' (1838); George Tucker, 'A Discourse on American Literature' (1838); 'The Inferiority of American Literature' (1840); William Cowper Scott, 'American Literature: The Present State of American Letters; The Prospect and Means of Their Improvement' (1845); Il Secretario, 'American Letters—Their Character and Advancement' (1845); William Gilmore Simms, 'Americanism in Literature' (1845); Anon., 'An Inquiry into the Present State of Southern Literature' (1856); Anon., 'Southern Literature' (1857). American literary history is underway in the periodicals long before Moses Coit Tyler's *A History of American Literature* (1878), Evert Augustus Duyckinck's *Cyclopaedia of American Literature* (1855), and Rufus Wilmot Griswold's three volumes: *The Poets and Poetry of America: With an Historical Introduction* (1842), *The Prose Writers of America with a Survey of the History* (1847), and *The Female Poets of America* (1849).

4 I am using 'discourse' and 'story' here in Chatman's senses of the 'how' and the 'what', the 'sjužet' and 'fabula' (19–20).

5 For 'anachronies', 'analepses', and 'prolepses', see Genette 33–85.

6 'The only way of expressing emotion in the form of art is by finding an "objective correlative"; in other words, a set of objects, a situation, a chain of events which shall be the formula of that *particular* emotion; such that when the external facts, which must terminate in sensory experience, are given, the emotion is immediately evoked' (T. S. Eliot, 'Hamlet and His Problems' 124–5).

7 On 'anisotropic time', and 'time with a dependable arrow', see Purdy 71. What is 'isotropic' exhibits 'equal physical properties or actions... in all directions' (*OED*).

8 James wrote this in a letter to Lilla (Cabot) Perry on 2 August 1914, two days before the outbreak of the First World War. The letter is now at Colby College, Waterville, Maine. I am grateful to Greg Zacharias of Creighton University for this quotation.

9 The most informative history of shifting attitudes towards time at the end of the nineteenth century remains Kern's. Kern makes much of a widening division between popular senses of time, present in increasingly oppressive ways in the world of work and transport, as 'made up of discrete parts as sharply separated as the boxed days on a calendar', and 'private time' whose 'texture was fluid' (33–4). There is an extent, however, as we shall see, to which he over-emphasizes this division, and especially the perception of public time as being anisotropic: James, for one, was not prepared to be hampered by 'simple common sense' notions of 'irreversible' time (29).

10 The relevant Bergson is in *An Introduction to Metaphysics*. He distinguishes there between 'two profoundly different ways of knowing a thing. The first implies that we move round the object; the second, that we enter into it. The first depends on the point of view at which we are placed and on the symbols by which we express ourselves. The second neither depends on a point of view nor relies on any symbol' (21).

11 As Kallen noted, after discussing this passage: 'James and Bergson are at one, then, in their repudiation of intellectualism, in their general temporalism' (46).

12 Landmark thinking on these issues is surveyed in Benjamin.

13 They are far from being, as Ward has it, an 'elaborate mechanical exercise' for the sake of it (163).

14 Henry James not only read H. G. Wells's *The Time Machine*, published three or four years before work began on *The Sense of the Past* in 1899, but had also solicited a copy. It is significant, on the brink of his own time-narratives, that in his letter to Wells James refers to his re-writing as he reads: 'It was very graceful of you to send me your book—I mean the particular master-piece entitled *The Time Machine*, after I had so *un*gracefully sought it at your hands....You are very magnificent. I am beastly critical—but you are in a still higher degree wonderful. I re-write you, much, as I read—which is the highest tribute my damned impertinence can pay an author' (29 January 1900, *HJL* 4: 132–3).

15 James may not have read McTaggart's essay, of course; although the journal *Mind*, in which it was published, was hardly unfamiliar to him: William James was one of its most frequent contributors. In any event, I am offering a family resemblance rather than seeking evidence for influence. That debates about time were raging in the early twentieth century is clear simply from Wyndham Lewis's attack on Bergson and his allies in *Time and Western Man*. Although published in 1927, Lewis devotes pages to haranguing Bergson as the 'creative source of the time-philosophy' (162), condemning him as 'the perfect philosophic ruffian, of the darkest and most forbidding description' (170).

16 Peirce defined time as 'the universal form of change' ('The Law of the Mind' 101).

17 McTaggart's views have come under attack from a number of critics. My concern here, however, is not with the credibility of his position but with

its significance as an index of seminal thought on the unreality of time for Henry James at the time he was writing 'The Jolly Corner'. For two challenges to McTaggart, see Findlay; Prior.

18 Einstein's 1905 writings were translated into English as *The Theory of Relativity: An Introductory Sketch Based on Einstein's Original Writing* (1920). The 1905 special theory of relativity was incorporated into *Relativity: The Special and the General Theory*, published in 1916, and translated into English four years later by Robert William Lawson (1920).

19 See Kern: 'With the special theory of relativity of 1905 Einstein calculated how time in one reference system moving away at a constant velocity appears to slow down when viewed from another system at rest relative to it, and in his general theory of 1916 he extended the theory to that of the time change of accelerated bodies....The general theory of relativity had the effect, figuratively, of placing a clock in every gravitational field in the universe' (19).

20 See Ringuette for a discussion of the relation between James's 'Is There Life After Death' (1910) and Peirce.

21 Bergson, on this point at least, writes in the tradition of Kant: 'Time is nothing but the form of inner sense, that is, of the intuition of ourselves' (*The Critique of Pure Reason* 77).

22 William James attributes the phrase 'specious present' to Edmund R. Clay's *The Alternative: A Study in Psychology* (1882): 'The present to which the datum refers is really a part of the past—a recent past—delusively given as being a time that intervenes between the past and the future. Let it be named the specious present' (167).

23 See Poulet (350–4) on James and American senses of time.

24 See Meyerhoff on the distinction between 'subjective' and 'objective' metrics (14).

25 'It is Bergson', Wyndham Lewis observed, 'who put the hyphen between Space and Time' (419).

26 Savoy simply takes the 'license' to 'assume, or perhaps even presume, that a fairly coherent "gay" man returns to New York' ('The Queer Subject of "The Jolly Corner"' 2).

27 For a discussion of the entrepreneurial aspects of the tale, see Benert.

28 'When we prepare for a crucial experiment, we review the situation and consider what would happen if our hypothesis were true and what would happen if it were false' (Chisholm 483).

29 See Savoy ('The Queer Subject of "The Jolly Corner"') for a queer positioning of Brydon's 'foreclosed opportunities' (7). Savoy also steps into the grammatical territory of the tale, but identifies past conditionals—'might have been met' (8)—which are actually present-perfects mired in complex modalities (even 'might have met' is far from an unproblematic past conditional once the force of the modal is felt).

30 For an illuminating reading of the gothic dimension of the tale, see Savoy 'The Queer Subject of "The Jolly Corner"'.

31 See Prior 10–18; David Lewis 87. Modal utterances and questions are closely related, however: 'questions may also be regarded as a means of conveying modality in so far as they may be defined semantically as the expression of a speaker's ignorance or doubt' (Perkins 111).

32   There are comprehensive treatments of modality and tense in three books by F. R. Palmer: *Modality and the English Modals, Mood and Modality*, and *The English Verb*. Also relevant are D. James; Visser; Denison; McCawley.

33   The argument is not that James read, or could have read, Jespersen, but that both writers are part of a climate of thinking in the early twentieth century about the nature of time. The first volumes of Jespersen's *A Modern English Grammar on Historical Principles* began to appear in 1909, a year after the publication of 'The Jolly Corner', and his *Growth and Structure of the English Language* was published four years earlier in 1905.

34   See also Reichenbach, *The Direction of Time* 269–70.

35   Spencer Brydon tests to the limit Bull's contention that 'hide and seek is not a game you can play successfully by yourself'(16). Norrman in charting James's fondness for 'chiastic inversion' (137) archly observes that 'normally, in literature, ghosts pursue the living, but in a typical "turning of the tables"-inversion Spencer decides to pursue the ghost' (145).

36   See my reading of the tale in Chapter 2.

37   Since Rosenzweig's article, the earlier (unsigned) 'A Tragedy of Error' (1864) has been attributed to James.

38   See Simpson.

39   In arguing that the 'story ends with perhaps the most successful social moment in James's work', Pippin is unwilling to embrace this irony (111).

40   An inversion of Queen Gertrude's advice to Polonius: 'More matter with less art'; *Hamlet* II ii 95.

41   Gosse expresses his views in *Aspects and Impressions* (17–53).

42   James began work on the novel in 1900 and abandoned it shortly afterwards until 1914. He dictated a 'First Statement (Preliminary)' for it in November 1914 and continued to dictate notes until May 1915, or so. These notes, together with the 'First Statement', can be found in *The Complete Notebooks of Henry James* (502–35).

43   Ralph's affinities here, on Underwood's account of romantic historicism at least, are with 'Romantic-era representations of history' and their frequent dependence 'on a special sense that sees or hears historical depth in the inanimate world' (237).

44   Ralph Pendrel occupies a dense intertextual space with complex temporal dimensions of its own. He looks back to Spencer Brydon from 1914 (when James resumed the writing of the novel) and forward from 1899 when *The Sense of the Past* was conceived, and both characters have a distant ancestry in the Clement Searle of 'A Passionate Pilgrim'. Fogel examines Searle's and Brydon's obsessions with an 'alternative life' but fails to mention Ralph Pendrel (152).

45   Kern's description of the process as an 'hallucination' (59) is a little flat-footed; and his reading of Pendrel as 'psychologically unbalanced' (60) is not legitimated by the text. See Williams for a concentration on the portrait, representation, and the imagination in the novel.

46   'The original version of *The Sense of the Past*, revised by the author in 1914…broke off in the middle of the scene between Ralph Pendrel and the Ambassador (Book III)' (Lubbock, ed., *The Sense of the Past* (291n). James dictated but did not revise the unfinished Book IV.

47 See Marshall on Ralph Pendrel's increasingly terrifying sensation of the 'wavering margin' (203) between his two identities and some of the intractable problems this presented for James.
48 See Purdy (83–93) on *The Time Machine* and *The Sense of the Past*.
49 Sicker, too, merges text and paratext in his interpretation.
50 In 1906, James instructed his publishers to tell the 'Compositors to *adhere irremoveably* to my punctuation & *never* to insert death-dealing commas' (Letter to Charles Scribner's Sons, 12 May 1906, *LL* 433).

Afterword

1 Hans Vaihinger (1852–1933) taught at the University of Halle from 1884 to 1906; his work forms a bridge, of a kind, between Kant and pragmatism. Many of his ideas were anticipated by Bentham in his *Theory of Fictions* (1814–32; but widely neglected until Ogden compiled the material in 1932); the confluence of Vaihinger's ideas with American pragmatism in *The Philosophy of 'As If'* (1911), however, has resulted in his work having a more powerful and wide-ranging impact than Bentham's.
2 The 'conception of a thing as a physical end', of each individual as a teleological entity, 'is only thinkable by the aid of reason....we have no insight into its objective reality...we do not know whether it is a mere logical fiction and an objectively empty conception (*conceptus ratiocinans*), or whether it is a rational conception, supplying a basis of knowledge and substantiated by reason (*conceptus ratiocinatus*)....For the conception of a physical end is altogether unprovable by reason in respect of its physical reality, which means that it is not constitutive for the determinant judgement, but merely regulative for the reflective judgement' (*The Critique of Judgement* 2: 48–9).
3 *King Lear* I i 90.

Works Cited

Aaron, Daniel. *The Unwritten War: American Writers and the Civil War*. London: Oxford UP, 1975.

Abrams, M. H. *The Mirror and the Lamp: Romantic Theory and the Critical Tradition*. New York: Oxford UP, 1953.

Adams, Henry. *The Education of Henry Adams*. 1907. *Novels, Mont Saint Michel, The Education*. New York, N. Y.: Literary Classics of the United States, 1983: 715–1192.

Agnew, Jean-Christophe. 'The Consuming Vision of Henry James'. *The Culture of Consumption: Critical Essays in American History, 1880–1980*. Ed. Richard Wightman Fox and T. J. Jackson Lears. New York: Pantheon, 1983: 67–100.

Alcott, Louisa M. *Hospital Sketches, and Camp and Fireside Stories*. Boston: Roberts Brothers, 1869.

Alderson, Bernard. *Andrew Carnegie: From Telegraph Boy to Millionaire*. London: Pearson, 1902.

'American Literature'. 1833. *AF* 1: 130–4.

Andreas, Osborn. *Henry James and the Expanding Horizon: A Study of the Meaning and Basic Themes of James's Fiction*. Seattle: Washington UP, 1948.

Aristotle. *Physics. A New Aristotle Reader*. Ed. J. L. Ackrill. Oxford: Clarendon, 1987: 81–131.

——. *Poetics. Ancient Literary Criticism: The Principal Texts in New Translations*. Ed. D. A. Russell and M. Winterbottom. Oxford: Clarendon, 1972: 85–131.

Arms, George. 'James's "The Birthplace": Over a Pulpit-Edge'. *Tennessee Studies in Literature* 8 (1963): 61–9.

Arnold, Matthew. 'To Marguerite—Continued'. *Poems*. London and New York: Dent and Dutton, 1965: 197–8.

Augustine, Saint, Bishop of Hippo. *The Confessions and Letters of St. Augustine*. AD 397. Trans. J. G. Pilkington. New York: Christian Literature, 1892.

Austin, J. L. *How to Do Things with Words*. William James Lectures, 1955. London: Oxford UP, 1976.

B. 'Literature of Virginia'. 1838. *AF* 1: 184–95.

Bachelard, *The Poetics of Space*. 1958. Trans. Maria Jolas. Boston, Mass.: Beacon, 1969.

Bacon, Delia. *The Philosophy of the Plays of Shakspere Unfolded*. Preface. By Nathaniel Hawthorne. London: Groombridge, 1857.

——. 'The Philosophy of the Plays of Shakspere Unfolded'. 1857. *AS:* 207–14.

——. 'William Shakespeare and His Plays'. 1856. *AS:* 169–99.

Banta, Martha. 'Men, Women, and the American Way'. *The Cambridge Companion to Henry James*. Ed. Jonathan Freedman. Cambridge, Cambridge UP, 1998: 21–39.

Barnum, P. T. *The Life of P. T. Barnum, Written by Himself, Phineas T. Barnum*. 1855. Urbana and Chicago: Illinois UP, 2000.

Barthes, Roland. 'The Discourse of History'. 1967. Trans. Stephen Bann. *Comparative Criticism* 3 (1981): 7–20.

Bataille, Georges. *Erotism, Death and Sensuality.* 1957. Trans. Mary Dalwood. San Francisco: City Lights, 1986.

Beebe, Maurice L. 'The Turned Back of Henry James'. *South Atlantic Quarterly* 53 (1954), 521–39.

Beerbohm, Max. *Letters to Reggie Turner.* Ed. Rupert Hart-Davis. London: Rupert Hart-Davis, 1964.

Bell, Ian F. A. *Henry James and the Past: Readings into Time.* Basingstoke: Macmillan, 1991.

——. *Washington Square: Styles of Money.* Twayne's Masterwork Studies. New York: Twayne, 1993.

Bell, Millicent. '"The Aspern Papers": The Unvisitable Past'. *Henry James Review* 10 (1989): 120–7.

Benert, Annette Larson. 'Dialogical Discourse in "The Jolly Corner": The Entrepreneur as Language and Image'. *Henry James Review* 8 (1987): 116–25.

Benjamin, A. Cornelius. 'Ideas of Time in the History of Philosophy'. *The Voice of Time: A Cooperative Survey of Man's Views of Time as Expressed by the Sciences and by the Humanities.* London: Allen Lane, 1968: 5–29.

Bennett, E. A. *Fame and Fiction: An Enquiry into Certain Popularities.* London: Grant Richards, 1901.

Bentham, Jeremy. *Theory of Fictions.* International Library of Psychology, Philosophy and Scientific Method. 1814–32. Ed. C. K. Ogden. London: Kegan Paul, 1932.

Bergson, Henri. *Creative Evolution.* 1907. Trans. Arthur Mitchell. Mineola, New York: Dover, 1998.

——. *An Introduction to Metaphysics.* 1903. Trans. T. E. Hulme. Introduction. Thomas A. Goudge. The Library of Liberal Arts. Indianapolis and New York: Bobbs-Merrill, 1949.

——. *Matter and Memory.* 1896. Trans. N. M. Paul and W. S. Palmer. New York: Zone, 1991.

——. *Time and Free Will: An Essay on the Immediate Data of Consciousness.* 1889. Trans, F. L. Pogson. 1910. Montana: Kessinger, 1966.

Bernard, Claude. *An Introduction to the Study of Experimental Medicine.* 1865. Trans. Henry Copley Greene. New York: Henry Schuman, 1949.

Bobinski, George S. *Carnegie Libraries: Their History and Impact on American Public Library Development.* Chicago: American Library Association, 1969.

'Books, Authors and Arts: Mr. James's New Short Stories'. Rev. of *The Better Sort,* by Henry James. *Republican* (Springfield, Mass.). 15 March 1903: 19.

Born, Brad S. 'Henry James's *Roderick Hudson*: A Convergence of Family Stories'. *Henry James Review* 12 (1991): 199–211.

Bradley, F. H. *Appearance and Reality: A Metaphysical Essay.* 2nd edn. Oxford: Clarendon, 1897.

——. *The Presuppositions of Critical History.* 1874. Ed. Lionel Rubinoff. Chicago: Quadrangle, 1968.

Bradley, John R. *Henry James's Permanent Adolescence.* Basingstoke: Palgrave – now Palgrave Macmillan, 2000.

Braudy, Leo. *The Frenzy of Renown: Fame and its History.* New York and Oxford: Oxford UP, 1986.

Bresnick, Adam. 'The Artist that Was Used Up: Henry James's "Private Life"'. *Henry James Review* 14 (1993): 87–98.

Bristol, Michael. *Shakespeare's America, America's Shakespeare*. New York: Routledge, 1990.

Brodhead, Richard R. *The School of Hawthorne*. New York and Oxford: Oxford UP, 1986.

Brooks, Van Wyck. *America's Coming-of-Age*. New York: Huebsch, 1915

Brown, Ivor and George Fearon, *The Shakespeares and the Birthplace*. Stratford-on-Avon: Fox, 1939.

Browning, Robert. 'Andrea del Sarto'. 1855. *The Selected Poetry of Browning*. The Signet Classic Poetry Series. Ed. George Ridenour. New York: New American Library, 1966.

——. *The Ring and the Book*. 4 vols. 1869. 2nd edn. London: Smith, Elder: 1872.

Brownson, Orestes A. 'Literature, Love, and Marriage'. 1864. *AF* 2: 218–35.

——. 'Specimens of Foreign Standard Literature'. Rev. of translations (Cousin, Jouffroy, and Constant), by George Ripley. 1838. *AS*: 72–4.

Buckle, Thomas. General Introduction. *History of Civilization in England*. 2 vols. 1856–61. *The Varieties of History from Voltaire to the Present*. Ed. Fritz Stern. 2nd edn. London and Basingstoke: Macmillan, 1970: 121–8.

Budd, Louis J. 'The Baconians: Madness through Method'. *South Atlantic Quarterly*, 54 (1955): 359–68.

Buitenhuis, Peter. *The Grasping Imagination: The American Writing of Henry James*. Toronto and Buffalo: Toronto UP, 1970.

Bull, Malcolm. *Seeing Things Hidden: Apocalypse, Vision, and Totality*. London and New York: Verso, 1999.

Burns, Allan. 'Henry James's Journalists as Synecdoche for the American Scene'. *Henry James Review* 16 (1995): 1–17.

Butler, Judith. *Gender Trouble: Feminism and the Subversion of Identity*. Thinking Gender. New York and London: Routledge, 1990.

Byron, George Gordon. Baron Byron. *Manfred: A Dramatic Poem*. London: John Murray, 1817.

Cannon, Kelly. *Henry James and Masculinity: The Man at the Margins*. Basingstoke: Macmillan, 1994.

Caramello, Charles. *Henry James, Gertrude Stein and the Biographical Act*. Chapel Hill, NC and London: North Carolina UP, 1996.

Carr, E. H. *What is History?* Harmondsworth: Penguin, 1964.

Carton, Evan. 'The Anxiety of Effluence: Criticism, Currency, and "The Aspern Papers"'. *Henry James Review* 10 (1989): 116–20.

Cash, W. J. *The Mind of the South*. The American Scene. New York: Alfred A Knopf, 1941.

Channing, Edward Tyrell. 'American Language and Literature'. 1815. *AF* 1: 23–8.

——. 'Reflections on the Literary Delinquency of America'. 1815. *AF* 1: 29–36.

Chatman, Seymour. *Story and Discourse: Narrative Structure in Fiction and Film*. Ithaca and London: Cornell UP, 1978.

Chisholm, Roderick M. 'The Contrary-to-Fact Conditional'. *Readings in Philosophical Analysis*. Ed. Herbert Feigl and Wilfrid Sellars. New York: Appleton-Century-Crofts, 1949: 482–97.

Church, Joseph. 'Writing and the Dispossession of Woman in *The Aspern Papers*'. *American Imago* 47 (1990): 23–42.

Clay, Edmund R. *The Alternative: A Study in Psychology*. London: Macmillan, 1882.

Cohen, Ed. *Talk on the Wilde Side: Towards a Genealogy of a Discourse on Male Sexualities*. New York and London: Routledge, 1993.

Collier, John Payne. *New Facts Regarding the Life of Shakespeare. In a Letter to Thomas Amyot*. London: Thomas Rodd, 1835.

Collingwood, R. G. *The Idea of History*. 1946. Oxford: Clarendon, 1956.

Conley, Tom. Introduction. 'For a Literary Historiography'. *The Writing of History*. By Michel de Certeau. 1975. Trans. Tom Conley. New York: Columbia UP, 1988: vii-xxiv.

Conn, Peter. *The Divided Mind: Ideology and Imagination in America, 1898–1917*. Cambridge Studies in American Literature and Culture. Cambridge: Cambridge UP, 1983.

Corelli, Marie. *The Plain Truth of the Stratford-on-Avon Controversy, Concerning the Fully-Intended Demolition of Old Houses in Henley Street, and the Changes Proposed to be Effected on the National Ground of Shakespeare's Birthplace*. London: Methuen, 1903.

——. *The Sorrows of Satan; or, The Strange Experience of one Geoffrey Tempest, Millionaire: A Romance*. London: Methuen, 1895.

Cowdery, Lauren T. 'Henry James and the "Transcendent Adventure": The Search for the Self in the Introduction to *The Tempest*'. *Henry James Review* 3 (1982): 145–53.

——. *The Nouvelle of Henry James in Theory and Practice*. Studies in Modern Literature. 47. Ann Arbor, Mich.: UMI Research Press, 1986.

Cox, James M. 'The Memoirs of Henry James: Self-Interest as Autobiography'. *Southern Review* 22 (1986): 231–51.

Dawson, Graham. *Soldier Heroes: British Adventure, Empire, and the Imagining of Masculinities*. London: Routledge, 1994.

De Certeau, Michel. *The Writing of History*. 1975. Trans. Tom Conley. New York: Columbia UP, 1988.

De Forest, John W. *Miss Ravenel's Conversion from Secession to Loyalty*. 1867. Ed. Gary Scharnhorst. Harmondsworth: Penguin, 2000.

Denison, David. *English Historical Syntax: Verbal Constructions*. London and New York: Longman, 1993.

Diffley, Kathleen. Ed. *To Live and Die: Collected Stories of the Civil War, 1861–1876*. Durham and London: Duke UP, 2002.

——. *Where My Heart is Turning Ever: Civil War Stories and Constitutional Reform, 1861–1876*. Athens and London: Georgia UP, 1992.

Donnelly, Ignatius. *The Great Cryptogram: Francis Bacon's Cipher in the So-Called Shakespeare Plays*. 2 vols. London: Sampson Low, 1888.

Donoghue, Denis. 'Attitudes Towards History: A Preface to *The Sense of the Past*'. *Salmagundi* 68–9 (1985–86): 107–24.

Doyle, Arthur Conan. *The Hound of the Baskervilles: Another Adventure of Sherlock Holmes*. London: George Newnes, 1902.

Duby, Georges. 'Private Power, Public Power'. *A History of Private Life: 2: Revelations of the Mediaeval World*. Ed. Georges Duby. Trans. Arthur Goldhammer. Cambridge, Mass.: and London, England: Belknap, 1988.

Duyckinck, Evert Augustus and George Long Duyckinck. *Cyclopaedia of American Literature*. 2 vols. New York: Scribner, 1855.

Dupee, F. W. *Henry James*. The American Men of Letters Series. London: Methuen, 1951.

Eakin, Paul John. *Fictions in Autobiography: Studies in the Art of Self-Invention*. Princeton, NJ: Princeton UP, 1985.

——. 'Henry James's "Obscure Hurt": Can Autobiography Serve Biography?' *New Literary History*, 19 (1987–88): 675–92.

Eco, Umberto. *Faith in Fakes: Travels in Hyperreality*. Trans. William Weaver. London: Minerva, 1995.

Edel, Leon. *Henry James: The Treacherous Years, 1895–1901*. 1969. New York: Avon, 1978.

——. *Henry James: The Untried Years, 1843–70*. 1953. New York: Avon, 1978.

Einstein, Albert. *Relativity: The Special and the General Theory: A Popular Exposition*. 1916. Trans. Robert William Lawson. London: Methuen, 1920.

——. *The Theory of Relativity: An Introductory Sketch Based on Einstein's Original Writings*. Trans. Henry Herman Leopold Adolf Brose. Oxford: Blackwell, 1920.

——. and Leopold Infeld. *The Evolution of Physics: The Growth of Ideas from the Early Concepts to Relativity and Quanta*. Cambridge Library of Modern Sciences. Cambridge: Cambridge UP, 1938.

Eliot, George. *Middlemarch*. 1871–72. Ed. W. J. Harvey. Harmondsworth: Penguin, 1965.

Eliot, T. S. 'Four Quartets'. 1935–42. *The Complete Poems and Plays of T. S. Eliot*. London: Faber, 1969: 169–98.

——. 'Hamlet and His Problems'. 1919. *Selected Essays, 1917–1932*. New York: Harcourt, 1932: 121–6.

——. 'On Henry James'. 1918. *The Question of Henry James*. Ed. F. W. Dupee. London: Allan Wingate, 1947: 123–33.

——. 'The Love Song of J. Alfred Prufrock'. 1917. *The Complete Poems and Plays of T. S. Eliot*. London: Faber, 1969: 13–17.

——. 'Preludes'. *The Complete Poems and Plays of T. S. Eliot*. London: Faber, 1969: 22–3.

Ellis, Henry Havelock and John Addington Symonds. *Studies in the Psychology of Sex*. Vol. 1: *Sexual Inversion*. London: Wilson and Macmillan, 1897.

Emerson, Ralph Waldo. 'The American Scholar'. 1837. *English Traits, Representative Men, and Other Essays*. London: Dent, 1908. 293–310.

——. 'History'. 1841. *Essays: First and Second Series*. London: Dent, 1906. 7–29.

——. 'Self-Reliance'. 1841. *Essays: First and Second Series*. London: Dent, 1906. 29–56.

——. 'Shakespeare; or, The Poet'. 1844. *AS*: 111–25.

——. 'Uses of Great Men'. 1844. *English Traits, Representative Men, and Other Essays*. London: Dent, 1908. 157–73.

Fahs, Alice. *The Imagined Civil War: Popular Literature of the North and South, 1861–1865*. Chapel Hill, NC and London: North Carolina UP, 2001.

Falk, Robert. 'Shakespeare in America: A Survey to 1900'. *Shakespeare Survey* 18 (1965): 102–18.

Feinstein, Howard M. *Becoming William James*. Ithaca and London: Cornell UP, 1984.

Findlay, J. N. 'Time: A Treatment of Some Puzzles'. 1941. *Essays on Logic and Language*. Ed. A. G. N. Flew. Oxford: Blackwell, 1951: 37–54.

Fitzgerald, F. Scott. *The Great Gatsby*. 1925. Harmondsworth: Penguin, 1950.

Flaubert, Gustave. Letter to Mademoiselle Leroyer de Chantepie. 18 March 1857. *Novelists on the Novel*. Ed. Miriam Allott. London: Routledge, 1965: 271.

Fogel, Daniel Mark. *Henry James and the Structure of the Romantic Imagination.* Baton Rouge: Louisiana State UP, 1981.

Follett, Wilson. 'Henry James and the Untold Story'. *Dial* 63 (6 December 1917): 579–81.

Foucault, Michel. *History of Sexuality.* Vol. 1. *An Introduction.* Trans. Robert Hurley. Harmondsworth: Penguin, 1978.

——. *Madness and Civilization: A History of Insanity in the Age of Reason.* Studies in Existentialism and Phenomenology. Trans. Richard Joseph Howard. London: Tavistock, 1967.

Fox, Levi. *In Honour of Shakespeare: The History and Collections of the Shakespeare Birthplace Trust.* Norwich: Jarrold and Sons; Stratford-upon-Avon: Shakespeare Birthplace Trust, 1972.

——. *Shakespeare's Birthplace: A History and Description.* Norwich: Jarrold, 1963.

Fradenburg, L. O. Aranye. 'Group Time: Catastrophe, Survival, Periodicity'. *Time and the Literary.* Essays from the English Institute. Ed. Karen Newman, Jay Clayton, and Marianne Hirsch. New York and London: Routledge, 2002: 211–37.

Frost, Robert. 'The Road Not Taken'. 1916. *The Poetry of Robert Frost.* Ed. Edward Connery Lathem. New York: Holt, Rinehart, 1969: 105.

Fussell, Paul. *The Great War and Modern Memory.* London: Oxford University Press, 1975.

Garber, Marjorie B. *Vested Interests: Cross-Dressing and Cultural Anxiety.* New York: Routledge, 1992.

Gard, Roger. Introduction. *Henry James: The Jolly Corner and Other Tales.* Harmondsworth: Penguin, 1990: 1–3.

Geertz, Clifford. *The Interpretation of Cultures: Selected Essays.* London: Fontana, 1993.

Genette, Gérard. *Narrative Discourse.* 1980. Trans. Jane E. Lewin. Oxford: Blackwell, 1980.

——. *Paratexts: Thresholds of Interpretation.* 1989. Trans. Jane E. Lewin. Cambridge: Cambridge UP, 1997.

Gilmore, David D. *Manhood in the Making: Cultural Concepts of Masculinity.* New Haven and London: Yale UP, 1990.

Gorak, Jan. *The Making of the Modern Canon: Genesis and Crisis of a Literary Idea.* Vision, Division, and Revision. London: Athlone, 1991.

Gordon, Lyndall. *A Private Life of Henry James: Two Women and His Art.* London: Vintage, 1999.

Gosse, Edmund. *Aspects and Impressions.* New York, Toronto, and Melbourne: Cassell, 1922.

Goulding, Captain. *An Essay Against too much Reading.* London: Moore, 1728.

Graham, Wendy. *Henry James's Thwarted Love.* Stanford, Calif.: Stanford UP, 1999.

Greenslade, William. *Degeneration, Culture, and the Novel, 1880–1940.* Cambridge: Cambridge UP, 1994.

Griffin, Susan M. 'Seeing Doubles: Reflections of the Self in James's *Sense of the Past*'. *Modern Language Quarterly* 45 (1984): 48–60.

Griswold, Rufus Wilmot. *The Female Poets of America.* Philadelphia: Carey, 1849.

——. *The Poets and Poetry of America: With an Historical Introduction.* Philadelphia: Carey, 1842.

——. *The Prose Writers of America with a Survey of the History*. Philadelphia: Carey, 1847.

Groesbeck, H. J. 'American Literature: Its Impediments'. 1835. *AF* 1: 168–74.

Gutterman, David S. 'Postmodernism and the Interrogation of Masculinity'. *Theorizing Masculinities*. Research on Man and Masculinities. Ed. Harry Brod and Michael Kaufman. Thousand Oaks, Calif. and London: Sage, 1994: 219–38.

Habegger, Alfred. *Gender, Fantasy, and Realism in American Literature*. New York: Columbia UP, 1982.

Habgood, Francis E. C. and R. L. Eagle. *The Stratford Birthplace: Reprinted from 'Baconia'*. London: The Bacon Society, 1940.

Hall, Richard. 'Henry James: Interpreting an Obsessive Memory'. *Journal of Homosexuality* 8 (1983): 83–97.

——. 'An Obscure Hurt: The Sexuality of Henry James'. Part 1. *New Republic*, 28 April 1979: 25–31.

——. 'An Obscure Hurt: The Sexuality of Henry James'. Part 2. *New Republic*, 5 May 1979: 25–9.

Halliwell-Phillips, James Orchard. *Illustrations of the Life of Shakespeare in a Discursive Series of Essays*. London: n.p., 1874.

——. *The Life of William Shakespeare. Including Many Particulars Respecting the Poet and his Family Never Before Published*. London: n.p., 1848.

——. *New Evidences in Confirmation of the Traditional Recognition of Shakespeare's Birth-Room, 1769–1777*. Brighton: private circulation, 1888.

——. *Outlines of the Life of Shakespeare*. Brighton: privately printed, 1881.

Halperin, John. 'Henry James's Civil War'. *Henry James Review* 17 (1996): 22–9.

——. *Novelists in their Youth*. London: Chatto and Windus, 1990.

Haralson, Eric. *Henry James and Queer Modernity*. Cambridge: Cambridge UP, 2003.

——. 'Iron Henry, or James Goes to War'. *Arizona Quarterly* 53 (1997), 39–59.

Hardy, Thomas. *Tess of the d'Urbervilles*. 1891. Harmondsworth: Penguin, 1978.

Harris, Neil. *Humbug: The Art of P. T. Barnum*. Chicago: Chicago UP, 1981.

Hart, Joseph C. *The Romance of Yachting*. 1848. *AS*: 140–50.

Hartstock, Mildred E. 'The Conceivable Child: James and the Poet'. *Studies in Short Fiction* 8 (1971): 569–74.

Haviland, Beverly. *Henry James's Last Romance: Making Sense of the Past and the American Scene*. Cambridge Studies in American Literature and Culture. Cambridge: Cambridge UP, 1997.

Hawthorne, Nathaniel. Letter to William D. Ticknor. 19 January 1855. *The Letters, 1853–1856*. Ed. Thomas Woodson, James A. Rubino, L. Neal Smith, Norman Holmes Pearson. The Centenary Edition of the Works of Nathaniel Hawthorne. 23 vols. Ohio: Ohio State UP, 1987: 17: 303–4.

——. *The Marble Faun; or, The Romance of Monte Beni*. 2 vols. Boston: Ticknor & Fields, 1860.

——. Preface. *The Philosophy of the Plays of Shakspere Unfolded*. By Delia Bacon. 1857. *AS*: 200–6.

——. 'Recollections of a Gifted Woman'. 1863. *AS*: 215–36.

Heath, James Ewell. 'Southern Literature'. 1834. *AF* 1: 164–7.

Hegel, Georg Wilhelm Friedrich. *The Philosophy of History*. 1822–23. Trans. J. Sibree. New York: Dover, 1956.

Hemingway, Ernest. *The Sun Also Rises*. New York: Scribner, 1926.

Hodgdon, Barbara. *The Shakespeare Trade: Performances and Appropriations*. New Cultural Studies. Philadelphia: Pennsylvania UP 1998.

Hoffmann, Charles and Tess Hoffmann. 'Henry James and the Civil War'. *New England Quarterly*, 72 (1989): 529–52.

Holland, Laurence B. *The Expense of Vision: Essays on the Craft of Henry James*. Baltimore and London: Johns Hopkins UP, 1982.

Holleran, James V. 'An Analysis of "The Birthplace"'. *Papers on Language and Literature* 2 (1966): 76–80.

Holly, Carol. *Intensely 'Family': The Inheritance of Family Shame and the Autobiographies of Henry James*. Madison, Wisc.: Wisconsin UP, 1995.

Holmes, Nathaniel. *The Authorship of Shakespeare*. 1866. *AS*: 247–55.

Horne, Philip. *Henry James and Revision: The New York Edition*. Oxford: Clarendon, 1990.

——. 'The Master and the "Queer Affair" of "The Pupil"'. *Henry James: The Shorter Fiction: Reassessments*. Ed. N. H. Reeve. London: Macmillan, 1997: 114–37.

Howard, David. 'Henry James and "The Papers"'. *Henry James: Fiction as History*. Critical Studies Series. Ed. Ian F. A. Bell. London: Vision, 1984: 49–64.

Howells, William Dean. Rev. of *Miss Ravenel's Conversion from Secession to Loyalty*, by J. W. De Forest. *Atlantic Monthly*, 20 (1867): 120–2.

——. *The Rise of Silas Lapham*. 1885. New York: Signet, 2002.

Hughes, H. Stuart. *Consciousness and Society: The Reorientation of European Social Thought, 1890–1930*. Brighton: Harvester, 1979.

Hunter, Robert E. *Shakespeare and Stratford-upon-Avon, A 'Chronicle of the Time': Comprising the Salient Facts and Traditions, Biographical, Topographical and Historical, Connected with the Poet and his Birth-Place; Together with a Full Record of the Tercentenary Celebration*. London: Whittaker, 1864.

Hyde, H. Montgomery. *Henry James at Home*. London: Methuen, 1969.

'The Inferiority of American Literature'. 1840. *AF* 1: 251–8.

'An Inquiry into the Present State of Southern Literature'. 1856. *AF* 2: 98–104.

Irving, Washington. 'The Boar's Head Tavern, East Cheap: A Shakesperian Research. 1820. *AS*: 32–41.

——. 'Stratford-on-Avon'. 1820. *AS*: 42–57.

Jacobson, Jacob. *Queer Desire in Henry James: The Politics of Erotics in* The Bostonians *and* The Princess Casamassima. Berliner Beiträge zur Anglistik. Bd. 7. Frankfurt am Main and Oxford: Peter Lang, 2000.

Jacobson, Marcia Ann. *Henry James and the Mass Market*. Alabama: Alabama UP, 1983.

James, D. 'Past Tense and the Hypothetical: A Cross-Linguistic Study'. *Studies in Language* 6 (1982): 373–403

James, Henry. 'The After-Season in Rome'. 1873. *CTWTC* 464–9.

——. 'Alfred de Musset'. Rev. of *Biographie de Alfred de Musset: sa Vie et ses Oeuvres*, by Paul de Musset. 1877. *LCFW* 596–618.

——. 'Alphonse Daudet'. 1883. *LCFW* 223–49.

——. 'The Altar of the Dead'. 1895. *CS* 4: 450–85.

——. *The Ambassadors*. 1903. Harmondsworth: Penguin, 1973.

——. 'American Letters'. 16 April 1898. *LCEL* 660–3.

——. 'American Letters'. 23 April 1898. *LCEL* 663–7.

——. 'American Letters'. 7 May 1898. *LCEL* 670–3.

——. *The American Scene*. 1907. *CTWGB* 351–736.

——. 'The Art of Fiction'. 1884. *LCEL* 44–65.

——. 'The Aspern Papers'. 1888. *CS* 3: 228–320.

——. 'The Author of Beltraffio'. 1884. *CS* 2: 865–910.

——. 'Balzac'. Rev. of *Balzac*, by Émile Fauget. 1913. *LCFW* 139–51.

——. *Beloved Boy: Letters to Hendrik C. Andersen*, 1899–1915. Introduction. Millicent Bell. Ed. Rosella Mamoli Zorzi. Charlottesville, VA: Virginia UP, 2004.

——. *The Better Sort*. London: Methuen, 1903.

——. 'The Birthplace'. 1903. *CS* 5: 441–95.

——. *The Bostonians*. 1886. Harmondsworth: Penguin, 1966.

——. 'The British Soldier'. 1878. *Henry James on Culture: Collected Essays on Politics and the American Social Scene*. Ed. Pierre A. Walker. Lincoln and London: Nebraska UP, 1999: 3–13.

——. 'Browning in Westminster Abbey'. 1890. *LCEL* 786–91.

——. 'A Chain of Cities'. 1875. *CTWTC* 497–512.

——. *The Complete Notebooks of Henry James*. Ed. Leon Edel and Lyall H. Powers. Oxford and New York: Oxford UP, 1987.

——. 'The Diary of a Man of Fifty'. 1879. *CS* 2: 453–84.

——. 'Dumas the Younger'. 1895. *Notes on Novelists*. London: Dent, 1914. 288–305.

——. 'Edmond Rostand'. 1901. *Henry James: Essays on Art and Drama*. Ed. Peter Rawlings. Aldershot and Vermont: Scolar and Ashgate, 1996: 516–37.

——. 'Eugene Pickering'. 1874. *CS* 2: 36–81.

——. 'A Few Other Roman Neighbourhoods'. 1909. *CTWTC* 486–96.

——. 'The Figure in the Carpet'. 1896. *CS* 4: 572–608.

——. 'Flickerbridge'. 1902. *CS* 4: 421–40.

——. 'Florentine Notes'. 1874. *CTWTC* 542–67.

——. 'Frances Anne Kemble'. 1893. *LCEL* 1069–97.

——. 'From Chambéry to Milan'. 1872. *CTWTC* 365–75.

——. 'From a Roman Note-book'. 1873. *CTWTC* 470–85.

——. 'The Future of the Novel'. 1899. *LCEL* 100–10.

——. 'Gabriele D'Annunzio'. 1904. Rev. of six English translations, 1898–1902. *LCFW* 907–43.

——. 'The Grand Canal'. 1892. *CTWTC* 314–35.

——. 'Gustave Flaubert'. Rev. of *Correspondance de Gustave Flaubert, Quatrième Série*. 1893. *LCFW* 295–314.

——. 'Guy de Maupassant'. 1888. *LCFW* 521–49.

——. *Hawthorne*. 1879. *LCEL* 315–457.

——. 'Henry James's First Interview'. 1915. *Henry James on Culture: Collected Essays on Politics and the American Social Scene*. Ed. Pierre A. Walker. Lincoln and London: Nebraska UP, 1999: 138–45.

——. 'Historical Novels'. Rev. of *The Household of Sir Thomas More* and *Jacques Bonneval, or The Days of the Dragonnades*, by Anne E. Manning. 1867. *LCEL* 1152–7.

——. 'Hubert Crackanthorpe: An Appreciation'. 1897. *Last Studies*. Hubert Crackanthorpe. *LCEL* 839–44.

——. 'In Warwickshire'. 1877. *CTWGB* 164–82.

——. Introduction. *Madame Bovary*. By Gustave Flaubert. 1902. *LCFW* 314–46.

——. Introduction. *Mine Own People*. By Rudyard Kipling. 1891. *LCEL* 1122–31.

——. Introduction. *The Tempest. The Complete Works of William Shakespeare*. Ed. Sidney Lee. 1907. *LCEL* 1205–20.

——. Introduction. *Two Young Brides*. By Honoré de Balzac. 1902. *LCFW* 90–115.

——. *Italian Hours*. London: Heinemann, 1909.

——. 'James Russell Lowell'. 1892. *LCEL* 516–40.

——. 'The Jolly Corner'. 1908. *CS* 5: 697–731.

——. 'The Lesson of Balzac'. 1905. *LCFW* 115–39.

——. Letter to Charles Eliot Norton. 25 March 1870. *LL* 32–5.

——. Letter to Charles Scribner's Sons. 12 May 1906. *LL* 432–3.

——. Letter to Edward Emerson. 4 August 1914. *LL* 540–3.

——. Letter to Henry James III. 15–18 November 1913. *HJL* 4: 800–4.

——. Letter to Henry James III. 7 April 1914. *HJL* 4: 806–7.

——. Letter to H. G. Wells. 29 January 1900. *HJL* 4: 132–3.

——. Letter to the Hon. Robert S. Rantoul. *The Proceedings in Commemoration of the One Hundredth Anniversary of the Birth of Nathaniel Hawthorne*. 10 June 1904. *LCEL* 468–74.

——. Letter to Jessie Allen. 19 September 1901. *HJL* 4: 202–4.

——. Letter to Mary Walsh James (mother). 26 March 1870. *LL* 36–8.

——. Letter to Thomas Sergeant Perry. 25 March 1864. *HJL* 1: 49–51.

——. Letter to Sarah Orne Jewett. 5 October 1901. *LL* 359–61.

——. Letter to Violet Hunt. 11 August 1903. *HJL* 4: 281.

——. Letter to Violet Hunt. 26 August 1903. *The Letters of Henry James*. 2 vols. Ed. Percy Lubbock. London: Macmillan and Co., Ltd, 1920: 1: 432–3.

——. Letter to William Dean Howells. 29 June 1900. *HJL* 4: 149–52.

——. 'Lichfield and Warwick'. 1872. *CTWGB* 67–81.

——. 'The Life of George Eliot'. Rev. of *George Eliot's Life*, by G. W. Cross. 1888. *LCEL* 994–1010.

——. 'A Little Tour in France'. 1877. *CTWTC* 735–51.

——. *A Little Tour in France*. 1884. *CTWTC* 1–277.

——. 'Livingstone's Last Journals'. Rev. of *The Last Journals of David Livingstone in Central Africa, from 1866 to his Death*. 1875. *LCEL* 1141–5.

——. 'London Notes'. 23 January 1897. *Henry James: Essays on Art and Drama*. Ed. Peter Rawlings. Aldershot: Scolar, 1996: 489–93.

——. 'London Notes'. 27 March 1897. *LCEL* 1394–9.

——. 'London Notes'. 5 May 1897. *Henry James: Essays on Art and Drama*. Ed. Peter Rawlings. Aldershot: Scolar, 1996: 505–11.

——. 'London Notes'. 31 July 1897. *LCEL* 1399–1406.

——. 'London Notes'. 21 August 1897. *LCEL* 1406–13.

——. 'London at Midsummer'. 1877. *CTWGB* 133–47.

——. 'The Long Wards'. 1916. *Henry James on Culture: Collected Essays on Politics and the American Social Scene*. Ed. Pierre A. Walker. Lincoln and London: Nebraska UP, 1999: 169–76.

——. 'Longstaff's Marriage'. 1878. *CS* 2: 296–325.

——. 'The Middle Years'. 1893. *CS* 4: 335–55.

——. *The Middle Years*. 1917. *HJA* 547–600.

——. 'A Most Extraordinary Case'. 1868. *CS* 1: 263–303.

——. 'Mr. and Mrs. James T. Fields'. 1915. *LCEL* 160–76.

——. 'Mr. Walt Whitman.' Rev. of *Drum-Taps*. 1865. *LCEL* 629–34.

——. *Notes of a Son and Brother*. 1914. *HJA* 239–546.

——. 'Notes on the Theatres'. 1875. *Henry James: Essays on Art and Drama*. Ed. Peter Rawlings. Aldershot: Scolar, 1996: 56–61.

——. 'The Novel in *The Ring and the Book*'. 1912. *LCEL* 791–811.

——. *The Novels and Tales of Henry James*. New York Edition. 24 vols. New York: Scribner, 1907–9.

——. 'Old Suffolk'. 1897. *CTWGB* 253–63.

——. 'Owen Wingrave'. 1892. *CS* 4: 256–90.

——. 'Pandora'. 1884. *CS* 2: 816–64.

——. 'The Papers'. 1903. *CS* 5: 542–638.

——. 'A Passionate Pilgrim'. 1871. *CS* 1: 543–611.

——. 'Pierre Loti'. 1888. *LCFW* 482–505.

——. 'The Point of View'. 1882. *CS* 2: 519–64.

——. 'Poor Richard'. 1867. *CS* 1: 149–208.

——. Preface. *Letters from America*. By Rupert Brooke. 1916. *LCEL* 747–69.

——. Preface. *Port Tarascon. The Last Adventures of the Illustrious Tartarin*. By Alphonse Daudet. Trans. Henry James. 1890. *LCFW* 249–53.

——. 'The Present Literary Situation in France'. 1899. *LCEL* 111–23.

——. 'The Private Life'. 1892. *CS* 4: 58–91.

——. 'The Real Thing'. 1892. *CS* 4: 32–57.

——. 'Recent Novels'. Rev. of *St. Simon's Niece*, by Frank Lee Benedict, *Buffets*, by Charles H. Doe, *Leah: A Woman of Fashion*, by Mrs. Annie Edwards, *Flamarande* and *Les Deux Frères*, by George Sand, and *Un Mariage dans le Monde*, by Octave Feuillet. 1876. *LCEL* 34–43.

——. 'Refugees in England'. 1915. *Henry James on Culture: Collected Essays on Politics and the American Social Scene*. Ed. Pierre A. Walker. Lincoln and London: Nebraska UP, 1999: 161–8.

——. *The Reverberator*. 1888. New York: Grove, 1979.

——. Rev. of *Azarian: An Episode*, by Harriet E. Prescott Spofford. 1865. *LCEL* 603–13.

——. Rev. of *The Correspondence of Carlyle and Emerson*.1883. *LCEL* 233–49.

——. Rev. of *Correspondence of William Ellery Channing*, D.D., and Lucy Aikin, from 1826 to 1842, ed. Anna Letitia Le Breton. 1875. *LCEL* 211–17.

——. Rev. of *The Earthly Paradise*, by William Morris. 1868. *LCEL* 1182–91.

——. Rev. of *England, Literary and Social, from a German Point of View*, by Julius Rodenberg. 1876. *LCFW* 950–2.

——. Rev. of *Ezra Stiles Gannett, Unitarian Minister in Boston, 1824–1871*, by William C. Gannet. 1875. *LCEL* 278–81.

——. Rev. of *Frülingsfluthen. Ein König Lear Des Dorfes. Zwei Novellen*, by Ivan Turgenev. 1874. *LCFW* 968–99.

——. Rev. of *George Sand, Sa vie et ses Oeuvres*, Vol. 3, by Vladimir Karénine. 1914. *LCFW* 775–98.

——. Rev. of *Hours of Exercise in the Alps*, by John Tyndall. 1871. *LCEL* 1357–62.

——. Rev. of *Ismailia: A Narrative of the Expedition to Central Africa for the Suppression of the Slave Trade, organized by Ismail, Khedive of Egypt*, by Sir Samuel Baker. 1875. *LCEL* 732–6.

——. Rev. of *Italian Journeys*, by William Dean Howells. 1868. *LCEL* 475–9.

——. Rev. of 'The Journals of the Brothers de Goncourt'. 1888. *LCFW* 404–28.

——. Rev. of *Légende des Siècles*, by Victor Hugo. 1877. *LCFW* 460–2.

——. Rev. of *Lettres d'Eugénie de Guérin*. 1866. *LCFW* 433–9.

——. Rev. of *Middlemarch. A Study of Provincial Life*, by George Eliot. 1873. *LCEL* 958–66.

———. Rev. of *Mon Frère et Moi: Souvenirs d'Enfance et de Jeunesse,* by Ernest Daudet. 1882. *LCFW* 213–23.

———. Rev. of *The Old Régime in Canada,* by Francis Parkman. 1874. *LCEL* 573–9.

———. Rev. of *Quatrevingt-treize,* by Victor Hugo, and its translation, *Ninenty-Three,* trans. Frank Lee Benedict, by Victor Hugo. 1874. *LCFW* 454–60.

———. Rev. of *The Schönberg-Cotta Family* (and a series of other novels), by Mrs. E. R. Charles. 1865. *LCEL* 826–9.

———. Rev. of *The Spanish Gypsy: A Poem,* by George Eliot. 1868. *LCEL* 941–58.

———. Rev. of *Two Men: A Novel,* by Elizabeth Stoddard. 1865. *LCEL* 614–17.

———. *Roderick Hudson.* 1875. Penguin: Harmondsworth, 1969.

———. 'A Roman Holiday'. 1873: *CTWTC* 413–30.

———. 'Roman Neighbourhoods'. 1873: *CTWTC* 447–63.

———. 'Roman Rides'. 1873. *CTWTC* 431–46.

———. 'The Science of Criticism'. 1891. *LCEL* 95–9.

———. *The Sense of the Past.* New York: Scribner, 1917.

———. 'She and He: Recent Documents'. 1897. *LCFW* 736–55.

———. 'Siena Early and Late'. Part 1, 1873; Part 2, 1909. *CTWTC* 513–32.

———. 'Sir Dominick Ferrand'. 1892. *CS* 4: 163–216.

———. *A Small Boy and Others.* 1913. *HJA* 3–238.

———. 'The Story of a Year'. 1865. *CS* 1: 23–66.

———. 'The Story-Teller at Large: Mr. Henry Harland'. Rev. of *Comedies and Errors,* by Henry Harland. 1898. *LCEL* 282–8.

———. 'The Third Person'. 1900. *CS* 5: 255–86.

———. 'Thomson's Indo-China and China'. Rev. of *The Straits of Malacca, Indo-China and China: or, Ten Years' Travels, Adventures, and Residence Abroad,* by J. Thomson. 1875. *LCEL* 1306–11.

———. 'A Tragedy of Error'. 1864. *CS* 1: 1–22.

———. 'The Tree of Knowledge'. 1900. *CS* 4: 220–34.

———. 'The Turn of the Screw'. 1898. *CS* 4: 635–740.

———. 'Two Old Houses and Three Young Women'. 1899. *CTWTC* 347–58.

———. 'Venice'. 1882. *CTWTC* 287–313.

———. 'Wells and Salisbury'. 1872. *CTWGB* 94–105.

———. *What Maisie Knew.* London: Heinemann, 1897.

———. *William Wetmore Story and His Friends.* 2 vols. Edinburgh and London: Blackwood, 1903.

———. *The Wings of the Dove.* Harmondsworth: Penguin, 1965.

———. 'Within the Rim'. 1917. *Henry James on Culture: Collected Essays on Politics and the American Social Scene.* Ed. Pierre A. Walker. Lincoln and London: Nebraska UP, 1999: 177–86.

———. *Within the Rim and Other Essays.* London: Collins, 1919.

James, William. 'Brute and Human Intellect'. 1878. *WJ1*: 910–49.

———. 'On a Certain Blindness'. c.1896. *WJ1*: 841–60.

———. 'Humanism and Truth Once More'. 1905. *WJ2*: 1193–1202.

———. Letter to Henry James. 4 March 1868. *The Correspondence of William James.* Vol. 1: *William and Henry, 1861–1884.* Eds. Ignas K. Skrupskelis and Elizabeth M. Berkeley. Charlottesville and London: Virginia UP, 1992: 36–7.

———. Letter to Henry James. 13 April 1868. *The Correspondence of William James.* Vol. 1: *William and Henry, 1861–1884.* Eds. Ignas K. Skrupskelis and Elizabeth M. Berkeley. Charlottesville and London: Virginia UP, 1992: 46–7.

——. 'The Moral Equivalent of War'. 1910. *WJ2*: 1281–93.

——. *A Pluralistic Universe*. Hibbert Lectures at Manchester College on the Present Situation in Philosophy. 1909. *WJ2*: 625–819.

——. *Pragmatism: A New Name for Some Old Ways of Thinking. Popular Lectures on Philosophy*. 1907. *WJ2*: 479–624.

——. *The Principles of Psychology*. 1890. Ed. George A. Miller. Cambridge, Mass.: Harvard UP, 1983.

——. 'The Sentiment of Rationality'. 1879. *WJ1*: 950–85.

——. 'On Some Mental Effects of the Earthquake'. 1906. *WJ2*: 1215–22.

——. 'On Some Omissions of Introspective Psychology'. 1883. *WJ1*: 986–1013.

——. *Some Problems of Philosophy: A Beginning of an Introduction to Philosophy*. 1911. *WJ2*: 979–1106.

——. *The Varieties of Religious Experience: A Study in Human Nature*. The Gifford Lectures on Natural Religion. Delivered at Edinburgh, 1901–2. 1902. *Writings, 1902–1910*. *WJ2*: 1–478.

Jeffords, Susan. *The Remasculinization of America: Gender and the Vietnam War*. Theories of Contemporary Culture. Vol. 10. Bloomington, Ind.: Indiana UP, 1989.

Jespersen, Otto. *Growth and Structure of the English Language*. Leipzig: Teubner, 1905.

——. *A Modern English Grammar on Historical Principles*. 4 vols. Heidelberg: Winter, 1909–31.

——. *The Philosophy of Grammar*. London: Allen and Unwin, 1924.

Jobe, Steven H. 'The Leon Edel Papers at McGill University'. *Henry James Review* 21 (2000): 290–7.

Jolly, Roslyn. *Henry James: History, Narrative, Fiction*. Oxford: Clarendon Press, 1993.

Jones, Vivien. *James the Critic*. London: Macmillan, 1985.

Joos, Martin. *The English Verb: Form and Meanings*. Madison and Milwaukee: Wisconsin UP, 1964.

Judd, Sylvester. *Margaret: A Tale of Real and Ideal*. 1845. London: Ward, Lock, & Tyler, 1874.

Kallen, Horace Meyer. *William James and Henri Bergson: A Study in Contrasting Theories of Life*. Chicago: Chicago UP, 1914.

Kant, Immanuel. *The Critique of Judgement*. 1790. Trans. James Creed Meredith. Rev. edn. Oxford: Clarendon, 1952.

——. *The Critique of Pure Reason*. 1781; 1786. Trans. Norman Kemp Smith. 2nd edn. London: Macmillan, 1990.

——. *Prolegomena to Any Future Metaphysics That Will Be Able to Come Forward as Science*. 1783. Trans. Paul Carus. Rev. James W. Ellington. Indianapolis: Hackett, 1977.

Kappeler, Susanne. *Writing and Reading in Henry James*. Foreword. Tony Tanner. London: Macmillan, 1980.

Kaplan, Fred. *Henry James: The Imagination of Genius: A Biography*. 1992. London: Sceptre, 1993.

Keats, John. 'Ode on a Grecian Urn'. 1820. *John Keats: Poetical Works*. Ed. H. W. Garrod. Oxford: Oxford UP, 1956: 209–10.

Kern, Stephen. *The Culture of Time and Space, 1880–1918*. Cambridge, Mass.: Harvard UP, 1983.

Kimmel, Michael S. *Manhood in America: A Cultural History*. New York and London: Free, 1996.

Kirby, David. 'The Sex Lives of the James Family'. *Virginia Quarterly Review* 64 (1988): 56–73.

Krafft-Ebing, Richard Freiherr von. *Psychopathia Sexualis: with Especial Reference to Contrary Sexual Instinct, a Medico-Legal Study*. 1886. 7th edn. Trans. Charles Gilbert Chaddock. Philadelphia and London: Davis, 1892.

Kramer, David. 'Masculine Rivalry in *The Bostonians*: Henry James and the Rhetoric of "Newspaper Making"'. *Henry James Review* 19 (1998): 139–47.

Kramnick, Jonathan Brody. *Making the English Canon: Print-Capitalism and the Cultural Past, 1700–1770*. Cambridge: Cambridge UP, 1998.

Lacan, Jacques. *The Seminar of Jacques Lacan. Book XI. The Four Fundamental Concepts of Psychoanalysis*. Ed. Jacques Alain Miller. Trans. Alan Sheridan. London and New York: Norton, 1981.

Lamb, Charles. 'On the Tragedies of Shakspere, Considered with Reference to his Fitness for Stage Representation'. 1818. *Poems, Plays and Miscellaneous Essays*. London: Macmillan, 1884: 220–40.

Landsberg, Alison. *Prosthetic Memory: The Transformation of American Remembrance in the Age of Mass Culture*. Columbia: Columbia UP, 2004.

Lawrence, D. H. Letter to Edward Garnett. 5 June 1914. *Novelists on the Novel*. Ed. Miriam Allott. London: Routledge, 1952: 289–90.

Lawrence, Herbert. *The Life and Adventures of Common Sense: An Historical Allegory*. 2 vols. London: Montagu Lawrence, 1769.

Le Clair, Robert C. *Young Henry James, 1843–1870*. New York: Bookman, 1955.

Leeming, David. *Stephen Spender: A Lifetime in Modernism*. New York: Holt, 1999.

Letter to the Editor. *The Times*. 10 April 1847: 7.

Letter to the Editor. *The Times*. 15 June 1847: 7.

Leverenz, David. *Manhood and the American Renaissance*. Ithaca and London: Cornell UP, 1989.

Levine, Lawrence W. *Highbrow /Lowbrow: The Emergence of Cultural Hierarchy in America*. The William E. Massey Sr. Lectures in the History of American Civilization. 1986. Cambridge, Mass. and London: Harvard UP, 1988.

Lewes, George Henry. *Problems of Life and Mind*. First series. 2 vols. London: Kegan, 1874–75.

Lewis, David. *Counterfactuals*. Oxford: Blackwell, 1973.

Lewis, R.W.B. *The Jameses: A Family Narrative*. London: Andre Deutsch, 1991.

Lewis, Wyndham. *Time and Western Man*. 1927. Beacon: Boston, 1957.

Limon, John. *Writing after the War: American War Fiction from Realism to Postmodernism*. New York: Oxford UP, 1994.

Linderman, Gerald F. *Embattled Courage: The Experience of Combat in the American Civil War*. New York: Free, 1987.

Lively, Robert A. *Fiction Fights the Civil War: An Unfinished Chapter in the Literary History of the American People*. Chapel Hill, NC: North Carolina UP, 1957.

Looney, Thomas. *'Shakespeare' Identified in Edward de Vere, the Seventeenth Earl of Oxford*. London: Palmer, 1920.

Lubbock, Percy. Preface. *The Sense of the Past*. By Henry James. London: W. Collins, 1917: v.

Lynn, Kenneth S. *William Dean Howells*. New York: Harcourt, 1971.

Macaulay, Thomas Babington. 'History'. 1828. *The Varieties of History from Voltaire to the Present*. Ed. Fritz Stern. 2nd edn. London and Basingstoke: Macmillan, 1970: 72–89.

McCawley, James D. 'Tense and Time Reference in English'. *Studies in Linguistic Semantics*. Ed. Charles J. Fillmore and D. Terence Langendoen. New York: Holt, 1971: 96–113.

McColley, Kathleen. 'Claiming Center Stage: Speaking Out for Homoerotic Empowerment in *The Bostonians*'. *Henry James Review* 21 (2000): 151–69.

McDonald, Henry. 'Nietzsche Contra Derrida: Two Views of Henry James's "The Birthplace"'. *Henry James Review* 11 (1990): 133–48.

Mach, Ernst. *The Science of Mechanics: A Critical and Historical Exposition of its Principles*. 1883. Trans. Thomas J. MacCormack. London: Watts, 1893.

Macherey, Pierre. *A Theory of Literary Production*. 1966. Trans. Geoffrey Wall. London: Routledge, 1978.

McManaway, James G. 'Shakespeare in the United States'. *PMLA* 79 (1964): 513–18.

McMurray, William. 'Reality in Henry James's "The Birthplace" '. *Explicator* 35 (1976): 10–11.

McTaggart, J. Ellis. 'The Unreality of Time'. *Mind* (new series) 68 (1908): 457–74.

McWhirter, David. *Desire and Love in Henry James: A Study of the Late Novels*. Cambridge: Cambridge UP, 1989.

——. Ed. *Henry James's New York Edition: The Construction of Authorship*. Stanford, Calif.: Stanford UP, 1995.

——. '"A Provision Full of Responsibilities": Senses of the Past in Henry James's Fourth Phase'. *Enacting History in Henry James: Narrative, Power, and Ethics*. Ed. Gert Buelens. Cambridge: Cambridge UP, 1997: 148–65.

——. 'Restaging the Hurt: Henry James and the Artist as Masochist', *Texas Studies in Literature and Language*, 33 (1991): 464–91.

Maher, Jane. *Biography of Broken Fortunes: Wilkie and Bob, Brothers of William, Henry, and Alice James*. Hamden, Connecticut: Archon, 1986.

Margolis, Anne T. *Henry James and the Problem of Audience: An International Act*. Studies in Modern Literature. No. 49. Ann Arbor, Mich.: UMI Research Press, 1985.

Marshall, Susan L. '"Framed in Death": *The Sense of the Past* and the Limits of Revision'. *Henry James Review* 10 (1989): 197–209.

Martin, Terence. *Parables of Possibility: The American Need for Beginnings*. New York: Columbia UP, 1995.

Marwick, Arthur. *The Nature of History*. London: Macmillan, 1970.

Masur, Louis P. Ed. *The Real War will Never get in the Books: Selections from Writers during the Civil War*. New York and Oxford: Oxford UP, 1993.

Matthiessen, F. O. *American Renaissance. Art and Expression in the Age of Emerson and Whitman*. London: Oxford UP, 1941.

——. *Henry James: The Major Phase*. New York: Oxford UP, 1944.

Mayne, Xavier. *Imre: A Memorandum*. Naples: English Book Press, 1906.

——. *The Intersexes: A History of Similisexualism as a Problem in Social Life*. Privately printed, 1908.

Meissner, Collin. *Henry James and the Language of Experience*. Cambridge: Cambridge UP, 1999.

Melchiori, Giorgio. 'Shakespeare and Henry James'. *Shakespeare Newsletter* 17 (1967), 56.

Melville, Herman. 'Hawthorne and his Mosses'. 1850. *AS*: 163–8.

Menand, Louis. *The Metaphysical Club*. London: Flamingo, 2001.

Mérimée, Prosper. 'The Venus of Ille.' 1837. *Carmen and Other Stories*. Trans. Nicholas Jotcham. World's Classics. Oxford: Oxford UP, 1989: 132–61.

Meyerhoff, Hans. *Time in Literature*. Berkeley and Los Angeles: California UP, 1955.

Miller, D. A. *The Novel and the Police*. Berkeley: California UP, 1988.

Miller, J. Hillis. *Hawthorne and History: Defacing It*. The Bucknell Lectures in Literary Theory. Oxford: Blackwell, 1991.

——. 'History, Narrative, and Responsibility: Speech Acts in "The Aspern Papers"'. *Enacting History in Henry James: Narrative, Power and Ethics*. Ed. Gert Buelens. Cambridge: Cambridge UP, 1997: 193–210.

Millgate, Michael. *Testamentary Acts: Browning, Tennyson, James, Hardy*. Oxford: Clarendon, 1992.

Mommsen, Theodor. 'Rectorial Address' (Berlin University). 1874. *The Varieties of History from Voltaire to the Present*. 2nd edn. Ed. Fritz Stern. London and Basingstoke: Macmillan, 1970: 192–96.

Morgan, David H. J. 'Theater of War: Combat, the Military, and Masculinities'. *Theorizing Masculinities*. Research on Man and Masculinities. Ed. Harry Brod and Michael Kaufman. Thousand Oaks, Calif. and London: Sage, 1994: 165–82.

Morse, James Herbert. 'The Native American Element in American Fiction: Before the War'. 1883. *AF* 3: 105–22.

——. 'The Native American Element in American Fiction: Since the War'. 1883. *AF* 3: 123–44.

Nakamura, Yoshio. 'The Significance of Fiction in Henry James's "The Birthplace"'. *Studies in English Literature*. The English Literary Society of Japan, 66 (1989): 255–69.

Nicoll, Allardyce. 'The First Baconian'. *Times Literary Supplement*. February 25, 1932: 128.

Niebuhr, Barthold Georg. Preface. *History of Rome*. 1811–12. *The Varieties of History from Voltaire to the Present*. 2nd edn. Ed. Fritz Stern. London and Basingstoke: Macmillan, 1970: 47–50.

Nietzsche, Friedrich Wilhelm. *Beyond Good and Evil: Prelude to a Philosophy of the Future*. 1886. *Basic Writings of Nietzsche*. Trans. and ed. Walter Kaufmann. New York: Modern Library, 1968: 3–146.

——. 'On the Genealogy of Morals'. 1887. *Basic Writings of Nietzsche*. Trans. and ed. Walter Kaufmann. New York: Modern Library, 1968: 439–602.

——. 'The Use and Abuse of History'. 1874. *The Complete Works of Friedrich Nietzsche*. 18 vols. Trans. Adrian Collins. Ed. Oscar Levy. Edinburgh and London: Foulis, 1909–13. 5: 3–100.

Norrman, Ralf. *The Insecure World of Henry James's Fiction: Intensity and Ambiguity*. London: Macmillan, 1982.

Novick, Sheldon M. *Henry James: The Young Master*. New York: Random House, 1996.

Oakeshott, Michael Joseph. *Experience and its Modes*. Cambridge: Cambridge UP, 1933.

O'Hara, Frank. *The Collected Poems of Frank O'Hara*. Ed. Donald Allen. Introduction. John Ashberry. Berkeley, Los Angeles, and London: California UP, 1995.

Osterweis, Rollin G. *The Myth of the Lost Cause, 1865–1900.* Hamden, Connecticut: Archon, 1973.

Palmer, F. R. *The English Verb.* 2nd edn. Longman Linguistics Library. London: Longman, 1974.

——. *Modality and the English Modals.* 2nd edn. Longman Linguistics Library. London: Longman, 1990.

——. *Mood and Modality.* Cambridge Textbooks in Linguistics. Cambridge: Cambridge UP, 1986.

Pattee, Fred Lewis. *The Feminine Fifties.* New York and London: Appleton-Century, 1940.

Paulding, James Kirke. 'National Literature' (1820), *AF* 1: 52–6.

Pearson, John H. *The Prefaces of Henry James: Framing the Modern Reader.* Pennsylvania: Pennsylvania State UP, 1997.

Pearson, Karl. *The Grammar of Science.* 1892. London: Dent, 1937.

Peirce, Charles Sanders. 'Issues of Pragmaticism'. 1905. *Collected Papers of Charles Sanders Peirce.* Ed. Charles Hartshorne, Paul Weiss, and Arthur W. Burks. 8 vols. Cambridge, Mass.: Harvard UP, 1931–58. 5: 293–313.

——. 'The Law of the Mind'. 1892. *Collected Papers of Charles Sanders Peirce.* Ed. Charles Hartshorne, Paul Weiss, and Arthur W. Burks. 8 vols. Cambridge, Mass.: Harvard UP, 1931–58. 6: 86–113.

Perkins, Michael R. *Modal Expressions in English.* Open Linguistics Series. London: Pinter, 1983.

Person, Leland S. 'Eroticism and Creativity in *The Aspern Papers*'. *Literature and Psychology* 32 (1986): 20–9.

——. 'James's Homo-Aesthetics: Deploying Desire in the Tales of Writers and Artists'. *Henry James Review*, 14 (1993): 188–203.

Pippin, Robert B. *Henry James and Modern Moral Life.* Cambridge: Cambridge UP, 2000.

Pope, Alexander. 'The Rape of the Lock: An Heroi-Comical Poem in Five Cantos.' 1714. *The Poems of Alexander Pope.* Ed. John Butt. London: Methuen, 1963: 217–42.

Posnock, Ross. *The Trial of Curiosity: Henry James, William James, and the Trial of Modernity.* New York: Oxford UP, 1991.

Poulet, Georges. *Studies in Human Time.* Trans. Elliott Coleman. New York: Harper, 1959.

Prior, A. N. *Past, Present, and Future.* Oxford: Clarendon, 1967.

Purdy, Strother B. *The Hole in the Fabric: Science, Contemporary Literature and Henry James.* Pittsburgh: Pittsburgh UP, 1977.

Quine, Willard Van Orman. *From a Logical Point of View: 9 Logico-Philosophical Essays.* Cambridge, Mass.: Harvard UP, 1953.

Raffalovich, Mark André. *Uranisme et unisexualité: Étude sur différentes manifestations de l'instinct sexuel.* Lyon, Paris, 1896.

Ranke, Leopold von. Preface. *Histories of the Latin and Germanic Nations from 1494–1514.* 1824. *The Varieties of History from Voltaire to the Present.* 2nd edn. Ed. Fritz Stern. London and Basingstoke: Macmillan, 1970: 55–8.

Rawlings, Peter. 'Grammars of Time in Late James'. *Modern Language Review* 98 (2003): 273–84.

——. 'Grotesque Encounters in the Travel Writing of Henry James'. *Yearbook of English Studies* 34 (2004): 171–85.

——. 'Henry James, Delia Bacon, and American Uses of Shakespeare'. *Symbiosis* 5 (2001): 139–58.

——. 'Henry James and "Brooksmith": Circumscribing the Task of Reading'. *Kyushu American Literature* (Japan) 38 (1997): 51–64.

——. 'Henry James and the Discourse of Organicism'. PhD thesis. University of Cambridge, 1991.

——. Ed. *Henry James: Essays on Art and Drama*. Aldershot: Scolar, 1996.

——. Introduction. 'Who Reads an American Book?' *AF* 2: xiii–xx.

——. 'A Kodak Refraction of Henry James's "The Real Thing"'. *Journal of American Studies* 32 (1998): 447–63.

——. 'Mythologies of Cultural Decline and Aspects of the Newspaper Industry'. *Studies in Languages and Cultures* (Kyushu University, Japan) 10 (1999): 161–78.

——. 'Pater, Wilde, and James: "The Reader's Share of the Task".' *Studies in English Language and Literature* (Kyushu University, Japan) 48 (1998): 45–64.

——. 'Resisting Death: Henry James's "The Art of Fiction"'. *Studies in Languages and Cultures* (Kyushu University, Japan) 9 (1998): 93–114.

——. 'Shakespeare Migrates to America'. *AS*: 1–28.

Reade, Brian. Ed. *Sexual Heretics: Male Homosexuality in English Literature from 1850–1900: An Anthology*. London: Routledge, 1970.

Reichenbach, Hans. *The Direction of Time*. Ed. Maria Reichenbach. Berkeley, Los Angeles, and London: California UP, 1971.

——. *Elements of Symbolic Logic*. New York: Dover, 1947.

Ringuette, Dana J. 'Imagining the End: Henry James, Charles Sanders Peirce, and the "Reach beyond the Laboratory-Brain"'. *Henry James Review* 20 (1999): 155–65.

Rivkin, Julie. *False Positions: The Representational Logics of Henry James's Fiction*. Stanford, Calif.: Stanford UP, 1996.

——. 'Speaking with the Dead: Ethics and Representation in "The Aspern Papers"'. *Henry James Review* 10 (1989): 135–41.

Roach, Joseph. 'Culture and Performance in the Circum-Atlantic World'. *Performativity and Performance*. Ed. Andrew Parker and Eve Kosofsky Sedgwick. New York and London: Routledge, 1995: 45–63.

Romero, Lora. *Home Fronts: Domesticity and its Critics in the Antebellum United States*. New Americanists. Durham, NC and London: Duke UP, 1997.

Roosevelt, Theodore. 'The Strenuous Life'. 1899. *The Strenuous Life: Essays and Addresses*. New York: Century, 1900: 1–21.

——. 'True American Ideals.' *Forum* 18 (1894–95): 743–50.

——. 'What "Americanism" Means'. *Forum* 17 (1894): 196–206.

Rose, Anne C. *Victorian America and the Civil War*. Cambridge: Cambridge UP, 1992.

Rosenzweig, Saul. 'The Ghost of Henry James: A Study in Thematic Apperception'. *Character and Personality* 12 (1943–44): 79–100.

Ross, Morton L. 'James's "The Birthplace": A Double Turn of the Narrative Screw'. *Studies in Short Fiction* 3 (1965): 321–28.

Rotundo, E. Anthony. *American Manhood: Transformations in Masculinity from the Revolution to the Modern Era*. New York: Basic, 1993.

Rowe, John Carlos. *Henry Adams and Henry James: The Emergence of a Modern Consciousness*. Ithaca and London: Cornell UP, 1976.

——. *The Other Henry James.* New Americanists. Durham, N.C. and London: Duke UP, 1998.

Salmon, Richard. *Henry James and the Culture of Publicity.* Cambridge: Cambridge UP, 1997.

Sarotte, Georges-Michel. *Like a Brother, Like a Lover: Male Homosexuality in the American Novel and Theater from Herman Melville to James Baldwin.* Trans. Richard Miller. Garden City, New York: Anchor, 1978.

Sartre, Jean-Paul. *Being and Nothingness: An Essay on Phenomenological Ontology.* 1943. Trans. Hazel E. Barnes. London: Methuen, 1969.

Saul, Jack. *The Sins of the Cities of the Plain; or, The Recollections of a Mary-Ann.* 2 vols. London: privately printed, 1881.

Savoy, Eric. 'Embarrassments: Figure in the Closet'. *Henry James Review* 20 (1999): 227–36.

——. 'The Queer Subject of "The Jolly Corner"'. *Henry James Review* 20 (1999): 1–21.

Schoenbaum, Samuel. *Shakespeare's Lives.* 2nd edn. Oxford: Clarendon, 1991.

Schwartz, Nina. 'The Master Lesson: James Reading Shakespeare'. *Henry James Review* 12 (1991): 69–83.

Scott, William Cowper. 'American Literature: The Present State of American Letters; The Prospect and Means of their Improvement'. 1845. *AF* 1: 318–30.

Secretario, Il. 'American Letters——Their Character and Advancement'. 1845. *AF* 1: 331–45.

Sedgwick, Eve Kosofsky. *Epistemology of the Closet.* London: Harvester Wheatsheaf, 1991.

——. *Tendencies.* London: Routledge, 1994.

Sicker, Philip. *Love and the Quest for Identity in the Fiction of Henry James.* Princeton, NJ: Princeton UP, 1980.

Silber, Nina. *The Romance of Reunion: Northerners and the South, 1865–1900.* Chapel Hill, NC and London: North Carolina UP, 1993.

Silverman, Kaja. 'Too Early/Too Late: Subjectivity and the Primal Scene in James'. *Novel* 21 (1988): 147–73.

Simms, William Gilmore. 'Americanism in Literature'. 1845. *AF* 1: 346–59.

Simpson, Lewis P. *Mind and the American Civil War: A Meditation on Lost Causes.* The Walter Lynwood Fleming Lectures in Southern History. Baton Rouge: Louisiana State UP, 1989.

Smith, Adam. 'The Principles which Lead and Direct Philosophical Enquiries; Illustrated by the History of Astronomy'. c.1750. *Essays on Philosophical Subjects.* Ed. Joseph Black and James Hutton. Dublin: n.p., 1795: 3–93.

Smith, William Henry. *Was Lord Bacon the Author of Shakespeare's Plays? A Letter to Lord Ellesmere.* London: Skeffington, 1856.

Snow, C. P. *The Realists: Portraits of Eight Novelists: Stendhal, Balzac, Dickens, Dostoevsky, Tolstoy, Galdós, Henry James, Proust.* London: Macmillan, 1978.

'Southern Literature'. 1857. *AF* 2: 129–41.

Sofer, Naomi Z. 'Why "different vibrations...walk hand in hand": Homosocial Bonds in *Roderick Hudson*'. *Henry James Review* 20 (1999): 185–205.

Spender, Stephen. *The Destructive Element: A Study of Modern Writers and Beliefs.* London: Jonathan Cape, 1935.

Stafford, William T. *Books Speaking to Books: A Contextual Approach to American Fiction.* Chapel Hill, N. C.: North Carolina UP, 1981.

——. 'James Examines Shakespeare: Notes on the Nature of Genius'. *PMLA* 73 (1958): 123–8.

Stern, Fritz. Introduction. *The Varieties of History from Voltaire to the Present*. 2nd edn. Ed. Fritz Stern. London and Basingstoke: Macmillan, 1970: 11–32.

Stevens, Hugh. *Henry James and Sexuality*. Cambridge: Cambridge UP, 1998.

Strychacz, Thomas. *Modernism, Mass Culture, and Professionalism*. Cambridge: Cambridge UP, 1993.

Symonds, John Addington. *A Problem in Modern Ethics: Being an Enquiry into the Phenomenon of Sexual Inversion, Addressed Especially to Medical Psychologists and Jurists*. London: privately printed, 1896.

Tanner, Tony. 'The Birthplace'. *Henry James: The Shorter Fiction: Reassessments*. Ed. N. H. Reeve. London, Macmillan, 1997: 77–94.

——. *Scenes of Nature, Signs of Men*. Cambridge: Cambridge UP, 1987.

Taylor, William R. *Cavalier and Yankee: The Old South and American National Character*. New York: Braziller, 1961.

Theweleit, Klaus. *Male Fantasies: Vol. 1: Women, Floods, Bodies, Histories*. 1977. Trans. Stephen Conway, Eric Carter, and Chris Turner. Minnesota: Minnesota UP, 1987.

——. *Male Fantasies. Vol. 2: Male Bodies: Psychoanalyzing the White Terror*. 1978. Trans. Chris Turner, Erica Carter, and Stephen Conway. Minnesota: Minnesota UP, 1989.

Thompson, Lawrence S. 'The Civil War in Fiction'. *Civil War History* 2 (1956): 83–95.

Thoreau, Henry David. *Journal*, 27 October 1857. *Consciousness in Concord: The Text of Thoreau's Hitherto 'Lost Journal', 1840–1841, together with Notes and a Commentary*. Ed. Perry Miller. Boston: Houghton, 1958.

Thorndike, Ashley. 'Shakespeare in America'. 1927. *AS*: 512–26.

Tintner, Adeline R. *The Book World of Henry James: Appropriating the Classics*. Studies in Modern Literature. No. 82. Ann Arbor, Mich. and London: UMI Research Press, 1987.

Tompkins, Jane. *Sensational Designs: The Cultural Work of American Fiction, 1790–1860*. New York and Oxford: Oxford UP, 1985.

Trilling, Lionel. *The Liberal Imagination: Essays on Literature and Society*. 1950. New York: Doubleday Anchor, 1953.

——. *The Opposing Self: Nine Essays in Criticism*. London: Secker and Warburg, 1955.

——. *Sincerity and Authenticity*. The Charles Eliot Norton Lectures. 1969–1970. Cambridge, Mass. and London, England: Harvard UP, 1972.

Tucker, George. 'A Discourse on American Literature'. 1838. *AF* 1: 202–20.

Twain, Mark. *Following the Equator: A Journey Around the World*. 1897. *AS*: 403–6.

——. and Charles Dudley Warner. *The Gilded Age*. London and New York: Routledge, 1874.

——. *Is Shakespere Dead?. From my Autobiography*. New York: Harper, 1909.

Tyler, Moses Coit. *A History of American Literature*. 2 vols. New York: Putnam, 1878.

Underwood, Ted. 'Romantic Historicism and the Afterlife'. *PMLA* 117 (2002): 237–51.

Vaid, Krishna Balder. *Technique in the Tales of Henry James*. Cambridge, Mass.: Harvard UP, 1964.

Vaihinger, Hans. *The Philosophy of 'As if': A System for the Theoretical and Religious Fictions of Mankind.* 1911. Trans. C. K. Ogden. 2nd edn. London: Routledge, 1935.

Very, Jones. 'Shakespeare'. 1839. *AS* 77–99.

Visser, F. T. *An Historical Syntax of the English Language.* 3 vols. Leiden: Brill, 1963–73.

Walter. *My Secret Life.* 11 vols. 1890–95. Ed. Gordon Grimley. London: Panther, 1972.

Walton, Priscilla L. *The Disruption of the Feminine in Henry James.* Toronto: Toronto UP, 1992.

Ward, J. A. *The Imagination of Disaster: Evil in the Fiction of Henry James.* Lincoln: Nebraska UP, 1961.

Warner, Anthony R. *English Auxiliaries: Structure and History.* Cambridge Studies in Linguistics. Cambridge: Cambridge UP, 1993.

Warner, Susan B. *The Wide, Wide World.* 1850. London: Clay, 1892.

Warren, Kenneth W. *Black and White Strangers: Race and American Literary Realism.* Chicago: Chicago UP, 1993.

Warren, Robert Penn. *The Legacy of the Civil War: Meditations on the Centennial.* New York: Random, 1961.

Weeks, Jeffrey. 'Inverts, Perverts, and Mary-Annes: Male Prostitution and the Regulation of Homosexuality in England in the Nineteenth and Early Twentieth Centuries'. *Hidden from History: Reclaiming the Gay and Lesbian Past.* Ed. Martin Duberman, Martha Vicinius, and George Chaubcey, Jr. Harmondsworth: Penguin, 1991: 195–211.

——. *Sex, Politics, and Society: The Regulation of Sex Since 1800.* Themes in British Social History. 2nd edn. London and New York: Longman, 1989.

Weiss, John. 'War and Literature'. 1862. *AF* 2: 189–201.

Wells, H. G. *The Time Machine.* 1894–95. *Selected Short Stories.* Harmondsworth: Penguin, 1958: 7–83.

Wescott, Glenway. 'A Sentimental Contribution'. *Hound and Horn* 7 (1933–34) 523–34.

West, Rebecca. *Henry James.* London: Nisbet, 1916.

Wheelwright, Julie. *Amazons and Military Maids: Women who Cross-Dressed in the Pursuit of Life, Liberty and Happiness.* London: Pandora, 1989.

White, Hayden. *The Content of the Form: Narrative Discourse and Historical Representation.* Baltimore and London: Johns Hopkins UP, 1987.

——. *Metahistory: The Historical Imagination in Nineteenth-Century Europe.* Baltimore and London: Johns Hopkins UP, 1973.

White, Richard Grant. 'The Anatomization of William Shakespeare'. 1884. *AS*: 332–56.

——. 'The Bacon–Shakespeare Craze'. *Atlantic Monthly* 51 (1883): 507–21.

——. 'Memoirs'. *The Works of William Shakespeare.* Ed. Richard Grant White. 12 vols. Boston: Little Brown, 1865: I: i–cxiii.

White, Thomas William. *Our English Homer; or, Shakespeare Historically Considered.* London: Sampson Low, 1892

Whitman, Walt. *Democratic Vistas.* 1871. *AS*: 282–3.

——. *Drum-Taps.* New York: Eckler, 1865.

——. 'Poetry Today in America—Shakspere—The Future'. 1881. *AS*: 317–31.

Wilkes, George. *Shakespeare from an American Point of View: Including an Inquiry as to his Religious Faith, and his Knowledge of Law; with the Baconian Theory Considered*. London: Sampson Low, 1877.

Williams, Susan S. 'The Tell-Tale Representation: James and *The Sense of the Past*'. *Henry James Review* 14 (1993): 72–86.

Wilson, Edmund. *Patriotic Gore: Studies in the Literature of the American Civil War*. London: Andre Deutsch, 1962.

——. *The Wound and the Bow: Seven Studies in Literature*. London: Allen, 1952.

Wordsworth, William. 'Ode: Intimations of Immortality from Recollections of Early Childhood'. *William Wordsworth's The Prelude, with a Selection from the Shorter Poems, the Sonnets, The Recluse, and The Excursion*. Ed. Carlos Baker. New York: Holt, 1954: 152–7.

X, Jacobus. *Crossways of Sex: A Study in Eroto-Pathology*. 2 vols. British Bibliophiles Society: Paris, 1904.

Young, Elizabeth. *Disarming the Nation: Women's Writing and the American Civil War*. Women in Culture and Society. Chicago: Chicago UP, 1999.

Young, G. M. *Portrait of an Age: Victorian England*. 2nd edn. Oxford: Oxford UP, 1953.

Zacharias, Greg W. 'James's Morality in *Roderick Hudson*'. *Henry James Review* 11 (1990): 115–32.

Zeigler, Wilbur Gleason. *It was Marlowe: A Story of the Secret of Three Centuries*. Chicago: Donohue, 1895.

Zwinger, Lynda. 'Bodies That Don't Matter: The Queering of "Henry James"'. *Modern Fiction Studies* 41 (1995): 657–80.

Index